Feeling as a Foreign Language

OTHER BOOKS BY ALICE FULTON

Sensual Math

Powers Of Congress

Palladium

Dance Script With Electric Ballerina

Feeling as a Foreign Language

The Good Strangeness of Poetry

ALICE FULTON

Graywolf Press

SAINT PAUL, MINNESOTA

Copyright © 1999 by Alice Fulton

Publication of this volume is made possible in part by a grant provided by the Minnesota State Arts Board through an appropriation by the Minnesota State Legislature, and by a grant from the National Endowment for the Arts. Significant support has also been provided by Dayton's, Mervyn's, and Target stores through the Dayton Hudson Foundation, the Bush Foundation, the McKnight Foundation, the General Mills Foundation, the St. Paul Companies, and other generous contributions from foundations, corporations, and individuals. To these organizations and individuals we offer our heartfelt thanks.

Published by Graywolf Press
2402 University Avenue, Suite 203
Saint Paul, Minnesota 55114
All rights reserved.

www.graywolfpress.org

Published in the United States of America

ISBN 1-55597-286-1

2   4   6   8   9   7   5   3   1

First Graywolf Printing, 1999

Library of Congress Catalog Card Number: 98-88484

Cover art: Hank De Leo, *Each Cell a Drunkard of Am (Robert Morgan)*, detail, 1984, collection of Thomas Lux

Cover design: Jeanne Lee

for Hank

Contents

Preamble

3

I PROCESS
Head Notes, Heart Notes, Base Notes

Screens: An Alchemical Scrapbook

11

II POETICS
Subversive Pleasures

Of Formal, Free, and Fractal Verse:
Singing the Body Eclectic

43

Fractal Amplifications:
Writing in Three Dimensions

61

III POWERS
The Only Kangaroo among the Beauty

Unordinary Passions:
Margaret Cavendish, the Duchess of Newcastle

85

Her Moment of Brocade:
The Reconstruction of Emily Dickinson
125

IV PRAXIS
Seed Ink

To Organize a Waterfall
173

V PENCHANTS
A Canon for Infidels

Three Poets in Pursuit of America
211

The State of the Art
227

Main Things
247

VI PREMISES
The Tongue as a Muscle

A Poetry of Inconvenient Knowledge
277

Feeling as a Foreign Language

Preamble

MY FIRST LESSON IN LITERARY MATTERS, AS IN SO many things, came from my mother. I was a child of six or seven when she told me I must never begin a letter with "How are you, I am fine." This phrase would identify me as a person of no imagination. Somehow she gave me to know that sentiments couched in threadbare words seem empty. Of course, the impulse to create a language commensurate to—or transcendent of—meaning is the driving force of poetry. From the mother tongue poets create a linguistic state that is both foreign and available to readers of the broader language in which it exists. Each poet creates an expatriate space, a slightly skewed domain where things are freshly felt because they are freshly said. In contrast to this good strangeness, how-are-you-I-am-fine was too at home in the vernacular. It lacked the shimmer and presence of the *unheimlich*, a word that translates literally as "unhomelike" but is understood to mean "uncanny." To my mind, *unheimlich* also suggests the undomesticated and eccentric (from the Greek *ekkentros*, "outside the center"). To be eccentric is to be at some remove from the cozy hearth of the familiar and well-received.

Sometimes a familiar saying disappears long enough to regain some good strangeness. A couple of weeks ago, I was describing the machinations of local administrators to my mother. "Tell them to go fry ice," she said in disgust. I hadn't heard that expression in twenty years. I could see the functionaries in question shaking a skillet of lightly breaded cubes, trying to cook them to a turn. The image was so suggestive of bureaucracies it made me smile. The platitude had become foreign and pictorial once again. Many common idioms have such vivid, literal origins, but their colorful beginnings are lost over time. Although we understand a *woolgatherer* to be a daydreamer, we no longer imagine someone wandering about the countryside harvesting bits of fleece from bushes or fences. In place of the little epiphany that accompanies literal to figurative translation, we have an unmediated grasp of an abstract meaning.

Mediation—in the form of resistance or interference—seems an important facet of the good strange or eccentric. And eccentricity seems a defining trait of postmodern aesthetics. As a form of novation, eccentric deviance is different, I think, from the originality of romanticism or the "make it new" credo of modernism. Both the concept of originality and poetry's ability to be "news that stays news" are construed as strengths, while deviance tends to be regarded as a weakness. Although the interests of these essays range from science to cultural politics, their understory posits eccentricity as a positive value, capable of injecting the foreign into the dully familiar.

"Screens: An Alchemical Scrapbook" considers the allure of linguistic, biological, electronic, and emotional veils. Such filters mediate between reader and page, heart and pulse, hacker and computer, private feelings and public façade. In doing so, they disturb transparency in uncanny ways. Two essays on fractal poetics look to chaos and complexity theory as touchstones for contemporary aesthetics. These pieces suggest that as free verse broke the pentameter, fractal verse can break the poem plane or linguistic surface.

A section called "The Only Kangaroo among the Beauty" takes its title from a letter by Emily Dickinson, who worried that she would be perceived as such an anomaly. Her anxiety was well-founded. In the late 1980s, one hundred years after her death, a scholar told me that Dickinson was "too eccentric" to foster a tradition. He was not alone in this opinion. In response, my essay on Dickinson's poetry considers aberrance as a source of power. Another essay in this section rediscovers an endearing seventeenth-century poet, Margaret Cavendish, the Duchess of Newcastle. Like Dickinson, Cavendish has been isolated rather than absorbed into any lineage or tradition. As I learned of the reception accorded her work, I was struck by the pathology of literary culture over the past 350 years. Her history testifies to a collusion of fear that regards female waywardness as a form of contagion and punishes singularity. I hope this essay might allow people to read Cavendish with new eyes and to recognize the self-protective agendas behind many critical judgments that pretend to disinterest.

Several years ago, I was invited to contribute to a special issue of poets writing about their own work. "'To Organize a Waterfall," written in response to this assignment, meditates on my own practice as a poet. It's followed by a section of essay-reviews. As reader and critic, I've tried to be as enthusiastic as honesty allows. In some cases, I've had to stretch imaginatively in order to engage with sensibilities utterly foreign to my own. Yet the better part of fairness is the willingness to move toward what is given rather than impose one's own aesthetic on a book. This approach—a sympathetic leaning toward the work coupled with patient rereading—is the one I've tried to realize.

Collections of reviews often limit their appraisals to acclaimed writers. I enjoy reading about established poets whose work I follow, but I'm also interested in learning of those who would have escaped my attention otherwise. To honor these impulses, I've included reviews of both laureled and lesser-known poets. In addition to the preference for high-profile subjects, collected reviews tend to favor poetry of the last fifteen minutes over poetry of the last fifteen years. There seems nothing inherently valuable about the newly published, however, and I've made no attempt to select recent rather than older pieces. What *have* I selected? Narrative, lyric, maximalist, baroque, Romantic, masculist, fractal, plain-style, environmentalist, feminist, and formalist poets number among the inclusions. (You can match those too-restrictive labels with the likeliest suspects.)

I earlier cited "patience" when describing my critical stance. Readers of fiction are propelled by the story's future developments: How will things turn out, what will become of the characters? Readers of poetry, on the other hand, develop a Zen gift for existing in the moment. No one reads poetry (including narrative poetry) to discover where the plot will settle. Poetry is neither future-driven nor teleological in spirit. The pleasure exists in the presence and texture of each line as each line is experienced. Which is to say: Fiction is about what happens next. Poetry is about what happens now. Immediacy is one of its hidden assets—immediacy as paradox, requiring a surrender to extemporal pleasures. That is why poetry remains a puzzle to the impatient. Yet rather than a riddle, poetry has the potential to be a subversive force. The last essay in the book, "A Poetry of Inconvenient Knowledge," invokes that possibility. It speaks to the difficult necessity of changing one's life—and words—so as to reflect rather than deflect one's ethos. Here, as throughout, I regard the tongue as a muscle capable of revising the world's alignments.

Alice Fulton, 1998

I

Process

Head Notes, Heart Notes, Base Notes

Screens:
An Alchemical Scrapbook

1. OCTOBER 1992, YPSILANTI, MICHIGAN: SUNSCREENS turn to smokescreens. The furnace, dormant since spring, fires up and fills the house with the snake cologne of burning mold. A fibrous resin from the Defiant woodstove thickens the air. This farmhouse, built in 1876, has no upstairs heat. My small study is warmed by a portable space heater—a nostalgic, homely looking object. Like many pre-high-tech appliances, it has a countenance: a metal grill that resembles a catcher's face guard shields its humming, blaze-orange element. When I first turn it on, a whiff of mortality fills the air: scent of vacuum and dust. The farmer's grain drier roars distantly; a month from now he'll fix a white electric star to its top. How radiant his utilitarian citadel will seem when crowned by that simplicity. Most of the farmers have day jobs. The lights of their tractors tunnel the fields after dark with the urgency of harvest; they peel out, do hairpin turns, wheelies, at the ends of the rows, worried about finishing or perhaps feeling the puissance of being their own boss. Pheasant cocks, driven from the harvested fields, squawk and fight over their new territory in our meadow. Mice take shelter inside; at night

their gnawing sounds like the scrape of scriveners' quills. Corn snakes wintering in the walls make a rope-through-dry-leaves rustling. The pock-pocking of shotguns signals hunters nearby. The house is swaddled by harvest in all of its guises: triumph and yield, realization and renunciation. After the committees of inertia, book blurs, wreck letters, I want to screen the day with the quiet that leads to words.

When I'm lost in the Thou-art-That of composition, the membranes dividing each from each dissolve; the separate self vanishes into an undifferentiated state, which—who knows—might be similar to the "suchness" of Buddhism. Yet to enter this seamlessness, I have to screen out distractions. The effort to do so creates new complications. We have two phone lines: one for ordinary calls and one for emergencies. Each phone rings with a different signal so we can tell them apart. The workaday phone is answered by a machine that's an intrusion in itself, a kind of electronic flypaper. As long as we have the emergency phone, we feel safe in turning off the machine attached to the nonemergency number. Going one step further, I also switch off the ringer of this workaday phone. As the days go by, I discover an odd fact: Even with the ringer off, the phone emits a vestigial trill when calls come in. As the quiet deepens, I can hear this tiny siren wherever I am in the house. At times, I wonder if I'm imagining the ghostly ringing. But no. My husband Hank hears it too.

I'm thinking about textures, dreams, mooncakes, and writing poems that remember the death of my nineteen-year-old niece, Laura, two years ago. Grace Lee, a Chinese American student, has given me a mooncake in celebration of the Autumn Festival. Traditionally associated with women, the Autumn Festival takes place when heat gives way to coolness, brightness to winter darkness, and the female principle ascends. A harvest fête, it is celebrated at night. People compose poems, tell stories, drink, and eat mooncakes made of lunar-colored flour. The cellophane wrapper of my mooncake features a yellow harvest moon, two tree peony blossoms, and a bar code. It says, "Made in Hong Kong by Tai Wing Wah Restaurant. Ingredients include Lotus Seed, Peanut Oil, Sugar, Flour." The wrapper enhances the pastry, as the moon is improved by cloud cover. Inside, there's an "oxygen absorber" packet, the desiccant packed with cameras. As I eat a dense sliver, I read about the structure of spider silk and how we dream to forget. It seems dreams are an erasure; a way to ease obsession; strategies for survival. Dreams are like writing.

When I need a break from the screen, I step to the window, see the cornstalks whittled into winter blond, a wizened forest against the unjustified margins of Midwestern sky. If the University of Michigan has a home game, I might see the silver football of the Goodyear blimp advertising itself in the blue and maize surround of sky and trees. But most of all, I like to see the old silo that anchors our backyard. The silo's glazed blocks are the size and shape of computer screens. Each terra-cotta tile is rich with variations of patina, tarnish. I name the colors: *warmly sorrel as a Guernsey, weary igneous, dun sunset, almost hemoglobin, hard hard cider, tiger lily, garnet lac.* Built to shelter grain from the elements, the silo has a run in its side like a laddered stocking where the grainshoot once stood. Previous owners must have used it as a target, because its blocks are riddled with bullet holes. Its cap has been sacrificed to the wind. Sometimes I leave my room and visit the silo. Climbing through its ripped side, I consider why some screens are more lovable than others. Why do I find it easy to admire the testy elegance of barbed wire? Easy to like the silo, a screen in the round. Can I extend any of this affection to electronic screens? Inside, the silo is cool as a root cellar, though its walls drip with ossified pitch, the furnace remnants of hot tar. Keats's personification of Autumn "sitting careless on a granary floor" comes to mind, though my appreciation of the silo does not, I think, arise from literature or a Romantic fascination with ruins. The silo has a sculptural loveliness. I think I hear the faint electronic summons of the phone, but it must be a wasp living—or dying—in the gauzy mortar of the blocks. And that sudden sound— pillowcases flapping on a clothesline, a row of ceremonial flags—must be low-flying Canadian geese. Looking up, I see the silo's open crown is sealed with clouds like boiled paraffin. Summer's paraclete. What farm wives poured on their preserves.

2. *Screen* descends, etymologically, from "shield": a safeguard or palladium. Like the element palladium, a screen is often silver. The Latin *corium*—"skin, hide"—is somewhere in its history also. Protective windscreens and sunscreens have to be transparent in order to work. But visibility, surface, is intrinsic to the shielding properties of the smokescreen or mask.

3. The veil is a prosthetic face. The electronic screen is a prosthetic mind.

The destruction of a prosthesis isn't as devastating as the destruction of what it replaces.

Which is why I'd like to have the option of veiling when I go out. I'd like to give readings from behind a scrim or screen. Isn't it time to revive the handheld parchment fan? Not the stare, but the glance, is revelatory. The space of between, where meaning is neither completely revealed nor completely concealed, is the space of possibility.

Men have natural veils, beards, which come from within and are painstakingly removed every day. Female veils are imposed from outside; they are cultural rather than natural: makeup. Women want to appear transparent though they are veiled: Makeup tries to be invisible.

Men usually have the option of removing their veils, but in some cultures, women do not. Enforced veiling is a sign of the sexual control of women by the state. It follows that violations of veiling are a means of disruption. Writing of Middle Assyrian Law, Gerda Lerner notes that when veils were worn only by respectable women, "a harlot who presumed to appear veiled on the streets was as great a threat to social order as was the mutinous soldier or slave."

The long hair and beards of poets are a form of veiling. Behind the veil lies something too shocking, too vigorous, too ghastly to be seen: disease, wounds, mourning. A veil can be a bandage. Or it can be erotic.

If I can't have a literal veil, I'd like some metaphorical screen, please.

4. Enhancing screens have the teasing quality of veils. The threat of opacity lingers within their meshes and shawls. They enforce distance between the viewer and a coveted resolution. Sublime by association, the enhancing screen is imbued with the qualities of the desirable it conceals. And in circular fashion, the screen bestows its power on whatever lies behind it. Reading through an enhancing screen of language, I spend more time with the work. The screen holds my attention more effectively than the bareness of clarity or the confusion of opacity.

> Sunset that screens, reveals—
> Enhancing what we see
> By menaces of Amethyst
> And Moats of Mystery.

EMILY DICKINSON, POEM 1609

5. Does the electronic screen have to be leaden? Why not screens that look like gems at rest? Amethyst. A little sunset in the house. A little blue-green algae. A little—you name it. Does technology have to be ugly to be functional? People aren't wild about the looks of their computers. Have manufacturers thought of this? Are they missing a chance to have computers fetishized as cars are? All other things being equal, would a Jaguar of computers sell better? Old radios—made of colorful Bakelite—are collectible. A friend whose field is artificial intelligence writes, "I do feel some nostalgia for my first home computer (a beautiful chrome-plated box in the basement)."

6. My antique Wang is as unprepossessing now as when I first acquired it, in 1983. Hank and I were renting an apartment in Ann Arbor, Michigan. We had taken the place because of its thirteen windows. We veiled most of them with Japanese rice-paper shades. My study was lit by tube lighting said to mimic sunlight and cure the winter desolations. But the high-tech wand was in itself a desolate-looking thing. We encased it in a Japanese paper lantern. The kitchen window was screened with matchstick blinds. A robin built her nest on the front porch that year, and peering through the tiny fissures of the matchsticks, I followed her progress. When a friend visited, I encouraged him to view the robin as I did, by pressing his eye to the hem of light between slats and making of the seam a frame. The oddity of this struck me later. Why didn't I raise the shade? Offering a guest a stingy slice of sight was like offering a stingy slice of cake. Yet the obstruction made the robin more elusive. Screened and piecemeal, she took on treasure. Picture windows are too easy. I like windows with mullions that frame the details and create peripheral compositions; they honor the margins.

We lived with three kinds of windows: transparencies that pulled in light; electronic screens that gave off light; and paintings that lived on light. The TV was a mirror window, darkly reflecting us when off and brightly distorting us when on. The opaque windows of the abstract paintings bestowed stasis on motion and substance on color. I was grateful to them for staying still. From reading, I raised my eyes to their nonreferential world; they were screens that didn't insist on narrative, figure, or landscape. They were absolute music. Their subject was paint just as poetry's was language. The dark peephole of my new Wang computer was something else again. The keyboard was quieter than a typewriter, though not as stealthy as a pen. The type was the spiky green of lawns raised on weed killer. From now on, I'd be writing in golf course, in Astro-Turf. I'd be writing in Emerald City.

7. What are the aesthetics of electronic screens? Superficially, these appliances bespeak a pragmatic world in which aesthetics have no place. But if I press that suggestion, the aesthetic residue of electronic screens unveils. Their aura is suburban: charcoal briquettes and nice driveways. Commercial: They resemble the tray table that opens to support the processed food served in the clouds. The screen connotes utilitarianism and industry: a home equipped with the latest resembles a museum of pavement, a gallery of wet macadam framed in plastic-composite. Electronic screens aspire to invisibility: Like the two-car attached garages of subdivisions, they are surfaces of strenuous neutrality. They long to disappear. And yet, the garage door has raised neutrality to visible—hence objectionable—heights. The trend in the more costly subdivisions is for side-facing garages. The middle classes don't want their houses annexed to enlargements of their computer screens.

8. Though many people contrive to hide their TVs, computers usually are allowed to see the light of day. Are they more aesthetically acceptable? Our own TV is housed

within an antique oak chimney cabinet: a screen for the screen. Isn't there an inherent vulgarity in hiding a high-tech intrusion within a nostalgic surround? Concealing the TV might show a certain insecurity in regard to taste. And yet, I don't veil the TV because I'm ashamed of owning one. I cover it because I think it's ugly. I can embrace modernism—in principle. But in practice, high-tech design holds associations—of office, commerce, Xerox—that oppress me. I also am repulsed by unintended suggestions of nature in high-tech design: the computer monitor on its stalk-like support resembles a skeletal insect. The "mouse" reminds me of a large waterbug rather than a furry rodent. I would like to hide my computer. It has as much aesthetic appeal as a window-unit air-conditioner or a NordicTrack. But computers, at this writing, are harder to conceal than TVs. There's the keyboard, the printer, the monitor, the mouse. Computers could be clothed. I see a large tea cozy with tassels on top. From the pragmatic point of view, a fire hazard. From the aesthetic? The well-dressed appliance is funnier than the naked.

9. Manufacturers, aware of the impersonality of technology, want the phrase "personal computers" to trip off the collective tongue. In fact, the adjective "personal" has crept like a blush through the language of advertising. Does fear of the impersonal lie behind this locution? I give you three smarmy sentences: "I want a personal pan pizza." "I want a personal trainer to help me achieve my personal best." "I want a personal computer." The words "I want" are auto-erotic. But it's "personal" that sticks in the craw. "Personal"

cloys. It's infantile. "Personal" infects computers with the warm fuzzies, a condition no appliance has had to bear before. "Personal" transforms cultural narcissism into a source of pride and self-affirmation. "Personal," it would appear, sells product.

10. Tools can be beautiful. But I don't think computers are destined to become lovely sensual presences. Thus begins their difference from books. There's a romance to the physicality of the book, a tactile pleasure to be had in its constructedness. Of all the objects associated with writing, books are potentially the most beautiful. Potentially, because books in numbers can look messy—even garish. My shelves layer the walls with horizons. Windows get in the way. The titles are an intoxication in themselves, suggesting compressed worlds, visible and at hand. Within the horizontal shelves blaze the slim verticals of the books. The room is a welter of stripes, a riot of primaries too hectic for my taste.

Readers often save a book's protective dust jacket from wear by removing it while reading. A friend of mine has disposed of the wraps entirely. His shelves are saturated with the garment-washed, wet stone glow of cloth bindings. It's as if the dust the jacket was meant to forestall has gentled the books. But I can't strip my books down to the spine. Taken together, the paper-wrapped books are a visual cacophony. Taken alone, a book in its wraps has more interest and texture than one without. It's an aesthetic version of the one/many problem.

11. Soon after the Wang arrived in 1983, I used it while working on a memoir. My resistance to writing the essay was private and weighty. After agonizing for days, I overcame andirons of resistance to pull forth—as if from my entrails, self-eviscerating—several finished pages. Toward the end of this day's work, absorbed, I touched a combination of keys and the Wang emitted a loud, unstoppable electronic scream. The screen was petrified in place. Hank had to pull the plug to get the computer to shut up, and I lost all of the day's writing. A friend who worked with Wangs said I'd hit "a screech bug." I don't have a good record with electric appliances. Is it possible that my own electromagnetic field upsets them? Are we physically incompatible?

12. I'm seduced by a book's ability to preserve physical traces of its readers. Readers of electronic books leave no ink behind in the margins. Though electronic books might allow for marginalia, the notes would be typed rather than handwritten, and they probably would not accumulate as the book passed through many readers' hands and minds. This last would be seen as an improvement. The marginal notes in library books serve as hecklers, upsetting the authority of the printed text, or as echoes, noisily parroting the meaning. But I'd miss the ink of them. As an adolescent, I discovered my sister's college texts in the attic. Sandy had been an English major. I feasted on *Jude the Obscure, Adam Bede, The Confessions of Saint Augustine, Immortal Poems.* And I devoured faddish, unassigned books—Ayn Rand's,

Kahlil Gibran's—with equal appetite. Sometimes the margins were wildcrafted with blue ballpoint notes in Sandy's hand. Between the pages of a paperback, I found a single red hair, unmistakably hers. A bookmark of the body, it seemed supernatural—recherché as the two recessive genes needed to express *auburn* and my sister.

13. I have a wardrobe of old, ink-covered clothes reserved for writing. Pen in hand, I'm a menace to the blank slate of everything in reach. The pen has become such a constant extension that I no longer remember I'm holding it. I stretch, and the movement is inscribed—on the sofa, the sheets, the cat. If invited to a literary costume party, I'd like to dress as Caddy Jellyby of *Bleak House,* whose "inky condition" parodies my state: "a jaded, and unhealthy-looking, though by no means plain girl, at the writing-table, who sat biting the feather of her pen, and staring at us. I suppose nobody ever was in such a state of ink. And, from her tumbled hair to her pretty feet, which were disfigured with frayed and broken satin slippers trodden down at heel, she really seemed to have no article of dress upon her, from a pin upwards, that was in its proper condition or its right place." Caddy serves as amanuensis to her mother, Mrs. Jellyby, a self-serving philanthropist and tireless generator of letters. In my reinscription, I cast Mrs. Jellyby as the draconian Muse. "Where are you, Caddy?" she says with a sweet smile. My copy of *Bleak House* belonged to my sister. Certain passages have been underwired with red ink, filaments delicate as hair.

14. Gatekeepers, judgmental structures, screens are invested with the power of entry and exclusion. They discriminate; censor; discern; play favorites. They have an agenda. They're critics. Or artists, functioning as silkscreens. In silkscreening, ink is forced—through a silk mesh with both pervious and impervious areas—onto a prepared ground. The artist's open and hidden interests are the blotchy screen through which the work is pressed.

15. October 1992: Well into work, I was floating around the silent house in a creative stupor, bumping into objects. Though the ringer was off, the phone continued its spectral trilling. We'd decided that the mechanism must vibrate slightly even when disconnected. The emergency phone was silent—as if all the fumble-fingered dialers of wrong numbers had entered a state of digital grace. I'd spoken to no one but Hank for who knows how long. In this somatic daze, I slumped in front of the screen and summoned my e-mail. Something from the English department appeared. What bureaucratic white noise—what evaluations, colloquia, surveys, forms—lay in wait? "What fresh hell is this?" I yawned, blasé as Dorothy Parker. But the adrenaline message on the screen pierced my nonchalance: My sister Pat was trying to reach us. It was urgent. I should call her immediately. I braced myself for some awful intelligence.

Pat had been phoning us for days. She'd been unable to get through because, as we soon discovered, the emergency phone had come unplugged by accident. As she talked, my mind filled with images like film rushes, nonsequential, nonverbal: Marleen, my sister Sandy's twenty-year-old daughter; a club in Argentina; disco dresses; drinks; a hold-up; film noir; smoke; gangsters; no shots fired. Marleen had lost consciousness. Marleen had died. Wait. No. A *health* club; tennis; juice drinks; a robbery; Marleen at the register; no shots fired. Marleen had lost consciousness. Marleen had died. Unbelief. Sandy's nineteen-year-old daughter Laura also had died suddenly, from natural causes, just two years earlier.

16. October 1992: When Laura died, Sandy and her husband George had tried to create a ceremony that would speak to that incommensurate loss. Everyone struggled to invent expressions for an event that had no precedent. Amateurs of mourning, we foundered in the new and terrible terrain. At Marleen's funeral, however, the sadness was magnified by a feeling of being over-rehearsed. We knew the ritual all too well. Familiarity—usually a comforting sensation—took on a horrific aspect. Repetition gathers its own significance: Recurring nightmares are the most frighteningly portentous.

While we were gathered for Laura's funeral, Marleen had shown everyone a photo album filled with snapshots of herself and her boyfriend, Mauro: bright occasions screened in laminate. Every time Mauro's name came up, Marleen would say, "I love him," with the same inflection: trusting, insouciant. Sometimes the voice tries to be a screen and fails. Sandy and George tried to sift the anguish from their voices, since their suffering would leave others at a loss. Though their composure was heroic, they sounded most distraught when asserting that they wouldn't be sad: Marleen was in heaven. The struggle between stoicism and emotion, between brave face and hysteria, creates pathos. The screen opens and closes. Burning and dodging. What's glimpsed in the hinge moment is most moving. *Burning in* increases the density of a photograph by exposing certain areas to extra light during enlargement. *Dodging* reduces the density of selected image areas by shading and masking the light. Both techniques create greater detail in the print.

Once women in mourning wore long black veils. These days, the face must serve as screen, and it fails. It leaks, rips, and before you know it, you're crying over your smile. At the wake, I felt sorry for Marleen being shown off when she was so dead. It was like being naked in front of everyone—except that she definitely would have looked better naked than dead. She was so attractive in life, and so unlike herself in death. In Scotland, a large head scarf is called a *screen*. I wanted to throw such a screen over her, anything to ease the exposure. But we don't do what we want to do on such occasions. Since Marleen's letters to my mother often began, "Hey Crazy Lady!" my mother wanted to put "Crazy Lady" in parentheses after "Grandma Fulton" when signing the funeral home's guest book. In deference to propriety, she refrained.

Funerals are mirror images of celebrations: They require announcements, programs, flowers, new outfits, photographs, and the preparation of a feast to be eaten afterward. On the day of Marleen's funeral, the sky glowed

like white organdy, silkscreening the light. Her handsome
Mauro spoke little English. His presence dramatized the
insufficiency of words. A little snow drifted down like pale
confetti. If funerals are inverse celebrations, this one was a
wedding.

17. A volatile folding word, *screen* encases dual meanings
within one another. *Screen* implodes and so allows its opposite to exist.

While the noun *screen* connotes an outer, visible layer,
the verb *to screen* means "to hide." Yet to screen a movie is to
show it, rather than obscure it. Screens are partitions that
conceal; but they also collapse into portability, revealing
all. As walls go, they're flimsy—temporary, nonweight-
bearing. When a screen is a sieve, it's both porous and im-
permeable: allowing and preventing passage. A screen can
be necessary or ornamental; solid or pierced. The opposing
definitions of *screen* remind me of stellar pairs, binary stars
in close proximity to one another orbiting about a common center of mass. Astronomers have noticed a feature
common to all binaries: The closer the two members lie to
one another, the more rapidly they swing about in their orbits. So *screen* oscillates under consideration.

18. November 1992: I called my mother. She said that last
Saturday was Laura's birthday. I remembered that we'd
been gathered to celebrate my mother's birthday when
Laura died.

This year on Laura's birthday, George and eight-year-
old Ali were in a bakery. Ali said, "Why don't we buy her a

cake?" So they did. My mother said, "It's better that they remember her birth than her death."

19. Iced with pastel Crisco, the glassed-in bakery cakes might remind a child of fairy tales. Snow White in her casket. The see-through slipper, poison-apple dramas. The wolf that huffs and puffs.

Breathing the hydrogenated fragrance of the bakery, of pastries dry and dainty as crumbs of marble dust. The cakes staring them down like frosted clocks. Considering. Thinking yes, why not celebrate her birth? Let them write "Laura" in a wreath of hemoglobin roses. Once home, the cake is an amazement of candles and mussed icing. Everyone inhales and thinks a wish. Everyone wishes that the radical hospitality of paradise has not been exaggerated. But no one has enough breath to extinguish the candles' little fiery bricks.

20. I wanted to write this in monument, but I just had ink.

21. I have a vested interest in the aesthetics of science. Since the sensibility of engineers and hackers affects the medium I use to compose my work, I'm curious about their worldview in particular. What tastes have informed and created computer culture? And what spoken or unspoken aesthetic makes itself felt in writer culture? Do the twain ever meet? Some of the same stereotypes have been used to characterize both groups: the mad scientist and mad poet; the science nerd and the bookworm.

"Elegance" is the most well-known component of

scientific aesthetics. The elegance of science is connected to simplicity, an investment that seems in conflict with science's ever-increasing complexity. Yet what seems elaborate to nonscientists can be a model of elegance to the expert. The hapless home computer user must purchase "upgrades" or find herself in possession of an obsolete system that cannot be repaired or replaced. Should her antiquated computer break, all of her files will become inaccessible. In order to keep up, she must spend hours installing and learning to use costly "improvements" upon a system that already seemed sufficient for her purposes. To me, the upgrades are extraneous: devised by manufacturers in order to sell more products. But to the virtuosos of hacking who created the novations, they are elegant.

In *The Second Self: Computers and the Human Spirit,* Sherry Turkle notes that hackers "built a computer culture around a widely shared aesthetic of simplicity, intelligibility, control, and transparency." The mainstream of American literature shares the same values. Most U. S. writers are adherents of the plain style, striving for transparency of surface and for meanings intelligible enough to be widely understood. Control is shown by a respect for craft or a revival of traditional forms. Turkle also points to hackers' fascination with recursive structures: the Escher stairway that climbs upward while folding back into itself, the Bach fugue that builds upon its inversions to end up where it began. In like fashion, postmodern literary works tend to be self-reflexive, "about" their own workings; rather than trying to awaken an emotive response in the reader, they create cerebral delight, the pleasure hackers locate in the Escher print or the fugue.

22. In the early '70s I had a radio show on a station owned by Rensselaer Polytechnic Institute (RPI). Like most of the djs, I was musically obsessed. The engineers, or "techies," on the other hand, were fixated on the station's broadcasting equipment, which they had built themselves, from the ground up. While I was on the air, an engineer would sometimes enter and gaze lovingly at the wall of bouncing meters and blinking lights—a sight that to my mind lacked the erotic halo of, say, a Martin D-28 guitar. Sometimes after a show we'd all go out to their restaurant of choice, the International House of Pancakes (IHOP), for a late dinner. The techies got to choose the restaurant because they owned the cars—rusty, oil-dribbling Volkswagens that smelled of sour milk and vinyl. Despite the marginal health of their vehicles, the engineers held an annual road rally. Rather than prizing the automobile's mechanism, they were excited by cars as a means of navigating a labyrinth under the constraint of rules and clues.

My future husband, Hank De Leo, was the station's program director and, unlike me, an RPI student. While at RPI, Hank had two roommates. The first, Strike Perlswigger, hoped to earn his living as a professional bowler. Strike seldom went to classes; he seemed to distill the requisite academic information from the thunderous air of the Troy Bowl, where he spent his days. Strike went from September to mid-November of 1970 without bathing. He evaded laundry by refusing to change his sheets or clothes. Many of the more gifted engineers ignored their own physicality. Flesh was not their concern. They were cerebral beings who one day would give birth to virtual reality and cyberspace. Learning of another student, Rob Rozecki, who also had roommate problems, Hank arranged to move in with him. Rob had very good hygiene; in fact, he was compulsively neat. He was besotted with Doris Day, and he knew every episode of *Star Trek* by heart. The engineers yearned for alternate worlds where technology reigned. As readers, they prized inventiveness—a sci-fi author's ability to resolve dilemmas without breaking self-created laws. Such writerly concerns as character and language were incidental. While many RPI students shared the *Star Trek* mania, Rob's former roommate, Claude Gideon, did not. Claude was obsessed with bridge. He never studied, but stayed up all night playing cards with a group of like-minded buddies. I'd never suspected that young men could be addicted to bridge—a game I associated with Junior League matrons. But bridge, like the road rally, offered the chance to master complex patterns while obeying clear-cut rules and working toward a trump.

More than simply serving as exemplars of dorky science nerds, these RPI engineers foreshadowed the values of computer culture. Their interest in mazes and the conquest of recondite structures would find its ideal expression in programming. Strike's apathy toward embodiment has been extended to the computer's body, whose physicality seems unimportant. Rob's Doris Day obsession was admittedly an uncommon affliction. Perhaps he was attracted to the reliability of her wholesome image and to her unavailability, which forestalled rejection. When Sherry Turkle asked hackers what they found in their relationship to the computer, their answers could be summarized as "safety." The relationship with the machine was more dependable than a relationship with a human being.

23. In my observation, writers are as fond of safety as engineers, though writers' quests for security take different forms. Hackers, according to Sherry Turkle, embrace "an ethic of total toleration for anything that in the real world would be considered strange." Writers are much less accepting. In fact, despite declarations of aesthetic risk-taking, writers seem afraid of nonconformity—on the page or the body. They limit their couture to camouflage. By courting invisibility, writers affect to transcend the superficiality of surface concerns. Instead of fashion innocents, they are disciples of a conservative, unspoken dress code that associates serious stature with earth tones. Better shabby than flashy. Better figuratively dead than literally red. The wish for plainness has no ethical dimension; the "Sackville-West Vest" from J. Peterman costs six times the price of the neon knit from Kmart. Romanticism tamed by folkloric elements is also a safe bet: All writers own those oatmeal-colored Irish fisherman sweaters.

While I'm being reductive, why not go all the way? If hackers are obsessives, writers are narcissists. If engineers are pragmatists, writers are connoisseurs—of wine, books, opera. Hackers gather at no-nonsense IHOP for physical sustenance; writers loiter in coffeehouses for imaginative fodder. Engineers decorate with Escher prints; writers choose Asian scrolls, Edward Hopper, Joseph Cornell. Engineers play bridge; writers play poker or blackjack. Hackers are Bach fans; writers are Rolling Stones fans. Hacking is the computer freak's drug. Drugs are the writer's drug: alcohol, nicotine, caffeine. The composite impression? Engineers are cerebral and analytical; writers are sensual and intuitive. And yet.

"When you are programming, you just build straight from your mind," a hacker tells Turkle. When lost in their work, writers also exist in a cyberspace of the mind, unaware of sensuality—screened from heat, cold, flies, hunger, darkness, e-mail, phone calls. A. R. Ammons, a poet who began as a scientist, ends his poem "Summer Session" with lines that acknowledge the biological and mechanistic underpinnings of imagination and unsettle the scientist/humanist binary:

> the head is my sphere:
> I'll look significant as I deal with
> mere wires of light, ghosts of
> cells, working there.

"I'll look significant" admits a self-conscious questioning of personal authority unknown to science. And rather than assert himself as prophet elect, a chosen conduit for the Muse, Ammons constructs the imaginative sphere in terms unknown to poetry: the poet's head as mysterious computer of flesh.

24. November 1992: My heart has always made me nervous. I don't like to contemplate my dependency on the common time it keeps so well, faithfully repolarizing itself between beats, muscling blood through the body. What an automaton the heart is. What a genius of insistence, mechanistic yet animate, the pulse like an insect trapped under the wrist's skin. Unthinking replication is a staple of the horrific. One ant might be an interesting subject for study, but thousands swarming together, identical, unfeeling, robotic, alive, would give many—give me—the creeps, the willies. The aesthetic deadliness of electronic screens arises in part from their likeness to one another: the thousands of computers as interchangeable as ants. And, like insects, computers raise questions concerning consciousness: At what point does a brain, "mere wires of light," come alive? When it becomes self-aware? When it shows a will to live? The heart scares me because I can feel its importance physically. Most of the body's major organs are more reticent: The brain hums along so quietly that the ancients believed thought lived in our noisy hearts. Now, of course, the heart symbolizes emotion, not analysis. Each beat offers another chance for revelation. Repetition can take on a powerful beauty if it manages variation while retaining the residue of its original meaning. The recurring lines in blues songs create fresh implications with each saying—unlike the drilling of the phone. After Marleen's funeral, we turned the ringer on again. Sandy called and told me about visiting her friend Rosa, who'd had a stroke and lost the ability to say anything other than "I love you." By shading

this phrase with different tones, Rosa managed to convey a wide range of emotion and meaning. She could say, "I love you" so that her family heard, for instance, "don't do that," "open the door," "I'm angry with you," or "I love you."

25. I once heard a psychologist remark that obsessive-compulsives were the most boring patients. I can see why. Yet the opposite is also true: Obsessions—because they hint at vast stores of passion and laser focus—are fascinating. Computer junkies are a source of concern: An Internet Addiction Group has formed to help the screenstruck. (This group "meets" onscreen, a choice that seems akin to holding an AA meeting in an open bar.) It's easy to imagine the lethal powers of electronic objects. Books, in contrast, seem more benign. "When you go to a bookstore after work, thus arriving home late at night, do you lie about where you have been, telling your spouse you were at a bar?" Tom Raabe asks in *Biblioholism: The Literary Addiction*, a book that parodies the self-help market. What's the term for someone who fetishizes the materiality of the book itself: who wants to crawl inside it, feed upon it, dwell in it? Bookworm? Bibliophile? Are there negative effects of book addiction? "I started reading *The Catcher in the Rye*, and I couldn't put it down until I got to the end. And I read it again. Then I held it between my hands. I put it against my face, and inhaled deeply, drinking in the aroma, that sort of faintly antiseptic smell of a new book, through my nostrils and my skin. And I felt: 'Here is a way . . .'" Mark David Chapman, the man who killed John Lennon, describes his favorite book.

26. November 1992: My heart has let me down more than once. I've learned a technical vocabulary to describe its fickleness: *syncope* (loss of consciousness), *prodrome* (sensations experienced in the seconds before fainting), *epinephrine* (adrenaline). The sudden deaths of my nieces sent me back to analyze my own medical history. When Laura died, doctors reassured Sandy that her other children were safe. They were wrong: Marleen. As soon as we returned from her funeral, Hank began researching the causes of sudden death in young adults. I began archiving the times I'd fainted or nearly fainted, scrutinizing the circumstances and adding to Hank's composite portrait of the undiagnosed condition. Along with necessary external details came unwanted images of the internal struggle to hold fast to consciousness. I remembered the times I'd fallen far into unbeing and come back terrified by a new knowledge of the nothing screen. How dreamlessly unlike sleep it was. How zero. I came back terribly impressed. Awareness has a sculptural, 3-D quality: The sensorium is experienced in the round, as if the depth, pitch, texture, taste, and scent of intelligibility were welded to the insides of our heads. I recalled the deflation of this sphere, the flattening of dimension to a screen of fiery pixels, snippets, vermiculite glittering, as vision swarmed to buzzing snow, a prodrome like the blizzard screen of no reception on TVs. Back came the loss of face that is loss of world, as I assembled my collection of helplessness.

In 1977, I almost passed out while trying to make a case for my aunt with her psychiatrist over the phone. "But my dear little girl . . ." he said, and the patriarchal maw of medical authority seemed to devour all the oxygen in the room. My aunt was at the mercy of this institutionalized egotism. For her sake, I fought to repress my anger and remain polite, an effort that almost made me black out. If I fainted, her shrink would brand me a hysteric. This realization kept me conscious while my mother's kitchen shifted and fizzed in place.

My nearest near-death experience occurred in grad school. I'd gathered my nerve and spoken to my advisors about the male domination of academe. "Women are motes of dust around here." I hadn't expected this pronouncement to be met with sympathy, but it was. "I think I'm going to faint," I said. Was this some kind of joke, the angels-of-desire-poetess swoon? I surprised them by dropping to the floor, deeply unconscious. I had every test available at the time, but the doctors were mystified.

This is just a short list of *losing it*. There were many other instances. To my own profile, I added those of Laura and Marleen. Laura had experienced a single episode of unconsciousness before the one that took her life. After the alarm sounded one morning, her roommate noticed that she was struggling to breathe. The paramedics were called; she was revived; tests were done; but as with me, nothing was found to be wrong. A year later, she died in her room, apparently while sleeping. The phone was ajar, and Sandy had wondered if she'd been trying to call for help. Before Marleen's sudden death during a hold-up, she had never lost consciousness.

As I reviewed these memories, Hank gazed at the computer screen, looking up abstracts on Medline, a database.

By searching under *cardiac, sudden death, syncope,* he came up with a huge list of articles. About half were available as abstracts on the computer. He read those and looked up others in the University of Michigan's medical library. He studied textbooks, seeking symptoms that matched the constellation surrounding Laura, Marleen, and me. By piecing details together, he was led to something called Jervell-Lange-Nielsen syndrome. But there was one confounding detail: The condition existed only in deaf children. Using this syndrome as a lead, Hank searched further on Medline and came up with four articles on an inherited disorder called Long QT syndrome. After reading these, he called Sandy and told her to be sure to have her doctor rule out this disorder. "I think I've found it," he said to me.

Long QT is a rare, genetic disease in which the electrocardiographs of some sufferers show an infinitesimally prolonged "QT interval," hence the condition's name. The medical histories of afflicted families reveal instances of fainting and inexplicable sudden death. In normal people, both exercise and the fight-or-flight mechanism cause a release of epinephrine (adrenaline), which increases the heart rate. In the case of long QT sufferers, however, an electrical defect prevents the heart from repolarizing after a massive influx of adrenaline. The resulting arrhythmia leads to fainting and in some cases cardiac arrest. Fainting episodes occur under physical or emotional stress. Loss of consciousness also is triggered by sudden noises, particularly if the subject is startled while sleeping. The articles recommended "that affected individuals avoid . . . exposure to abrupt auditory stimuli. This can be accomplished by eliminating alarm clocks, door bells, and phone ringing from the household." Hank speculated that the phone had startled Laura from a nap; this would explain why it had been found ajar. In Marleen's case, as in mine, the emotional component of the disease was telling. The literature cited instances of children in the nineteenth century who dropped dead while being scolded in school. Fainting resulted from a feeling of powerlessness; it was a response to an oppression that allowed for neither fight nor flight. Like a hold-up. Like misogyny. "But I can't be right," Hank concluded. "I'm not a doctor."

When Sandy relayed Hank's suspicion to her cardiologist, he said it was as if a light went on. Apparently Hank had diagnosed the disorder, and he couldn't have done so without the computer. The condition can be treated with beta blockers, drugs that protect the heart by building a chemical screen in the body. They block the beta reception sites so that epinephrine cannot reach them and make the heart race. Some beta blockers work only on the heart, and some cross the blood-brain barrier, a screening device that allows certain chemicals into the brain while refusing others. But these are clumsy descriptions of intricate effects, beyond current comprehension. *Behold, I shew you a mystery; We shall not all sleep, but we shall all be changed.*

27. Consider the leafiness of books, the peeling that is reading. Consider the peeling that is writing. By the end, I feel exfoliated.

Writing this, I was blinded by the paper, the screen, the events recounted. The material called for shades. Called for language to screen the emotional loudwork. Language as acoustic shadow: an area that inexplicably retains its reticence despite a great noise nearby.

28. I wanted to write this in diamond, but I just had blood. I used the hand's most important attribute, opposition, to hold the pen, scissors, glue. I marred the page, wrist pulsing against the notebook's cool seersucker, its ticking checking my drifting sentences and chilling my recklessness. I used paper sacrificed from the gold fingerprints inside trees: high acid foolscap with no watermark, I see, holding to the light a scrap of flimsy, its edges grunged with dust.

1995

II

~~

Poetics

Subversive Pleasures

Of Formal, Free, and Fractal Verse: Singing the Body Eclectic

For the past three years, there's been a critical outburst against the "formlessness" of much contemporary poetry. This critical bias defines and defends a narrow notion of form, based largely on a poem's use of regular meter. J. V. Cunningham defined form more generously as "that which remains the same when everything else is changed. . . . The form of the simple declarative sentence in English is the same in each of its realizations." Hence, by changing the content of any free verse poem while retaining (for example) its irregular meter and stanzaic length, one can show its form. And if a poem's particular, irregular shape were used again and again, this form eventually might be given a name, such as "sonnet."

It seems to me that good free and formal verse have a lot in common. In fact, I'd venture to say that both are successful in proportion to their approximation of one another. Often, a metered poem contains several lines so irregular we might as well call them free. The poems of Donne, Blake, Dickinson, and Hopkins are frequently polyrhythmic, and substitutions of one metrical foot for another are common in both classical and Romance verse forms. We know that perfectly regular rhythm is a sure sedative to the ear. It follows that the variations rather than the regularities of metered verse give the work of its great practitioners a signature charm. On the other hand, vers libre frequently contains an underlying beat that comes close to regular measure. Richard D. Cureton, writing on the prosody of free verse, observes: "If we are intersted in the rhythmic structure of a poetic text, the appropriate question is not *Is this text rhythmic?* but *At what level and to what degree is this text rhythmic?*"

Regular meter is pleasing because we can readily anticipate the rhythm of the lines to come. The pleasure lies in having our expectations fulfilled. Irregular meter, on the other hand, pleases because it delivers something unforeseen, though, in retrospect, well-prepared for. Free verse is most compelling when most rhythmic: The poet must shape the irregular rhythms of language to underscore, contradict, or in some way reinforce the poem's content. Occasional lapses into regular meter frame the more jagged lines and help the reader appreciate their unpredictable music. For example, when a long iambic line is followed by a spondee or two, the rhythms are thrown into high relief. It's a little like placing a swatch of red next to a swatch of green: When juxtaposed, these complements increase each other's vibrancy.

Prosody provides a comprehensive means of discussing traditional metered verse. But free verse is seldom subjected to any such systematic analysis in our literary magazines. There is, however, an insightful and growing body of literature by scholars of prosody, linguistics, and musicology on the rhythms of free verse. I think of Stephen Cushman's book *Williams and the Meaning of Measure* (which in advancing our understanding of Williams's prosody advances our understanding of free verse); Charles O. Hartman's *Free Verse, An Essay on Prosody*; Grosvenor W. Cooper and Leonard B. Meyer's work on musical rhythm; linguist Ray Jackendoff's model of hierarchical structure in language as applied to music; David Stein and David Gil's linguistic insights concerning prosodic structures; phonologist Elizabeth Selkirk's study of the relationship between sound and structure; Donald Westling's syntactic theory of enjambment, which he calls "grammetric scissoring"; and Richard D. Cureton's analysis of the "myths and muddles" of traditional scansion. However, to judge from their opinions, many of the critics, essayists, and poets holding forth in our literary journals are unaware of such studies, and consequently, of any of the newer theories of prosody. As reviewers, they are content to describe the content of the poems and praise the poet's skillful use of blank verse. If the poet does not write in blank verse, or in any of the more obvious metrical forms, the poems simply are not scanned. It's as if the reader, upon scanning two lines and finding dissimilar rhythms, gives up the search and regards the poem as a formless mass of words. I'd argue, however, that all poems have a shape—whether it's pleasing or perceptible to the reader is something else. It's time that we, as poets, readers, and critics, begin to discern and analyze the subtle, governing structures of free verse and to talk more about its operative tropes.

Rather than placing the emphasis upon the formal

devices of regular rhyme and meter, why not consider the whole panoply of design and pattern? As J. V. Cunningham noted, "A poem is a convergence of forms. It is the coincidence of forms that locks in the poem." Prosody is too specific an instrument to describe all the pattern-making possibilities of verse. To devote our analytical energy and aesthetic passion solely to metrical form is to deny the existence (and importance) of the myriad structural options available. At the very least, responsible formal analysis must define the details it chooses to disregard.

What are some of the formal schemes awaiting our investigation? As a beginning, we might look at the smaller linguistic units that influence or enlarge a text, such as allusions, puns, apostrophes, and pronouns with their function of insinuating gender. Or we could dissect the poem's larger governing organization: its rhetorical questions, conceits, virtuoso listings, registers of diction, and lineations. Cushman effectively argues that Williams wrote a prosody of enjambment, a counterpointing of visual line and syntactic unit. We might analyze the poem's enjambment within a syntactic-grammatical context, or consider its use of resistent or resolved line-breaks. As Cureton notes, enjambments alone can dramatize the "curve of emotion" in the text, from relaxation to tension to resolution. It's also important to consider the poem's visual form on the page, which changes the way we hear the words. Is the use of white space mimetic, abstract, or temporal; do such effects serve to emphasize or to defamiliarize the line? We also should be attentive to the poem's use of reiterative devices such as epanalepsis (ending a sentence with its own opening words—*Leaves of Grass* has many examples), refrain, chorus, or repetend (a repetition that occurs irregularly or partially, as in Delmore Schwartz's poem "Do the Others Speak of Me, Mockingly, Maliciously"). And, as Jonathan Holden has pointed out, we can regard many contemporary poems as analogues that borrow their form from letters, horoscopes, TV listings, fugues, etc. The deep logic of a poem may be based upon such concepts as the microcosm moving toward macrocosm; the linkage of opposites (oxymoron); stasis; dynamism; and equilibrium. Because English, unlike the Romance languages, does not contain a multitude of rhymes, we need to appreciate and make use of aural difference rather than similitude. French and Spanish poetry can afford to value sameness of sound, but we must value the variety of our word endings, which contribute so much to the irregular texture and attendant richness of our language. With this in mind, we might consider the orchestration of verse through echo (assonance, consonance, irregular rhyme, front rhyme, half-rhyme, accords, and so on). It's also interesting to analyze the operative rhetorical strategies, such as paralipsis (a passing over with brief mention in order to emphasize the suggestiveness of what was omitted) and parataxis (placing words or phrases next to one another without coordinating connections). In rhythm, we could turn our attention to the use of accentual or syllabic verse, to irregular meter that enforces content (i.e., the tension of strong-stress rhythms or the relaxation of pyrrhic, atonic lines). If we wish to be more ambitious, Cureton's theory of hierarchical scansion provides a formal mechanism for representing comparable rhythmic shapes at different linguistic levels. (The major levels are narrative, syntactic, and phonological.) We also could consider the formal devices of asyndeton (omission of conjunctions, common in the work of A. R. Ammons or May Swenson, for example) and its opposite, poly-syndeton (repetition of conjunctions).

The last two devices, though opposite in principle, both have the effect of making the content more vivacious and emphatic. In fact, I hope that discussions of form will lead to considerations of content. Without this obligation, formalism becomes a comfortable means of avoiding re-sponsibility for what is being said. It's safer to speak of metrical finesse or blunders than to appraise the subjects poets choose. In too many reviews, I find lengthy *descriptions* of content, which do little more than paraphrase. Descrip-tive criticism is fine as a place to begin, but few critics go on to question why particular subjects continue to be chosen (while other topics suffer poetic banishment). Brave criti-cism might ask, what is this subject's value to me, as reader? And, what worldviews, values, or secular mythologies are implicit in the poet's stance? Surely we must consider the cultural assumptions questioned or supported by the text, as well as the style in which these concerns are voiced.

Quantum physics teaches us that the act of measuring changes what is being measured. It follows that the act of measuring language (by putting it into regular meter) must change what is being said. Part of the resistance toward metered verse is coupled with a belief that passion or sin-cerity evaporates when the poet takes to counting stresses and feet. I'd contend that the content of metered poems can, at times, take on a greater urgency by means of a regular rhythm. The exigencies of form foster such careful choices that each word can become a palimpsest of implication. In fact, I value the qualities of rhythm and multidimensional language in all poetry, whether the meter is regular or not. If it is true (and I'm not sure it is) that the poetry of social commitment is often written in irregular meters, perhaps this is because the poets write from a tradition other than that of English prosody. We should respect the richness of such cultural contexts. It is ethnocentric to regard traditional English prosody as the one sure means of writing poetry. Such a stance also fails to consider the changes our language underwent in becoming American.

Several critics have lamented the repose of free verse into stylistic plainness. Mary Kinzie has even coined a new literary term, "the rhapsodic fallacy," which speaks to the problem. Kinzie's position is too complex to summarize here, but the rhapsodic fallacy describes, in part, the equation of a prosaic style with authenticity of engagement. The observation is an important one. Have we forgotten that the plain style represents a conscious aesthetic choice, rather than a simple outpouring of pure feeling? The word *style* itself points to language as a selective construct. As such, flat-style poetry is no more "sincere" or "engaged" than are the constructs of metered verse. And when the majority of poets choose to write in a given style, one suspects it is becoming a convention, as well as an artful device. (However, free verse is not to be equated with plain style or any other calcified aesthetic. If it were, there would be nothing free about it.) Perhaps readers are bored by the plethora of poems in simple language; perhaps they feel manipulated by the poet's guileless pose. As a solution to the monotony of flat-style poetry, Mary Kinzie calls for a return to "those forms associated with the eighteenth century: formal satire, familiar epistle, georgic, pastoral . . ." Lamenting the blurring of high and low styles into "the low lyrical shrub" that is contemporary poetry, she would have poets write in clearly delineated genres. This stance supposes that by segregating high style from low and by restricting subject one may write "heart-piercing" poetry, to borrow Kinzie's adjective. But hearts are subjective entities, steadfast only in their refusal to be reliably pierced by aesthetic programs—that's the great thing about them! They remain willful little blobs, despite our best efforts at persuasion.

Robert Hillyer's *In Pursuit of Poetry* classifies the language of verse into two styles: "the rhetorical, heightened and dignified, and the conversational, informal and familiar. . . . Each has its dangers as well as its virtues; the first may become bombastic, the second prosaic." I don't agree that the language of verse falls neatly into binary registers of diction. If so, where would Chaucer or Shakespeare land in the aesthetic shakedown, combining as they do the dignified with the familar, the high with the low? To my mind, great work is large enough to include a multiplicity of styles, tones, and subjects. However, our attention for the moment is on the two styles Hillyer describes rather than the wide diversity of work he excludes. I think his description of the dangers common to high and low styles holds true. Poets are just as likely to write rhapsodic epics that ring false as they are to write fallacious, plain-style lyrics. If Mary Kinzie's program should catch on, we'd undoubtedly see vast numbers of insufferable "genre" poems, written to fit the bill. Isn't this what happened in the eighteenth century?

Perhaps the impulse for simplicity began as a corrective when the formal post–World War II poem was felt to have degenerated (through imitation and overuse) into a polished veneer of language. The veneer might have been gold plate or marble, but everyone suddenly felt a yen for solid oak—or Formica. And for the past twenty years the majority of poets have forsaken the primrose path for the plain one, which now begins, in its turn, to feel like an aesthetic shortcut.

In the largest terms, the search for a style is a search for a language that does justice to our knowledge of how the world works. According to one ordering of the canon, poetry has consistently reflected the worldviews of its age. Thus, in the Middle Ages, when everyone believed the world was created and run by a divine being, and earthquakes were viewed as a result of God's intervention (rather than of shifting plates), poetry mirrored the religious hierarchy. Dante's conception of the world as a series of spheres—the enormous heavens, the crystalline planets, the earth's elements, and the seven circles of hell—gave everyone a proper place, from king to serf. Newtonian physics replaced the hierarchical model with a physics of ordinary matter ruled by mathematical laws. And the literary climate of the early eighteenth century mirrored the harmony of a universe seen as a great, logical clock. The lawful and orderly cosmos was taken for proof of God's presence and goodness. Christian Wolff evolved the first system of German Rationalism from aspects of Newton's *Principia*. And the idea of Nature as order (prominent in *Principia*) also influenced such representative eighteenth-century literature as Pope's "Essay on Man." Later in the century, the rise of democracy, which posits an equality between parts of the social machinery, found expression in an enthusiasm for the simpler modes of folk poetry. And by the early nineteenth century, Wordsworth's "Preface to Lyrical Ballads" argued for the democratic readmission of "rustic" speech and subjects into English poetry.

Just as Newton shattered the medieval hierarchical conception of the world, modern physics has smashed Newton's mechanistic clockwork. Modernism may indeed have been a true reflection of Einstein's physics. He, after all, never accepted quantum theory and held to the old-fashioned hope that a realistic vision of the world could be congruent with the quantum facts. In his autobiography, he states, "I still believe in the possibility of a model of reality—that is, of a theory which represents things themselves and not merely the probability of their occurrence." If we substitute "ideas" for "probability," we have a restatement of Williams's famous "No ideas but in things."

However, Niels Bohr's claim that there is no deep reality represents the prevailing view of contemporary quantum physics. Bohr insisted, "There is no quantum world. There is only an abstract quantum description." Physicist N. David Mermin summed up Bohr's antirealist position by stating, "We now know that the moon is demonstrably not there when nobody looks." Perhaps popular literature and culture have made people aware of this and other quantum theories, such as the view that reality consists of a steadily increasing number of parallel universes; that consciousness creates reality; or that the world is twofold, consisting of potentials and actualities. Heisenberg's uncertainty principle, which forbids accurate knowledge of a quantum particle's position and momentum, is certainly well known. A truly engaged and contemporary poetry must reflect this knowledge. As a body of literature it might synthesize such disparate theories into a comprehensive metaphor for the way the world appears to us today. Or it may be that synthesis and unity are fundamentally premodern concepts. In this case, a fragmentary, diffuse literature is the perfect expression of our world knowledge. In a sense, our search for a language mirrors science's search for a quantum reality. As Nobel laureate Richard Feynman remarked, "I think it is safe to say that no one understands quantum mechanics. Do not keep saying to yourself, if you can possibly avoid it, 'but how can it be like that?' Nobody knows how it can be like that." This reluctance to attempt meaning is clearly reflected in postmodern literature and deconstruction, where "meaning" is no longer the issue.

Perhaps it shouldn't surprise us, then, that the term *free verse* has lost its meaning and become a convenient catchall whereby any piece of writing with wide margins may be defended as poetry. Pound's advice was to "compose in the sequence of the musical phrase, not in sequence of a metronome." He didn't say poetry should have no music at

free verse had to begin w verse
Benoit Mandelbrot

all. And founding mother Amy Lowell preferred the term
"cadenced verse" to vers libre, noting that "to depart satis-
factorily from a rhythm it is first necessary to have it."
Frost, of course, thought that writing free verse was like
playing tennis without a net. But surely the Net-Nabbing
Freeform Tennis Club would waste no time in inventing
another restriction. They might move the game indoors,
use the walls as obstacles, and call their new sport "rac-
quetball." In the same way, when free verse absconded with
the net, it created other means of limitation. The best
poets of free verse work long and hard to structure their
poems. But as readers and critics, we have been slow in
finding ways to discern and discuss the orders of their irregular form. But form *is* regularity, you might protest. If
so, how much regularity constitutes pattern and structure?

Perfect Euclidean forms occur rather rarely in nature.
Instead we find a dynamic world made up of quantities
constantly changing in time, a wealth of fluctuations—
such as variations in sunspots and the wobbling of the
earth's axis. The mathematician Benoit Mandelbrot observed that "25 or 30 years ago, science looked at things that
were regular and smooth." In contrast, he became intrigued
by what are called chaotic phenomena: the occurrence of
earthquakes; the way our neurons fire when we search our
memories; patterns of vegetation in a swamp; price jumps
in the stock market; turbulence in the weather; the distrib-
ution of galaxies; and the flooding of the Nile. Mandelbrot saw similarities in shapes so strange that fin de siècle
mathematicians termed them "pathological" and "mon-

Earlier scientist investigates regularity rules [handwritten margin note]

Euclid's lines, planes, and spheres are individual — fractals replicate the big in the small is infinite complexity [handwritten top note]

sters." These earlier scientists never supposed that such "monstrous" shapes bore any relation to reality. Mandel-brot, on the contrary, believed they described nature much better than ideal forms. He found that certain chaotic structures (including the preceding list) contained a deep logic or pattern. In 1975, he coined the word *fractals* (from the Latin *fractus,* meaning "irregular or fragmented") to de-scribe such configurations. (Pound's injunction to "break the pentameter" is nicely implicit in the term.)

To put it simply, each part of a fractal form replicates the form of the entire structure. Increasing detail is re-vealed with increasing magnification, and each smaller part looks like the entire structure, turned around or tilted a bit. This isn't true of the classical Euclidean forms of lines, planes, and spheres. For example, when a segment of a cir-cle is subjected to increasing magnification it looks increas-ingly like a straight line rather than a series of circles. But a fractal form has a substructure (we might say a subtext) that goes on indefinitely, without reposing into ordinary curves. The bark patterns on oak, mud cracks in a dry riverbed, a broccoli spear—these are examples of fractal forms: irregular structures containing just enough regular-ity so that they can be described. Such forms are, at least to my perception, quite pleasing. Like free verse, they zig and zag, spurt and dawdle, while retaining an infinite complex-ity of detail. (In contrast, formal verse travels at a regular pace and is less dynamic, less potentially volatile.) The fas-cination of these intricate forms ("the fascination of what's difficult," you might say) indicates that we don't

non objective art is fractal
asymmetry   turbulence

need an obvious or regular pattern to satisfy our aesthetic or psychological needs. Nonobjective art, which often reflects the fractal patterns of nature, makes the same point. In fact, asymmetrical or turbulent composition may be the essence of twentieth-century aesthetics.

There are two kinds of fractals: geometric and random. The geometric type repeats an identical pattern at various scales. As a corollary, imagine a poem structured on the concept of the oxymoron. The linkage of opposites on the smallest scale might appear in antonymic word usage; on a larger scale in one stanza's ability to oppose or reverse the form and content of another; and at the grandest scale in the poem's overall form becoming a paradoxical or self-reflexive contradiction of content. Thus far, the poem could be a sonnet or an ode. After all, ordered forms about chaos were rather popular in the eighteenth century. But let's suppose that the poem's rhythm is also oxymoronic: that a smooth, regular line is purposefully followed by a rambunctious or jagged utterance. If repeated throughout, this juxtaposition would constitute the poem's metrical form. Random fractals, to consider another possibility, introduce some elements of chance. In the composition of poetry, this could be as simple a factor as opening a book at random and using the metrical pattern happened upon as a contributing factor in the verse.

In his essay "How Long Is the Coast of Britain?" Mandelbrot showed that a coastline, being infinitely long with all of its microscopic points and inlets, is best treated as a random fractal rather than an approximation of a straight line. While complication is characteristic of coastlines, there is also a great degree of order in their structures, which are self-similar. A self-similar mechanism is, formally speaking, a kind of cascade, with each stage creating details smaller than those of the preceding stages. As Mandelbrot writes, "Each self-similar fractal has a very specific kind of unsmoothness, which makes it more complicated than anything in Euclid." Fractal form, then, is composed of constant digressions and interruptions in rhythm.

Scientists are just beginning to uncover all the events, things, and processes that can be described through fractals. Clouds follow fractal patterns. (Incidentally, you'll notice that the previous sentence is composed of three trochaic feet, with one extra stressed syllable at the beginning. How regular! And irregular.) Since fractals can be illustrated by means of computer graphics, it's possible to *see* the basic fractal properties in all their intricacy and beauty.

Mandelbrot's discoveries could change the way we look at the world, and, by extension, the way we look at poetry. Certainly the discovery of order within the turbulent forms of nature should encourage us to search for patterns within the turbulent forms of art. Fractal form may allow a more precise measure of those poetic shapes that aren't governed by the strategies of prosody. Though it's been around for over one hundred years (if one counts Whitman), in regard to free verse we're a little like people who've never seen a two-dimensional image and can't, at first, ascertain that the shapes in photographs form faces or bodies. We must develop our ability to recognize subtle, hidden, and original patterns as well as the time-honored (and more obvious) metrical orders of prosody. And we might pay more attention to the irregularities of traditional formal verse, the freedoms and deviations within a context of similitude and correctness. After all, deviance can't exist without an orderly context from which to differ.

Since free verse has become a misnomer, perhaps we could use the irregular yet beautifully structured forms of nature as analogues and call the poetry of irregular form *fractal verse*. Its aesthetic might derive from the structural limitations of self-similar fractal form. I offer the following as a tentative exploration of fractal precepts: Any line when examined closely (or magnified) will reveal itself to be as richly detailed as was the larger poem from which it was taken; the poem will contain an infinite regression of details, a nesting of pattern within pattern (an endless imbedding of the shape into itself, recalling Tennyson's idea of the inner infinity); digression, interruption, fragmentation and lack of continuity will be regarded as formal functions rather than lapses into formlessness; all directions of motion and rhythm will be equally probable (isotropy); the past positions of motion, or the preceding metrical pattern, will not necessarily affect the poem's future evolution (independence).

Poems are linguistic models of the world's working. Now our knowledge of form includes the new concept of manageable chaos, along with the ancient categories of order and chaos. If order is represented by the simple Euclidean shapes of nature and by metered verse, chaos might be analogous to failed free verse and gibberish. (It's somehow reassuring that chaos is still with us, evident in natural forms that show no underlying pattern). And manageable chaos or fractal form might find its corollary in fractal poetry. One thing seems certain: Our verse should be free to sing the wildly harmonious structures that surround and delight us, the body eclectic, where botany ends and milkweed begins.

1986

Poems are linguistic models of the world's working.

Fractal Amplifications: Writing in Three Dimensions

Uring the last quarter of the twentieth century, science has turned away from regular and smooth systems in order to investigate more chaotic phenomena. Rather than being divided into the classical binaries of order and entropy, form now can be regarded as a continuum expressing varying degrees of the pattern and repetition that signal structure. As architect Nigel Reading writes, "Pure Newtonian causality is an incorrect (finite) view, but then again, so is the aspect of complete uncertainty and (infinite) chance." The nature of reality now is "somewhere . . . between." ("Dynamical Symmetries") It occurs to me that this shift in focus makes itself felt within literature as postmodernism. In any case, the poetry I am calling "fractal" shares many defining traits of that contested term: postmodern. Since other contemporary poetries show a greater allegiance to romantic, confessional, or formalist traditions, fractal aesthetics describe—or predict, if you will—only one feature of the topography. I say "predict" because I hope these remarks will suggest future vistas. When poets address aesthetics, their own work inevitably shades their views. I write from perceptions of where my poems have lately been and where they're likely headed.

Earlier drafts of this essay included a few exemplary poems by contemporaries, but these specific instances became points of contention as readers argued with my choices and proposed their own. Perhaps this was inevitable: The short poems suitable for inclusion in an essay cannot illuminate the maximalist aesthetic I describe. And since I am proposing a largely untried poetics, a poetics more emergent than existent, few examples are available. The insistence on examples, moreover, seems a way of saying, "Is this a real poetics, or did you make it up yourself?" The honest answer, unwelcome as it might be, is that I am in the process of making it up, in and from the whole cloth of my poems. There is no fractal school of poets at this writing. Such a group will exist only if readers imagine or build, identify or locate, the representative works themselves. Before declaring a poem "fractal," I suggest that you ask whether comic, bawdy, banal, or vulgar lines are spliced to lyrical, elegiac, or gorgeous passages. Ask whether resistant (dense) surfaces are juxtaposed with transparent (lucid) areas. Those features seem fundamental. They offer an obvious place to begin.

~~

In the seventies, the mathematician Benoit Mandelbrot found that certain structures once thought to be "chaotic" contained a deep logic or pattern. The communication between roots and leaves; the oscillations of cotton futures;

the movement of spiraling funnel galaxies; the branching of arteries and veins; and the curved, nonlinear structure of space-time itself are examples of chaotic phenomena found to contain fractal designs. Mandelbrot coined the word *fractals* (from the Latin *fractus*, meaning "irregular or fragmented") to describe such configurations. In my 1986 essay, "Of Formal, Free, and Fractal Verse: Singing the Body Eclectic," I suggested that science's insights concerning turbulence might help us to describe traits common to the poetry of volatile (rather than fixed) form. I proposed that we view the eccentric yet beautifully structured forms of nature as analogues and call the poetry of irregular form *fractal verse.*

Just as fractal science analyzed the ground between chaos and Euclidean order, fractal poetics could explore the field between gibberish and traditional forms. It could describe and make visible a third space: the nonbinary *in-between.* Consider water. At low temperatures, it is fully ordered in the form of ice; at higher temperatures it becomes fluid and will not retain its shape. The stage between ice (order) and liquid (chaos) is called the transition temperature. Fractal poetics is interested in that point of metamorphosis, when structure is incipient, all threshold, a neither-nor. Over the past decade, scientists have come to view fractals as particular instances within the larger field of complexity theory. While retaining the term *fractal poetry*, I hope to suggest ways in which complexity theory might amplify the possibilities of such a poetics. (A poem is not a complex adaptive system: The comparison is analogical, not literal.)

My tentative 1986 prospectus for postmodern fractal poetry suggested that digression, interruption, fragmentation, and lack of continuity be regarded as formal functions rather than lapses into formlessness and that all shifts of rhythm be equally probable. Of course, disjunction also informed high modernist aesthetics. Postmodernism seems more an elaboration of that tradition than a wholly new formation. The new always contains aspects of the old: Novation springs from the existent. Hand-me-downs are recombined, and during the process freshness (a strange entity that might seem wrong or counterintuitive at first) seeps in. Perhaps it's nothing new to say that newness is a composite. Rather than elide this truism, however, postmodernism rejects originality and stresses the inevitability of appropriation in creative work. The prefix *post* signals a foundational debt and an unabashedly reactive position that departs from a modernist make-it-new credo.

Common sense, moreover, suggests that contemporary work must be inflected by the pressures of its day regardless of the poet's willed intentions. Even a strenuous attempt to duplicate a previous aesthetic would fall into the temporal gap and become, at best, ventriloquism. Difference is a given. Describing that shift—the changes in poetry's metabolism across generations and time—is an ongoing project for scholars and poets. Recent scholarship has suggested alternative modernisms that enlarge the view. In this essay, however, Pound's well-known "A Few Don'ts by an Imagiste" and Eliot's *The Waste Land* will serve as high-profile reference points. Pound and Eliot, more than any other literary figures, have defined literary modernism dur-

Ugh!

ing the twentieth century. Pound's directives were the catechism of poetry workshops during the sixties and seventies. As a result, his precepts possibly have exerted a greater effect on contemporary poetry than they did on the poetry of his own day.

~~

In *Hidden Order*, John H. Holland writes that complex systems possess "a dynamism" that is different from the static structure of a computer chip or snowflake, which are merely complicated. Complex systems are balanced on the edge of chaos, where the components "never quite lock in place, and yet never quite dissolve into turbulence either." A rainforest, the immune system, the economy, and a developing embryo are examples of complex adaptive systems. In poetics, Holland's "dynamism" makes itself felt in eccentric forms that share broad similarities, in contrast to more "static" received forms with specific similarities. This essay describes those broadly similar traits and calls the poetry that shares them "fractal." Lest my descriptions seem to imply otherwise, I must assert that aesthetics are not a progress narrative: It isn't getting better all the time. It's getting different all the time.

On the ground between between set forms and aimlessness a poem can be spontaneous and adaptive—free to think on its feet rather than fulfill a predetermined scheme. In a departure from Romantic ideals, fractal aesthetics suppose that "spontaneous" effects can be achieved through calculated as well as ad libitum means. Thus "spontaneity" does not refer to a method of composition but to linguistic gestures that feel improvisatory to the reader. Riffing and jamming, rough edge and raw silk—such wet-paint effects take the form of long asides, discursive meanderings, and sudden shifts in diction or tone. By such means "spontaneity" becomes a structural component of the poem.

Complex adaptive systems do not seek equilibrium or try to establish balance; they exist in unfolding and "never get there." As Holland says, "the space of possibilities is too vast; they have no practical way of finding the optimum." Like complex systems, fractal poetry exists within a vast array of potentialities: It is a maximalist aesthetic. High modernism also was much of a muchness. At 433 lines, *The Waste Land* may not be a long poem by today's standards, but it is long when compared with the imagist poems of its time. Perhaps *The Cantos,* at roughly 23,000 lines, offers the best prefiguration of contemporary maximalism. In any case, the high modernist impulse toward length seems different in kind from the spirit informing today's long poem.

For at least part of his career, Pound espoused a modernist renaissance that would draw on the example of rightly governed past cultures. His aesthetics were imbued with his sense of historicity, a backward gaze that became increasingly elegiac as his discouragement gained force. Modernist maximalism, as practiced by Pound and Eliot, was a structure of depletion: The poem spent itself as a gesture of mourning—for lost civilizations and mythologies. Its exhaustion was nihilistic in spirit, much ado about nothing ("I can connect / Nothing with nothing," *The*

Waste Land; "emptiness is the beginning of all things," "Canto 54"). To risk a generalization, their modernism beautifully encountered what-is-not and gave ample voice to absence. The postmodern poem, on the other hand, is an architecture of excess; it spends itself by reveling in the plethora of what-is. Its exhaustion is celebratory—or hedonistic, grasping. With the A-bomb's ashes for its grim confetti, it means to carpe diem all night long, whistling in the dark context of impending (rather than ended) apocalypse. Built from presence, it has a life wish. Taken together, the two modernisms resemble a twentieth-century lost and found.

Although a fractal poem might offer transcendence at the local level—in a line, a phrase—like a complex adaptive system it does not try to sustain a sublime optimum throughout. Its high lyric passages might be juxtaposed with vulgar or parodic sections; its diction can range from gorgeous to caustic. These oscillations occur with no change of speaker since fractal poetics is not a voice-based aesthetic. Williams's variable foot arose from his observation that "the iamb is not the normal measure of American speech." And Pound stipulated that poetry's language must "depart in no way from speech save by a heightened intensity (i.e., simplicity)." Poetry must contain "nothing that you couldn't, in some circumstance, in the stress of some emotion, actually say. Every literaryism, every book word, fritters away a scrap of the readers' sense of the poets' sincerity." (Of course, Pound did not take his own advice. But hundreds of poets did—and do.) "Naturally," he added, "your rhythmic structure should not destroy the shape of your words, or their natural sound, or their meaning."

Fractal poetics has dispensed with fidelity to the "normal" and the "natural," to "simplicity" and "sincerity." Instead of reproducing speech, the poem makes a sound-unto-itself; its music is not so much voiced as built. Even the most "sincere" or "natural" poem is a means, however unwitting or disavowed, of manipulating the reader. Fractal verse heightens the distinction between art and life rather than creating an insincere sincerity. Marjorie Perloff describes it splendidly: "Whereas Modernist poetics was overwhelmingly committed, at least in theory, to the 'natural look,' . . . we are now witnessing a return to *artifice,* but a 'radical artifice,' to use Lanham's phrase, characterized by its opposition, not only to 'the language really spoken by men' but also to what is loosely called Formalist (whether old or new) verse, with its elaborate poetic diction and self-conscious return to 'established' forms and genres. Artifice, in this sense, is less a matter of . . . elaboration and elegant subterfuge, than of the recognition that a poem . . . is a *made thing*—contrived, constructed, chosen. . . ." (*Radical Artifice*)

Fractal form might counter such "natural" effects as breaking lines on nouns and verbs; it might favor music that unhinges rather than reinforces the poem's content. Such effects call attention to themselves, and in doing so they highlight the "radical artifice" that is the poem's surface and disrupt its transparency. Diction, surface textures, irregular meters, shifts of genre, and tonal variations take center stage as defining formal elements. Function words (articles, conjunctions, prepositions) assume schematic importance. The content of fractal poetry's form (yes, the *content* of *form*) also dismantles assumptions concerning "the natural." Form's subversive or reactionary possibilities are recognized rather than denied.

Holland's *Hidden Order* notes that when reading formal structures we decide to call some aspects irrelevant; we agree to ignore them: "This has the effect of collecting into a category things that differ only in the abandoned details." The form of Petrarchan sonnets, for instance, differs only in those structural aspects we choose to overlook. We focus on the identical rhyme scheme, the iambic pentameter, the "turn" at line nine. We examine properties that define the sonnet and disregard properties that fall outside of this definition. Fractal poetics is composed of the disenfranchised details, the dark matter of Tradition: its blind spots, recondite spaces, and recursive fields.

When structure is imbued with substance, when form carries freight, the poem need not resort to polemical narrative or didactic anecdote as a means of airing its engagements. Its "political" explorations, structurally embedded, can retain subtlety. The gender of pronouns and the relation of linguistic figure and ground can provide a formal means of addressing cultural visibility and negation. Punctuation, rather than effacing itself, can become a glyph of implication (as the leveling, democratic colon does in the poetry of A. R. Ammons, for instance).

The emphasis on ground rather than figure necessarily

changes the poem's point of view. If *The Waste Land* were written from the perspective of the woman who says, "My nerves are bad to-night," the resultant work might resemble Adrienne Rich's "Snapshots of a Daughter-in-Law." "*You! hypocrite lecteur!—mon semblable,—mon frere!*" Eliot quotes from the Preface to *Fleurs du Mal.* "The argument, *ad feminam,* all the old knives / that have rusted in my back, I drive in yours, / *ma semblable, ma soeur!*" Rich revises. Rather than conversing with *The Waste Land,* it seems to me that Rich enacts a radical reversal of ground by placing one of Eliot's peripheral "voices" at the center of her poem.

There are two kinds of fractals: geometric and random. The geometric type, by repeating an identical pattern at various scales, suggests new dimensions of figure and ground. The fractal's smaller parts replicate the form of the entire structure, turned around or tilted a bit, and increasing detail is revealed with increasing magnification. My long sequence, "Give," can be seen as a fractal reimagining of the Daphne and Apollo legend from Ovid's *Metamorphoses.* In my telling, the story changes scale; the myth is blown up: enlarged and exploded. Daphne, who was voiceless in Ovid, is given words. And after she is turned into a tree, the subjugated, silent laurel speaks—literally speaks— to the human intrusion into nature. Ovid's bit players— victimized Daphne and the violated tree—are magnified and given starring roles.

To say that the politics of masculist high modernism were different from those in the previous paragraphs is to understate. Rather than culturally inflected icons and scripts, Eliot and Pound viewed archetypes and mythology as revelations of "essential drives": universal, *natural* truths whose meanings apply across time and place. They identified the loss of such mythology with spiritual bankruptcy. The feminist postmodern poem, on the other hand, seeks to discredit the pandemic power of myth. It questions the assumption of "naturalness" surrounding, for instance, heterosexuality, human sway over animals and planet, woman's association with nature and man's with culture. The loss of such "natural" truths is seen as a potential source of spiritual gain.

Of course, postmodern aesthetics do not automatically assume "high" art to be more interesting than "low." I find the engagement with popular culture to be somewhat troublesome and contradictory, however. Attention is a form of homage. And our fascination as a culture has fed upon commercial art throughout the twentieth century. "Serious," "composed," contemporary music, for instance, has been neglected to such a degree that we lack an adjective to describe it. Throwing euphemism to the winds, I refer to it as *un*popular music. Such music is less commodified, clearly, than popular genres. It also is of high quality and deserving of more notice. If fractal poetics means to honor the margins and illuminate the fringes—the quirky handmade rather than the slickly mass-produced, the bit players and backdrop rather than the spectacle and principals—*un*popular art, though redolent of "high" culture, must be part of its subject. The example of music extends to the visual arts and to literature. Whatever is complex and underinvestigated must become the starring subject.

And yet. The implications of popular culture—and the

engines of its power—have come under scrutiny only recently. Rather than exclude the popular, fractal aesthetics
want to understand its magnetism—and sometimes richness. "Consider the way of the scientist rather than the way
of the ad agent," Pound advised. Fractal poetics considers
both. Neither elitist nor populist, it exists on a third
ground between "high" or "low" terrains, resistant to
those classifications. Like the components of complex systems, the poems' inclusions neither lock into position nor
dissolve into turbulence.

~~

The structure of complex adaptive systems is determined
by internal models. In like fashion, the fractal poem's
growth and resolution are activated by self-determined im-
peratives rather than by adherence to a traditional scheme.
But how does the inner imperative of fractal verse differ
from the organic form of free verse? In 1912, Pound stated
the organic credo as succinctly as his Romantic predeces-
sors or the Black Mountain poets who succeeded him: "I
believe in an 'absolute rhythm,' a rhythm, that is, in poetry
which corresponds exactly to the emotion or shade of
emotion to be expressed."

Though modernism has come to be associated with
discontinuity, Pound seemed to regard *The Waste Land* as a
model of cohesive design. In a letter of praise to Eliot he
admonished himself for "never getting an outline" in his
own poems. For me, the wholeness of *The Waste Land* arises
from its singleness of tone and symbolic coherence. Its

polyphonic voices wear a gray membrane of irony; the sensibility throughout is measured and austere. There are no petards. Nothing funny or vulnerable is to be found in its shifting lines. Eliot's rhetoric never veers into confession or exposition. Fractal poetry, on the other hand, splices satiric and lyrical, elegiac and absurd lines without casting a unifying tonal veil over the mélange. But the distance between the mod and the post- is nowhere more evident than in their respective stands toward the symbolic. Contemporary poetry prefers metaphoric to symbolic encodings. A poem as self-consciously and determinedly allusive as *The Waste Land* would seem old-fashioned if written today; the water/desert trope, heavyhanded and shopworn.

Modernist discontinuity tended to be grounded in mimesis and realism. Its disjunctions sought to replicate the mechanistic quality of urban life and the beginning of the age of information (as figured by telephone, film, and radio). Rather than mirroring its age, fractal disruption functions as a Zen slap, awakening readers from the spell of the "sincere" voice. It contrasts transparent lines with less "genuine" dictions, and the disparate tones vibrate like complementary colors, highlighted by proximity. The poem thrums with bone-conduction music as registers vibrate in concert with unlikenesses spliced nearby.

Both organic and fractal form compare poetry to structures in the natural world. Organic form, however, extends this prizing of nature to imitations of the "natural" speaking voice. Fractal poetry, as we have seen, regards voice as a construct: a consciously made assemblage of dictions, meters, rhetorics, gestures, and tones. Whereas organicism insists upon wholeness and smoothness of thought, fractal poetry regards interruption, artifice, disjunction, and raggedness as facets of its formal vocabulary. In practice, these differences mean that the textures of fractal poetry will be more turbulent than those of organic free verse. A fractal poem might establish iambic pentameter only to break it with rudely dissonant effects. It locates structure in disruption and allows new (or old) forms to emerge as the poem proceeds.

Organic aesthetics, by definition, try to match the poem's cadence with its emotional content. Feelings must be expressed in a "natural" speaking voice, lest they sound stilted or become inaccessible. If the verse is truly organic (and *The Cantos* is not) its language will vanish into meaning when read rather than linger opaquely on the page as an indecorous reminder that poems are made of words. Fractal aesthetics, in contrast, refract the poem's surface in order to make its linguistic materiality more evident. As free verse broke the pentameter, fractal verse breaks the poem plane.

The poem plane is analogous to the picture plane in painting: a two-dimensional surface that can convey the illusion of spatial depth. Painters use perspective, colors, texture, and modeling to suggest three dimensions on the flat canvas. If objects are painted progressively smaller and closer together they will seem to recede. Space also can be suggested by juxtaposing oncoming warm colors with introverted cool ones. By alternating thickly textured impasto with turpentine-thinned washes, the artist can create opaque areas of positive space and radiant glazes of negative space. Objects of the same scale can be modeled differently to create depth: a hard-edged rendering will appear nearer than a hazy one.

A composition's rhythm sometimes depends on repeating picture planes through multiple zones of recession until the painting gives credence to spaces ungoverned by the laws of physics. In Poussin's *The Funeral of Phocion*, for instance, the picture plane is repeated as walls, buildings, and hills recede toward the final backdrop of sky. John Canaday describes the effect this way: "A second series of planes at an angle to the picture plane is suggested first by the side plane of the stone wall at the right. We enter the picture from the lower left and move across it, but are kept from moving out by the tall tree at the right and by this plane of the wall, which is turned to deflect the 'current' of our movement back into the picture. It is not noticeable that this plane is, in fact, a distortion of true perspective...."

The eye moves from left to right across the painting until a tree and a plane of wall at the far right rebound the gaze back into the picture. In poetry, a justified flush-right margin (instead of the usual flush-left alignment) will halt the eye abruptly, almost rudely, stranding the gaze in an unbidden white surround before deflecting it leftward and into the next line. Such a "distortion" underscores the poem's constructedness; it also offers a subtle formal means of reinforcing content.

The motion of reading is horizontal and vertical: Our eyes skim across and edge down the flat planes of print. Poetry has held language to this single plane rather than using linguistic properties as a means of constructing three-dimensional space. "To be fractal a form must be . . . between dimensions," notes Nigel Reading. Just as paint fosters illusions of proximity and distance on canvas, words can suggest spatial depth on paper. A fractal poem can do this by shifting its linguistic densities: The poem's transparent, "easy" passages impart the sensation of negative space; they vanish into meaning when read rather than calling attention to their linguistic presence. More textured language, on the other hand, refuses to yield its mass immediately. The eye rests on top of the words, trying to gain access, but is continually rebuffed. Such (relatively) opaque sections assume the solidity of positive space. By juxtaposing transparent with textured passages, fractal poetry constructs a linguistic screen that alternately dissolves and clouds.

Planes of varying densities move us into and out of the poem, as if it were a field of three dimensions. We gaze "through" thin lines and are deflected to the surface by "showier," distracting, dense language. This modulating depth of field allows us to experience the poem as a construct of varying focal lengths. Such palpable architectonics also create an awareness of the poem as thing-in-itself rather than conduit for meaning. I've used the words *transparent* and *textured* to describe two broad effects. Perhaps it's worth noting that transparent lines are not drawn solely from simple, lyric registers. They also can be forged of exposition, reportage, platitudes, advertisements, or clichés. What they have in common is lucidity. And textured passages are not composed only of arcane, difficult words. Density need not be leaden or dull. "Texture" can be built, for instance, from sequined, wooly, stippled, flannel, marbled, glittery, or drippy linguistic registers. Resistance is key.

What I'm suggesting is that poetry take advantage of a synesthesia that attributes physicality (color and texture) to language. For me, and I think for many linguistically addicted people, words have an unignorable materiality. It is not only the meaning of words that holds my attention, but their sensual, and especially tactile, presence. Passages can have an ultrasuede nap, like the velour finish of a petal, or they can feel prickly as hairbrushes. I am bored by poetry contructed solely of thin, homogenous tones because it reads like a field of gray plaster. I think most readers possess some degree of synethesia. Fractal verse develops this ability to feel language as a 3-D tactile surround. Perhaps its greatest urgency exists in its potential for limbic awakening.

Of course, *The Cantos* also can be read as "planes in relation." Yet that staggering poem does not create a sense of three-dimensional space; it splices disparate people and places so that readers can draw inferences from the allusive montage. Pound modeled his poem plane on the ideogram or concrete picture, and *The Cantos* strives for a uniform degree of concretion rather than a plate techtonics of transparent and textured passages. "Don't use 'dim lands of peace,'" he famously advised. "It dulls the image. It mixes an abstraction with the concrete. It comes from the writer's not realizing that the natural object is always the *adequate* symbol." Pound's later practice—in which the "natural object" became a preexistent text spliced into the poem— was more complex than his early theory would lead one to suppose. Poetry-writing textbooks and workshops over the past thirty years have taken his injunction to "go in fear of abstraction" at face value, nonetheless. In the grammar school of imagism, contemporary poets learn that "dim lands" imply "peace." This might be a useful place to begin, but it's a facile place to end up.

Rather than excise stale portmanteaus, fractal poetry might use empty rhetoric sardonically, as a means of splintering the "sincere" voice that was a modernist value. Abstractions are arguably the most rarified words because they have no relation to a specific physical object. In fractal poetics, abstractions are not forsworn as redundant explications of self-sufficient concrete symbols; rather, the abstract becomes a valuable realm in itself, a means of adding ether, gassiness, fumes, breath to the poem's corporate mix. By adjoining abstract with concrete pigments, poets are afforded another method of refracting the poem plane.

~~

As soon as one begins to analyze or dissect a poem's formal components, the poem is no longer organic or "whole." This is why organicism seems the antithesis of formalism. And it explains why organic free verse never developed a vocabulary with which to describe its formal properties.

Although fractal poetry does not adhere to a predetermined scheme, it offers a terminology (planes, surface, canopy, textures, transparency, opacity, obverse, metabolism, understory, cluster, supercluster, limbic . . .) that is descriptive of its structure. The vocabulary used to describe form changes the way that we think of form. And changes in thinking emerge as changes in the work.

The New Critics believed poems rended by formal analysis were reconstituted within the readers' improved understanding. Rather than stressing the retrievable wholeness of separate parts, fractal poetics investigate—and prize—the spaces *between* the parts. In *Chaos: Making a New Science*, James Gleick writes, "One simple but powerful consequence of the fractal geometry of surfaces is that surfaces in contact do not touch everywhere. . . . The bumpiness at all scales prevents that. . . . It is why two pieces of a broken teacup can never be rejoined, even though they appear to fit together at some gross scale. At a smaller scale, irregular bumps are failing to coincide." The excerpt hints at concepts dear to fractal aesthetics: surfaces, touch, bumpiness, scale, brokenness, irregularity, and failure.

Failure might seem an unlucky inclusion, but with it I mean to suggest not only a relinquishment of subter*fusion* but a taste for subterfuge in the guise of accidents, pratfalls, slippage, and mistakes. I have two copies of *The Waste Land*. One is a recent, clean edition. The other, the one I favor, is a used paperback remastered by the marginal scribbling of some eager, previous reader. One comment refers to "the lonely, arid *dessert* within," and the phrase's connotations are more interesting than the "right" words would have been. Fractal poetry is enthralled by such failures and fallshorts, such improving accidents. "Plan addiction with Hank," I find on a to-do list. And in a letter, "I'll have it to you by the end of the mouth." Lengthy, scholarly notes at the end of poems (as in *The Waste Land* or Marianne Moore's books) predate this sense of the absurd. Unless such notes become creative works in themselves (a parodic means of undoing the poem's precious gestures, for instance), they remain a mod trait.

Marjorie Perloff noted that the poetry of "radical artifice" is not to be confused with formalist verse, which depends on established forms and genres and whose artifice is based on elaboration and elegance. I would add that poetry in received forms can be likened to standard mathematics (calculus, say, or linear analysis) in which the value of the parts adds up to the value of the whole. That is, the strength of a metered poem's lines adds up to the poem's strength as whole. The disjunctive shifts of fractal poetry, however, are akin to nonlinear interactions in which the value of the whole cannot be predicted by summing the strength of its parts. A fractal poem might contain purposely insipid or flowery lines that would be throwaways if taken out of context. When juxtaposed with other inclusions, however, these debased lines establish a friction or frame greater than their discrete presence would predict.

Complex systems tend to recycle their components. A rainforest, for instance, captures and reuses critical resources as a means of enriching itself. Fractal poetry likewise makes use of recurring cluster words, limbic lines, or canopy stanzas as a means of creating depth. (*Cluster* being an aggregation of stars with common properties; *limbic* connoting emotion and motivation; *canopy* casting a shade over all.) Unlike the villanelle or sestina's recycling, fractal repetition does not appear at a predetermined place within a set scheme. The poem is more dynamic and turbulent because its repetitions have an element of ambush. Readers experience the consolation of pattern without being able to anticipate the moment of return. Such recycling, at once surprising and reassuring, can occur throughout a poem, book, or body of work. (Dickinson's recurring vocabulary comes to mind.)

Skeptical readers might think, *Dickinson? What is she doing here?* And, *poets have always used repetition.* I can only say again that newness is a composite. Dickinson—with her broken syntax and maximal dashes—is a fractal forebear. And though all structures rely on repetition, poets have not used recycling in conjunction with the other effects I've described. Novation also is created by context and label: Free verse was written before the modernists popularized the term, yet twentieth-century unrhymed poetries of variable meter sound like none other.

Although this might be the maximalist talking, I sense there is much more to say. My intent here has been more visionary than critical: That is, I've described an incipient poetics, one that I feel forming as I write and read. I've taken the liberty of devising a vocabulary as necessary. Rather than existing territories, I've looked toward unmet horizons. Generalizations must be customized to particular poets since each turns on her own axis. Each builds her emancipations by hand. That such freedoms can speak to one another is my fair calculation: that difference can be tempered by affinity. I leave the compass of that conversation to you.

1997, 1998

III

Powers

The Only Kangaroo among the Beauty

Unordinary Passions:
Margaret Cavendish, the
Duchess of Newcastle

I'VE BEEN A POET FOR TWENTY-THREE YEARS, AND I don't cry easily. I've seen poetry at home in its inky T-shirt and at large in its designer dress. I've done time in poetry boot camp and at the top of Parnassus. I've joined workshops held in funeral parlors and delegations to the People's Republic of China. I've raised consciousness, figuratively, in the presence of famous feminist poets and lost consciousness, literally, in the presence of renowned Romantic poets. I've been dressed down by colleagues with thought disorders; I've received an honorary doctorate. I've awoken in an artist colony to find excrement smeared over my bathroom by a rejected fellow. I've overheard three men poets, celebrated for their sensitive verse, describe my rape: "You hold her hands behind her back while I fuck her and Nameless shoves his fist up her ass." I've been a poet for twenty-three years, I've seen poetry at home in its sour sneakers, at large in its power suit, and I don't cry easily. So I was surprised to find myself moved to tears while reading a poem by Margaret Cavendish, the Duchess of Newcastle.

At one time I might have bought into the fiction of dispassionate criticism. However, it now seems disingenuous to elide the emotional components of evaluation: the hysterical rancor that fuels vitriolic reviews, the critic's crush on beloved works. I've come to think that the deepest engagement is possible only when a reader falls for a poet's work, finding there a home away from home, self away from self. Whereas I once might have mistrusted the slippery slope of this position, I now mistrust appraisals that would lop off the critic's affective life. This is not to dismiss analysis or theory. Statements of feeling (*this poetry is exhausting; this poetry is exhilarating*) that fail to investigate the cause of emotive effects are irresponsible and naive. By exploring the poem's form and content, by locating it within an ongoing struggle of tradition, we might understand how emotion couched in language attains durability. I would like to understand the indelible feeling that traveled across three and a half centuries of belittlement and neglect to break my voice as I read.

～

I recently joined a reading group composed of scientists and humanists. At our last meeting, a professor of linguistics admitted to "falling in love with" Margaret Fuller, the nineteenth-century feminist. I was delighted by his choice of words. It is unscholarly to own up to crushes. I was in the grip of one myself, but everyone expects gooey thinking from poets. "I'm in love with Margaret Cavendish, the Duchess of Newcastle," I admitted. Margaret Cavendish was all I wanted to talk about, really. Every conversation that night put me in mind of her or her work. Like all lovers, I prize the traits that others have despised in her: her gaucheness and original style; her guileless pursuit of fame; her eccentricity. Her goodness. I respect and would defend this Duchess for her courage, honesty, intrepidness, intellect, fairness, charm, innocence, and common sense. Her goodness. But if these strengths and felicities of character were not amply evident in her poetry, their presence in her life would hold much less interest for me. Had her poetry proved unworthy, I would not have succumbed to what I'm calling "love."

Margaret Cavendish's poetry deserves emphasis because it has been sacrificed to her legend, and her legend has been founded on the laziness of hearsay and the wickedness of misogyny for 350 years. She has had her defenders, of course. Now that I know her, I am fond of her champions. I think better of Charles Lamb for deeming her "the thrice noble, chaste, and virtuous . . . original-brain'd, generous Margaret Newcastle." And I think less of Samuel Pepys, who disliked her because she was "so unordinary." Her detractors' opinions, when scrutinized, tend to dissolve into gossip. They certainly show little evidence of any comprehensive engagement with her work. Although recent scholarship has been far more responsible than the wholesale bludgeonings meted out by literary history, today's attention seems to gravitate toward her prose and plays. In fact, I could find no serious appraisal of Margaret Cavendish's poems by a critic whose primary field is poetry.

Although poems are included in several of Cavendish's sixteen books, her debut publication, *Poems and Fancies,* devotes itself most fully to verse. I've spent a few weeks poring over a reproduction of the 1653 first edition, my progress slowed to the luxurious basking pace of poetry by the book's antiquated typeface: its ambiguous "s" and "f" that blur *wise* to *wife*. Since very few people have read her work, my wish is to guide readers toward some of the stronger poems and to suggest their singular merits. It is possible to read Cavendish's verse for its intriguing representations of seventeenth-century folkways or science. Such an approach has its own value and necessity, but it begs the foundational question of quality: Why are these good poems? By what means do they create pleasure, and yes, emotion? How do they exist within the context of their epoch and the broader spectrum of aesthetics?

When considered within the nexus of the seventeenth century, Margaret Cavendish's poems bear some resemblance to those of George Herbert and Richard Crashaw. As this comparison suggests, she wrote two different sorts of verse: One is kin to the simplicity of Herbert; the other shares the grotesque sensibility of Crashaw. The first sort is uncontrived in the best sense of the word; the second is contrived in ways that disturb the reader's sense of proportion and taste. Cavendish is not a religious poet, however, and this fact alone assures that any likeness to Herbert or Crashaw will be full of difference.

Whereas Herbert's simplicity is worshipful and austere, Cavendish's plain style is heretical and rustic. Her work is more roughly spun than his; her diction and phrasing more impulsive and fauve. Ragged syncopation and slant rhymes enliven her surfaces, while details of seventeenth-century manners and customs sweeten the content. Her finest poems, impassioned by an artless eloquence, bespeak an innocence of "craft" in the sense of wiles or manipulation. In *Sociable Letters* (1664), she noted, "some may say that if my understanding be most of Sheep and a Grange it is a beastly understanding. My answer is I wish Men were as Harmless as most Beasts are, then surely the World would be more quiet and happy than it is." Her imagery often arose from her knowledge of farming, and she also drew upon the female spheres of housewifery or, as in the following excerpt, fashion.

> I *Language* want, to dresse my *Fancies* in,
> The *Haire's* uncurl'd, the *Garments* loose, and thin;
> Had they but *Silver Lace* to make them gay,
> Would be more courted then in *poore array*.
> Or had they *Art*, might make a *better show*;
> But *they are plaine*, yet cleanly doe they goe.
> The world in *Bravery* doth take delight,
> And *glistering Shews* doe more attract the *sight*;
> And every one doth honour a rich Hood,
> As if the *outside* made the *inside* good.
> And every one doth bow, and give the place,
> Not for the *Man's sake*, but the *Silver Lace*.
> Let me intreat in my poore Bookes behalfe,
> That all may not adore the Golden Calf.
> Consider pray, *Gold* hath no life therein,
> And *Life* in *Nature* is the richest thing.

Her deepest subject is not man's relation to God, but man's relation to the natural world. Her poems challenge

Hobbes's assertion of man's preeminence, especially as revealed in his manipulation of language. "All creatures may do as much;" she wrote, "but by reason they do it not after the same manner or way as man, man denies they do it at all, which is very hard; for what man knows whether fish do not know more of the nature of water, and ebbing and flowing, and the saltness of the sea? or whether birds do not know more of the nature and degrees of air, or the cause of tempests? ... For, though they have not the speech of man, yet hence doth not follow that they have no intelligence at all. But the ignorance of men concerning other creatures is the cause of despising other creatures, imagining themselves as petty gods in nature." (*Philosophical Letters*, 1664) By stressing the materiality of the human state and the mysterious divinity of the creaturely world, Cavendish posits a radical reversal of grounds: "And for the *Mind*, which some say is like *Gods*, / I do not find, 'twixt *Man*, and *Beast* such odds ..." ("Of Humility"). The intensity of her fellow feeling, coupled with her freshness and guilelessness, makes her a poet of great charm and genuine moral weight.

When evaluating untried poets, T. S. Eliot suggested that we ask not, "are they great?" but, "are they *genuine?*" ("What is Minor Poetry") The word *genuine*, however, has come to suggest a rhetoric of sincerity that is by no means hard to simulate. In his essay "The Metaphysical Poets," Eliot noted that Herbert's simplicity had been "emulated without success by numerous modern poets." The trend continues in contemporary poems that mistake the simplistic for the simple and equate straightforward syntax, modesty of tone, and ordinary language with the genuine. Thus threadbare sentiments and sedentary ethics may be touted as "deeply felt" as long as they are plainly put. Many poets today, perhaps most, strive for such transparency, but the choice is more symptomatic of aesthetics than of ethics or character. The word *genuine*, however, connotes integrity and scruples; it suggests an authenticity of feeling and a depth of purpose that is unrelated to ease of understanding or clarity of surface. In her ambivalent essay on Cavendish, Virginia Woolf allowed that "the vast bulk of the Duchess is leavened by a vein of authentic fire." But how does one assess the "authentic" or "genuine" without slipping into critical fallacies that suppose themselves privy to the poet's unstated motives? I think one can begin by asking what the poet has to gain or lose from the stand she has taken. If a poet risks the ridicule, scorn, abuse, and contempt of her age, I suspect I'm in the presence of "the genuine."

Cavendish was not only the first English woman to write for publication, she was an ardent feminist whose sense of justice extended, as we will see, to the natural world. That she has been punished for her crimes in favor of humanity is beyond question. In *Margaret the First,* biographer Douglas Grant notes that her compassion made her "speak out of turn in a century when cruelty to animals was all too common." Her empathy surely was strengthened by her identification with beasts as fellow sufferers. In 1667, she was conflated with an animal in John Lacy's adaptation of *The Taming of the Shrew.* Cynthia M. Tuerk notes that Lacy's "Sauny the Scott" retains Shakespeare's names for all the characters with the exception of the shrew, whom he christens "Margaret." Tuerk speculates that Lacy transformed "the controversial Duchess of Newcastle" into "the plain-speaking, scolding 'Petticoate Devil' who must be tamed into submission through the use of brutality and violence."

Seventeenth-century misogyny was founded, in part, on Plato's conception of woman as an animal possessed of bodily life but bereft of reason and intellect. Cavendish recognized man's assertion of sovereignty as a self-serving belief that condoned the subjugation of nature and, by extension, women. Although her poems do not openly analogize animals to women, her prose and plays frequently present the comparison. In *Divers Orations* (1662), she wrote that women "live like bats or owls, labor like beasts, and die like worms." She worried that women "should grow irrational as idiots by the dejectedness of our spirits, through the careless neglects and despisements of the masculine sex to the female, thinking it impossible we should have either learning or understanding, wit or judgement; as if we had not rational souls as well as men; and we out of a custom of dejectedness think so too, which makes us quit all industry towards profitable knowledge . . . for we are kept like birds in cages, to hop up and down. . . . We are shut out of all power and authority . . . our counsels are despised and laughed at; the best of our actions are trodden down with scorn by the overweening conceit men have of themselves, and through a despisement of us." (*Philosophical and Physical Opinions*, 1663) Rather than arguing for woman's superiority to beasts, however, Cavendish argued that man, too, was an animal, and that animals were man's creaturely equals.

Although Cavendish's feminist stand attracted much spitefulness, her empathy for otherness lends authority to her finest poetry. "A Dialogue of Birds," which I will excerpt, humanizes animals by endowing them with voices, emotions, and thought. Rather than the treacle and cuteness portended by such personification, the poem has the dignified purity of the ballads Cavendish loved to sing. Its songlike qualities predict the work of another self-educated "nature" poet, Robert Burns.

Both Cavendish and Burns have a canny eye for country details; both press the vernacular into a tumultuous prosody; both strike an ingenuous, forthright tone. Yet Cavendish's poems are less playful and bantering than Burns's; their empathy is different in kind, more sober. Burns's "To a Mouse" recounts that creature's trials with winsome specificity before concluding: "Still thou are blest compared wi' me! / The present only toucheth thee." He then invokes memory and anticipation as sources of human suffering unknown to mice. Cavendish would make no such claim. Among beliefs she wished repealed was "That no Beast hath remembrance, numeration, or curiosity." ("The Animal Parliament") In Burns's poem, moreover, the plowman-speaker informs the mouse of its own hardships. "A Dialogue of Birds," on the other hand, affords animals the agency and eloquence of testimony. The human observer is out of the picture, and this effacement assures that pity for animals does not devolve into self-pity. The matchless poignancy of Cavendish's animal poems can be attributed to the absence of human agendas, as well as to the exactitude and freshness of the depiction. Witness, in the opening passage, how the image of the lark torquing its small force skyward is effectively extended to the corkscrew vibrato of its song.

A Dialogue of Birds

As *I* abroad in *Feilds,* and *Woods* did walke,
I heard the *Birds* of severall things did talke:
And on the *Boughes* would *Gossip, prate,* and *chat,*
And every one discourse of *this,* and *that.*
I, said the *Larke,* before the *Sun* do rise,
And take my flight up to the *highest Skies:*
There sing some *Notes,* to raise *Appollo's* head,
For feare that *hee* might lye too long a *Bed.*
And as *I* mount, or if descend downe low,
Still do *I* sing, which way so ere *I* go.
Winding my *Body* up, just like a *Scrue,*
So doth my *Voice* wind up a *Trillo* too.
What *Bird,* besides my selfe, both flyes and sings,
Just tune my *Trilloes* keeps to my *flutt'ring Wings.*
    I, said the *Nightingale,* all night do watch,
For feare a *Serpent* should my *young ones* catch:
To keep back sleep, *I* severall *Tunes* do sing,
Which Tunes so pleasant are, they *Lovers* bring
Into the *Woods;* who listning sit, and mark:
When *I* begin to sing, they cry, *hark, hark.*
Stretching my *Throat,* to raise my *Trilloes* high,
To gaine their praises, makes me almost dye.
    Then comes the *Owle,* which saies, here's such a doe
With your sweet *Voices;* through spight cries *Wit-a-woo.*

In *Winter*, said the *Robin*, *I* should dye,
But that *I* in good warm house do flye:
And there do pick up *Crummes*, which make me fat,
But oft am sear'd away with the *Pusse-cat.*
If they molest me not, then *I* grow bold,
And stay so long, whilst *Winter Tales* are told.
Man superstitiously dares not hurt me,
for if *I* am kill'd, or hurt, *ill Luck* shall be.

   The *Sparrow* said, were our *Condition* such,
But *Men* do strive with *Nets* us for to catch:
With *Guns*, and *Bowes* they shoot us from the *Trees*,
And by small *Shot*, we oft our *Lifes* do leese,
Because we pick a *Cherry* here, and there,
When, *God* he knowes, we eate them in great feare.
But *Men* will eat, untill their *Belly* burst,
And *surfets* take: if we eat, we are *curst.*
Yet we by *Nature* are revenged still,
For eating over-much themselves they kill.
And if a *Child* do chance to *cry*, or *brawle*,
They strive to catch us, to please that *Child* withall:
With *Threads* they tye our *legs* almost to crack,
That when we *hop* away, they pull us back:
And when they cry *Fip*, *Fip*, strait we must come,
And for our paines they'l give us one *small Crum.*

   I wonder, said *Mag-pye*, you grumble so,
Dame Sparrow, we are us'd much worse *I* trow.
For they our *Tongues* do slit, their *words* to learne,
And with the *paine*, our food we dearely earne.

   Why, say the *Finches*, and the *Linnets* all,
Do you so prate *Mag-pie*, and so much baule?
As if no *Birds* besides were wrong'd but you,
When we by *cruell Man* are injur'd to.

For we, to learn their Tunes, are kept awake,
That with their *whistling* we no rest can take.
In *darknesse* we are kept, no *Light* must see,
Till we have learnt their *Tunes* most perfectlie.
But *Jack-dawes*, they may dwell their houses nigh,
And build their *Nests* in *Elmes* that do grow high:
And there may *prate*, and flye from place to place;
For why, they think they give their *House a grace*.

     Lord! said the *Partridge, Cock, Puet, Snite*, and *Quaile,*
Pigeons, Larkes, my *Masters*, why d'yee raile?
You're kept from *Winters Cold*, and *Summers heat*,
Are taught new *Tunes*, and have good store of meat.
Having a *Servant* you to wait upon,
To make your *Cages* cleane from *filth*, and *Dung:*
When we *poore Birds* are by the dozens kill'd,
And luxuriously us eate, till they be fill'd:
And of our *flesh* they make such cruell wast,
That but some of our *Limbes* will please their tast.
In *Wood-cockes thighes* they onely take delight,
And *Partridge wings*, which swift were in their flight.
The smaller *Lark* they eate all at one bite,
But every part is good of *Quaile*, and *Snite*.
The *Murtherous Hawk* they keep, us for to catch,
And learn their *Dogs*, to *crouch*, and *creep*, and *watch:*
Untill they have *sprung* us to *Nets*, and *Toiles*,
And thus *poore Creatures* we are made *Mans* spoiles.
Cruell Nature! to make us *Gentle, Mild:*
They *happy* are, which are more *feirce*, and *wild.*
O would our *flesh* had been like *Carrion, course,*
To eate us onely *Famine* might inforce.
But when they eate us, may they surfets take,
May they be *poore*, when they a Feast us make.

The more they eate, the *leaner* may they grow,
Or else so *fat*, they cannot stir, nor go.

O, said the *Swallow*, let me mourne in *black*,
For, of *Mans cruelty I* do not lack:
I am the *Messenger* of *Summer warme*,
Do neither pick their *Fruit*, nor eate their *Corne;*
Yet they will take us, when alive we be,
I shake to tell, *O horrid Cruelty!*
Beate us alive, till we an *Oile* become.
Can there to *Birdes* be a worse *Martyrdome?*
O Man, O Man, if we should serve you so,
You would against us your *great Curses* throw.
But *Nature, shee* is good, do not her blame:
We ought to give her thankes, and not exclaime.
For *Love* is *Natures* chiefest *Law* in *Mind*,
Hate but an *Accident* from *Love* we find.

Over the next two pages, the titmouse chides the other birds for neglecting their "Home-Affaires," and heeding this call to domesticity, they set about gathering spilled corn, newly sown seed, ripe cherries, and ant eggs, with which to feed their chicks. Their flight home is likened to men returning from market, joined by "a Troop of Neighbors." The birds' communal activities—their need to eat, breed, and exchange information—imply their kinship with the human. Embodiment is the leveling factor: We are alike in our ineluctable physicality, and this debt to materiality creates equity. Once in their nests, the birds carol a hymn asking God for a fine tomorrow. The view of the age was that man's immortal soul established his supremacy to nature. In constructing birdsong as prayer, Cavendish suggests that the natural world also communes with God and partakes of divinity by means of unorthodox worship. The poem's closure finds in sleep—with its intimations of mortality—a denominator both common and consoling. In a lovely simile, the ebbing of birdsong is compared to a gradual closing of eyes:

> At last they *drousie* grew, and heavie were to *sleep*,
> And then instead of singing, cried, *Peep, Peep.*
> Just as the *Eye*, when *Sense* is locking up,
> Is neither open wide, nor yet quite shut:
> So doth a *Voice* still by degrees fall downe,
> And as a *Shadow*, wast so doth a *Sound*.
> Thus went to rest each *Head*, under each *wing*,
> For *Sleep* brings *Peace* to every *living thing*.

"John Clare was the nearest thing to the 'natural poet' for whom primitivists had been searching ever since the mid-eighteenth century," the *Norton Anthology* (6th edition) asserts. The naif-seekers need not have waited so long: In Margaret Cavendish they could have had their innocent. Yet the unstudied rudeness of her work would not have pleased "the primitivists" in pursuit of a happy savage, painting idyllic naturescapes. Although "A Dialogue of Birds" has something of the sweetness of Clare's verse, Cavendish generally is a far more disturbing poet. "Twas pity that in this Titanic continent where nature is so grand, Genius should be so tame," Emerson remarked of his own day and place. Cavendish's genius was of the untamed variety; her expressiveness, as we shall see, exceeds the rules of decorum and aesthetics. Yet these violations awaken uncanny emotions—from grief to repugnance—and are largely responsible for the force of her poems.

~~

"Nobody, so far as I know, not even an eighteenth-century minor poet, could imagine any connection between events in the mind of a cricket and those in the mind of the human," Lewis Thomas writes. Robert Burns's "To a Louse," with its comic ruminations on extermination, hardly counts. Fast forwarding to the nineteenth century, there is John Clare's fanciful portrayal of "Insects" who are free of "labours drudgery." Clare's poem says more about human misery and envy, however, than it does about the "tiney loiterer on the barley's beard." "I will begin to feel better about us," Lewis Thomas concludes, ". . . when we finally start learning about some of the things that are still mystifications. Start with the events in the mind of a cricket, I'd say, and then go on from there." ("Crickets, Bats, Cats, & Chaos") Several of Margaret Cavendish's poems start in such places—the minds of birds, stags, or hares—and go on to suggest sympathetic connections between animal and human intelligences. Her poems, like John Clare's, are fearlessly anthropomorphic. But her assignment of human traits illuminates the animals' sentience rather than the human pysche.

Within the context of scientific inquiry, the dangers of anthropomorphizing are well-rehearsed. In poetics, the *pathetic fallacy*, a term coined by John Ruskin in 1856, describes the projection of human traits onto the nonhuman. With a nod toward Ruskin, the bulk of twentieth-century aesthetics has dismissed the anthropomorphic gesture as inherently sentimental. Postmodern poetry, for its part, doesn't worry about the pathetic fallacy; its concerns are other and elsewhere. But science's fear of the anthropomorphic continues, and that caution begins to seem overdetermined. Perhaps our closeness to animals frightens us into asserting difference. We do tend to subjugate any version of ourselves that is not completely to our liking. There is, moreover, some sleight of mind or doublethink at the heart of the scientific argument. The projection of human traits onto animals is said to distort objectivity: We cannot assume that they are like us. Animal experiments, however, are founded on just that assumption. The similitude that creates the test's value also creates the ethical dilemma. If animals are enough like us to inform us of ourselves, how can we maim and kill them in order to secure that information? Surely if animals can serve as models for the human, humans can serve as models for the animal. To anthropomorphize is to acknowledge rather than disavow the inflection of human experience upon investigations of nonhuman life. Human experience, after all, is the only kind we have.

In "The Hunting of the Stag," Cavendish uses personification to blur the distinction between human and animal. The poem begins by describing the deer's marvelous physicality: "his *Legs* were *Nervous,* and his *Joynts* were strong." Like Narcissus, the stag is given to admiring his reflection in a brook, "Taking such *Pleasure* in his *Stately Crowne,* / His

Pride forgets that *Dogs* might pull him downe." Although Cavendish no doubt thought of Charles I when composing those lines, the poem does not become an allegory of the death of kings. Just as the absence of moralizing makes John Clare's verse all the more enchanting, the absence of symbolism makes Cavendish's poems more heartfully profound. How tiresome it would be read the stag as a stand-in for some loftier idea, and how refreshing it is to read him as a deer, expressing his own value or dearness. The poem takes the scenic route, meandering into a fascinating catalogue of trees that does nothing to deepen the tropes or advance the narrative. The stag wanders into a shady wood where "*slender Birch* bowes head to *golden Mines.*" (*"Good Mines are found out by the* Birches *bowing,"* a side note ingenuously tells us.) The forest also holds:

> Small *Aspen Stalkt* which shakes like *Agues* cold,
> That from perpetuall *Motion* never hold. . . .
> The weeping *Maple,* and the *Poplar* green,
> Whose *Cooling Buds* in *Salves* have healing been. . . .
> And *Juniper,* which gives a pleasant smell,
> And many more, which were too long to tell.

The stag's epicurean palate charts his course through winter-savory and cowslips to the ultimate succulence of the farmer's wheat blades. After a fine feed, he is discovered and pursued by the field's owner, his dogs, and other men who "for sport did come." The stag leaps into a river and tries to swim invisibly as a fish: "But out alas, his Hornes too high do shew." His proud antlers give him away, and the hunters' watery reflection undoes his earlier image of noble materiality: "*Feare* cuts his *Breath* off short, his *Limbs* do shrink, / Like those the *Cramp* doth take, to bottom sink." The deer struggles until "His *Heart* so heavie grew, with *Griefe*, and *Care*, / That his small *Feet* his *Body* could not beare." At the end, he defiantly faces the hunters: "But *Fate* his *thread* had spun, so downe did fall, / Shedding some *Teares* at his own *Funerall*."

Weeping animals probably make modern readers uneasy. But the unvarnished closure has its own rude power; its nakedness moves beyond sentimentality into poignancy. The stag's self-mourning—venial, vulnerable—is terribly human. The final rhyme contrasts the ritualized grief of a funeral to the ritualized killing of the hunt. The disproportion—between the stag's prizing of his life and the men's disdain of it, between communal formalized mourning and the animal's lonely death—creates pathos.

Earlier the hunters were compared to boys who "when *Mischiefe* takes not place, / Is out of *Countenance*, as with *disgrace*." An endearing trait of Margaret Cavendish was her tendency to be thrown "out of countenance" by social occasions. Cavendish's loyal maid, Elizabeth Toppe, described her in a prefatory letter: "You were always Circumspect, by Nature, not by Art; . . . your Ladiship is naturally bashful, & apt to be out of Countenance, that your Ladiship could not oblige all the World." But some accounts suggest "out of countenance" as a euphemism for what could happen to Cavendish in unsympathetic company. She admitted to being afflicted with "bashfulness" from childhood. "It hath many times obstructed the passage of my speech, and perturbed my natural actions, forcing a constraintedness, or unusual motions," she wrote. John Evelyn's wife described her conversation as "terminating commonly in nonsense, oaths, and obscenity," and Dorothy Osborne wrote that Cavendish's friends were at fault "to let her go abroad." Douglas Grant writes that "when confronted by Mrs. Evelyn, coldly eyeing her from behind the mask of modest conventional housewife, Margaret's demon seized command, translating her into the affected, grimacing creature whom her guest was later to deride." Sir Walter Scott portrayed her as "an entire raree show . . . a sort of private Bedlam hospital."

Such testimonies make me wonder whether she might have suffered from Tourette's syndrome, a neurological disorder characterized by sudden, meaningless movements or vocalizations. These tics can include eye blinking; squinting; lip smacking; neck jerking; shoulder shrugging; arm flailing; nail biting; foot stomping; barking; coughing; hissing; humming; stuttering; sudden changes of voice tone, tempo, or volume; the utterance of short meaningless phrases; and, most famously, coprolalia, the compulsion to swear or use socially unacceptable words. The "forbiddenness" of a given expression compels sufferers to say it, against their will. Tics can vanish for long periods of time; thus Cavendish could have been symptom-free when she first attracted the attention of her adoring husband, the dashing Marquis of Newcastle.

Tourette's syndrome can induce some spectacularly bizarre behavior, but I wouldn't want such a "diagnosis" to efface a more important—and more evident—explanation for the imaging of Cavendish as literary embarrassment. It seems to me that she serves as a dumping ground for repressed anxieties concerning reputation and authority. Philosopher Robert Paul Wolff writes that the most common reason for acknowledging claims of authority, "taking the whole of human history, is simply the prescriptive force of tradition. The fact that something has always been done in a certain way strikes most men as a perfectly adequate reason for doing it that way again." Despite recurring *outré* movements, the authoritative mainstream of literary culture, shaped by "the prescriptive force of tradition," emphasizes seemliness, conventionality, and patrilineage. My reading persuades me that fears concerning the transgression of such traditions have been displaced onto Margaret Cavendish. Her views, indeed, her entire self-definition, were—and are—culturally incorrect. She championed women's rights; opposed cruelty to animals; argued for religious freedom; dismissed witchcraft, alchemy, and astrology as unfounded superstitions. She also trespassed on the male preserves of writing and science.

Although Cavendish's critics ostensibly thought about her, their own reputations were a large part of the subject. From the start, her radically independent style evoked fear of contamination by association. Although she was the first woman invited to visit the Royal Society, the fashionable center of scientific discussion, some members opposed the invitation for fear that her presence would attract mockery. Of Cavendish's book *Nature's Pictures,* biographer Kathleen Jones writes: "Although women could identify with the characters in Margaret's tales they hesitated to defend her in case they too were branded as 'ridiculous.'" (*A Glorious Fame*) Through the centuries, she has been treated as a contagious site liable to infect writers who ventured a close association. In 1758, Horace Walpole opined that her brain was "diseased with cacoethes scribendi." Those who did venture to write about her used a condescending rhetoric as germ barrier or hid behind a surgical mask of satire.

Virginia Woolf notes that Cavendish became a bogey with which to frighten clever girls. The technique worked all too well. Woolf's several renditions of the Duchess are amusing yet frightened pieces of writing. While acknowledging her "wild, generous, untutored intelligence," Woolf compares Cavendish to "some giant cucumber" spreading itself "over all the roses and carnations in the garden" and choking them to death. The genteel flowers snuffed out by this overbearing, phallic vegetable are, I would suggest, such exemplars of acceptable feminine behavior as Katherine Philips, "the Divine Orinda." Philips declared writing "unfit for the sex to which I belong" and became sick with shame after her work was "inadvertently" published. She was, not accidentally, the reigning poetess of Cavendish's moment.

"Margaret's whole attitude to poetry flouted decorum," writes Douglas Grant. "Her real fault in Dorothy Osborne's eyes was an offense against taste." The dismissive appraisals by those who have never read her work; the longevity of gossip; the spread of calumny as good copy; the critical opinions founded on hearsay; the knee-jerk authority of "prescriptive tradition"; the ridicule occasioned by bravery are frightening. Cavendish's role as designated whipping girl of English literature is frightening. The fearful derision and hostility directed at her for three and a half centuries should be retargeted toward the literary culture that created her reception.

Philosopher Mary Midgley offers sobering thoughts on the suasions of false evidence. "Even people who know perfectly well that the so-called *Protocols of the Elders of Zion* were deliberately forged by the Czarist police still find no difficulty in accepting them as evidence. The dark vision is too vivid to be doubted; its force is its warrant. What we see out there is indeed real enough; it is our own viciousness, and it strikes us with quite appropriate terror. And by an unlucky chance, while it remains projected, there is no way to weaken or destroy it. Persecution and punishment of those to whom it is attributed do not soften it at all; . . . Hence the strange insatiability of persecution, the way in which suspicion seems to grow by being fed. . . . The joint repressed aggression of a whole populace makes up a very powerful motive for communal crimes, such as . . . witchhunts." (*Wickedness*)

~~

"I am as fearefull as a Hare . . . only my courage is, I can heare a sad relation, but not without griefe, and chilnesse of spirits," Cavendish wrote. The comparison of herself to a hare suggests the degree of sympathy she felt with hunted prey. Joy Williams writes, "Hunters have a tendency to call large animals by cute names—'bruins,' and 'muleys,' 'berryfed blackies,' and 'handsome cusses' and 'big guys,' thereby implying a balanced jolly game of mutual satisfaction between hunter and the hunted—*Bam, bam, bam, I get to shoot you and you get to be dead.*" ("The Killing Game") In like fashion, the abundantly sane Cavendish was nicknamed "Mad Madge." It was a short journey from being outspoken or "out of countenance" to being declared out of her mind.

"The Hunting of the Hare," reprinted here in full, is the poem that moved me to tears. Of course, emotions are irreproducible results. You could read the poem to your closest companion, as I did, and not be moved as I was. No doubt my entire life prepared me to be stricken at a given point. Not just life, but the intrinsic sinews of DNA before lived experience began. (I wasn't alone in my emotion, though. When I looked at my husband, he was wiping his eyes.)

The Hunting of the Hare

Betwixt two *Ridges* of *Plowd-land,* lay *Wat,*
Pressing his *Body* close to *Earth* lay squat.
His *Nose* upon his two *Fore-feet* close lies,
Glaring obliquely with his *great gray Eyes.*
His *Head* he alwaies sets against the *Wind;*
If turne his *Taile,* his *Haires* blow up behind:
Which *he* too cold will grow, but *he* is wise,
And keeps his *Coat* still downe, so warm *he* lies.
Thus resting all the day, till *Sun* doth set,
Then riseth up, his *Reliefe* for to get.
Walking about untill the *Sun* doth rise,

Then back returnes, down in his *Forme he* lyes.
At last, *Poore Wat* was found, as he there lay,
By *Hunts-men*, with their *Dogs* which came that way.
Seeing, gets up, and fast begins to run,
Hoping some waies the *Cruell Dogs* to shun.
But they by *Nature* have so quick a *Sent*,
That by their *Nose* they race, what way *he* went.
And with their deep, wide *Mouths* set forth a *Cry*,
Which answer'd was by *Ecchoes* in the *Skie*.
Then *Wat* was struck with *Terrour*, and with *Feare*,
Thinkes every *Shadow* still the *Dogs* they were.
And running out some distance from the *noise*,
To hide himselfe, his *Thoughts* he new imploies.
Under a *Clod* of *Earth* in *Sand-pit* wide,
Poore *Wat* sat close, hoping himselfe to hide.
There long he had not sat, but strait his *Eares*
The *Winding Hornes*, and crying *Dogs* he heares:
Starting with *Feare*, up leapes, then doth he run,
And with such speed, the *Ground* scarce treades upon.
Into a great thick *Wood he* strait way gets,
Where underneath a *broken Bough he* sits.
At every *Leafe* that with the *wind* did shake.
Did bring such *Terrour*, made his *Heart* to ake.
That *Place* he left, to *Champion Plaines* he went,
Winding about, for to deceive their *Sent*.
And while they *snuffling* were, to find his *Track*,
Poore *Wat*, being weary, his swift pace did slack.
On his two *hinder legs* for ease did sit,
His *Fore-feet* rub'd his *Face* from *Dust*, and *Sweat*.
Licking his *Feet*, he wip'd his *Eares* so cleane,
That none could tell that *Wat* had hunted been.
But casting round about his *faire great Eyes*,

The *Hounds* in full *Careere he* neere him 'spies:
To *Wat* it was so terrible a *Sight*,
Feare gave him *Wings*, and made his *Body* light.
Though weary was before, by running long,
Yet now his *Breath* he never felt more strong.
Like those that *dying* are, think *Health* returns,
When tis but a *faint Blast*, which *Life* out burnes.
For *Spirits* seek to guard the *Heart* about,
Striving with *Death*, but *Death* doth quench them out.
Thus they so fast came on, with such loud *Cries*,
That *he* no hopes hath left, no *help* espies.
With that the *Winds* did pity *poore Wats* case,
And with their *Breath* the *Sent* blew from the *Place*.
Then every *Nose* is busily imployed,
And every *Nostrill* is set open, wide:
And every *Head* doth seek a severall way,
To find what *Grasse*, or *Track*, the *Sent* on lay.
Thus quick Industry, that is not slack,
Is like to Witchery, that brings lost things back.
For though the *Wind* had tied the *Sent* up close,
A *Busie Dog* thrust in his *Snuffling Nose*:
And drew it out, with it did foremost run,
Then *Hornes* blew loud, for th' *rest* to follow on.
The *great slow-Hounds*, their throats did set a *Base*,
The *Fleet swift Hounds*, as *Tenours* next in place;
The little *Beagles* they a *Trebble* sing,
And through the *Aire* their *Voice* a round did ring?
Which made a *Consort*, as they they ran along;
If they but *words* could speak, might sing a *Song*,
The *Hornes* kept time, the *Hunters* shout for *Joy*,
And valiant seeme, *poore Wat* for to destroy:
Spurring their *Horses* to a full *Careere*,

Swim Rivers deep, leap Ditches without feare;
Indanger *Life,* and *Limbes,* so fast will ride,
Onely to see how patiently *Wat* died.
For why, the *Dogs* so neere his *Heeles* did get,
That they their sharp *Teeth* in his *Breech* did set.
Then tumbling downe, did fall with *weeping Eyes,*
Gives up his *Ghost,* and thus poore *Wat he* dies.
Men hooping loud, such *Acclamations* make,
As if the *Devill* they did *Prisoner* take.
When they do but a *shiftlesse Creature* kill;
To hunt, there needs no *Valiant Souldiers* skill.
But *Man* doth think that *Exercise,* and *Toile,*
To keep their *Health,* is best, which makes most spoile.
Thinking that *Food,* and *Nourishment* so good,
And *Appetite,* that feeds on *Flesh,* and *blood.*
When they do *Lions, Wolves, Beares, Tigers* see,
To kill poore *Sheep,* strait say, they cruell be.
But for themselves all *Creatures* think too few,
For *Luxury,* with *God* would make them new.
As if that *God* made *Creatures* for *Mans meat,*
To give them *Life,* and *Sense,* for *Man* to eat;
Or else for *Sport,* or *Recreations* sake,
Destroy those *Lives* that *God* saw good to make:
Making their *Stomacks, Graves,* which full they fill
With *Murther'd Bodies,* that in sport they kill.
Yet *Man* doth think himselfe so gentle, mild,
When *he* of *Creatures* is most cruell wild.
And is so *Proud,* thinks onely he shall live,
That *God* a *God-*like *Nature* did him give.
And that all *Creatures* for his sake alone,
Was made for him, to *Tyrannize* upon.

Did I say emotions were irreproducible results? Silly me. On TV last night a relaxation therapist described a test conducted on rabbits. The animals were fed a high-fat diet in order to determine its relation to arteriosclerosis. When the rabbits were "autopsied" (the flimsiest shade of misgiving passed over the therapist's face as he said the word), one group proved to have healthy arteries. This was mystifying since all the animals had received exactly the same food. Upon investigation, a single difference came to light: The healthy rabbits had been cared for by a graduate student who stroked them when she fed them. (At this, a doctor serving as audience smiled benignly: Isn't that sweet.) Of course, the experiment had to be conducted several times in order to verify the findings. After a sufficient number of rabbits had been caressed and vivisected, the study concluded that *compassion lowers cholesterol.*

At last a sound argument for loving kindness. Let's be merciful and lower each other's cholesterol. The experiment also gave a reproducible effect (healthy arteries) stemming from an emotive cause (compassion). *Compassion?* Wouldn't *duplicity, selfishness, coldness, calculation* better describe the experiment's character? The listening doctor's sappy smile made me suspect a connection between sentimentality and synecdoche. To feel selectively, responding with fuzzy feelings to one aspect of an event while repressing any troubling emotions stirred by other aspects is, I submit, sentimental.

~~

Lewis Thomas observed that much of the current environmental concern is based on self-interest rather than concern for nature, "that vast incomprehensible meditative being." Margaret Cavendish consistently took Nature's side. "Dialogue with an Oake" finds a tree arguing with Man, who is about to cut it down. Throughout the poem, Man unwittingly testifies to human greed, which he conflates with Man's "divine nature." The poem concludes with an ironic comment on Man's perversity and narcissism: Only if the Oake desires the afterlife of harvest, in which it would be transformed into a ship or house, will Man recognize his likeness in the tree and spare it from harvest.

Cavendish wrote a series of Dialogues in which two players argue opposing sides of a question. Her gift for seeing the recessive, yin slant of things, the ground rather than the figure, helped her to complicate these polarized conversations. Thus Darknesse tells Earth that the Sun is responsible for night: "*I do not part you, he me hither sends, / Whilst Hee rides about, to visit all his Friends.*" Hate depicts Love as self-serving: "*Love loves Ambition, the Mind's hot Fire, / And Worlds would ruine, for to rise up higher.*" And Ignorance says that Learning "Doth nought but make an *Almes-tub* of the *Braines.*" Cavendish's penchant for reversals arose not from a contrarian temperament but from her feelings of alterity and the specious arguments used to enforce that position. Notions of what constitutes "natural" behavior always have been invoked as a means of controlling women's lives. Cavendish turned the argument against itself, writing, "It is not only uncivil and ignoble, but unnatural for men to speak against women and their liberties." (*Divers Orations*, 1662) Many of her poems unsettle assumptions of hierarchy. "A Dialogue betwixt Wit, and Beauty" questions superiority founded on skin color:

> *Mixt Rose*, and *Lilly*, why are you so proud,
> Since *Faire* is not in all *Minds* best allow'd?
> *Some* like the *Black*, the *Browne*, as well as *White*,
> In all *Complexions* some *Eyes* take delight . . .

The Dialogues show Cavendish's scientific intelligence, a cast of mind that assumed as little as possible and pressed the given explanations. Her skepticism led her to mistrust superficial perceptions and to critique the evidence of the senses. Using magnetism to exemplify counterintuitive truths, she wrote: "What *Eye* so *cleere* is, yet did ever see / Those *little Hookes*, that in the *Load-stone* bee" ("It is hard to believe, that there are other Worlds in this World.") Passion makes us advocates: In the grip of emotion we cling wholeheartedly to one position, and other sides of the argument are lost to us. As if in recognition of this, the Dialogues sometimes warp binary thinking by arguing both positions convincingly. Alterity implodes as agency is exchanged between equally convincing speakers. Readers are forced to acknowledge the power of both claims and to establish within the paradox of opposing truths a third, indeterminate space that differs from the fixed positions of dichotomous thinking.

Cavendish objected to standard measures of intelligence, noting that man may have "a different knowledge from beasts, birds, fish, worms, and the like and yet be no wiser or knowing than they; for different ways in knowledge make not knowledge more or less, no more than different paths enlarge one compasse of ground." Her passion for equity extended beyond social and humanitarian contexts to notions of the sublime. Paradise was "Equinoctiall" ("Of a Garden"); and "a consecrated place" was one where trees "grew in equall space." ("Of an Oake in a Grove") One of her loveliest works, "The Motion of Thoughts," uses Euclidean tropes of measurement to describe the light of cognition and the self-referential neural networks that give rise to consciousness. The poem begins with a nature walk that in Romantic fashion leads to an epiphany.

The Motion of Thoughts

Moving alone, mine *Eyes* being fixt
Upon the *Ground,* my *Sight* with *Gravell* mixt:
My *Feet* did walke without *Directions* Guide,
My *Thoughts* did travell farre, and wander wide;
At last they chanc'd up to a *Hill* to climbe,
And being there, saw things that were Divine.
    First, what they saw, a glorious *Light* to blaze,
Whose *Splendor* made it painfull for the *Gaze:*
No *Separations,* nor *Shadowes* by stops made,
No *Darknesse* to obstruct this *Light* with *Shade.*
This *Light* had no *Dimension,* nor *Extent,*
But fil'd all places full, without *Circumvent;*
Alwaies in *Motion,* yet fixt did prove,
Like to *Twinkling Stars* which never move.
This *Motion* working, running severall waies,

Did seeme a *Contradiction* for to raise;
As to it *selfe*, with it *selfe* disagree,
Is like a *Skeine* of *Thread*, if 't knotted bee.
For some did go strait in an even *Line*,
But some againe did crosse, and some did *twine*.

Lewis Thomas describes the mechanism of thought as follows: "Predictable, small-scale, orderly, cause-and-effect sequences are hard to come by and don't last long when they do turn up. Something else almost always turns up at the same time, and then another sequential thought intervenes alongside, and there come turbulence and chaos again. When we are lucky, and the system operates at its random best, something astonishing may suddenly turn up, beyond predicting or imagining."

Yet at the last, all severall *Motions* run
Into the first *Prime Motion* which begun.
In various *Formes* and *Shapes* did *Life* run through,
Life from *Eternity*, but *Shapes* still new;
No sooner made, but quickly pass'd away,
Yet while they *were*, desirous were to stay.
But *Motion* to one *Forme* can nere constant be,
For *Life*, which *Motion* is, joyes in varietie.
For the first *Motion* every thing can make,
But cannot add unto it selfe, nor take.
Indeed no other *Matter* could it frame,
It *selfe* was all, and in it *selfe* the fame.
Perceiving now this fixed *point* of *Light*,
To be a *Union*, *Knowledge*, *Power*, and *Might*;
Wisdome, *Justice*, *Truth*, *Providence*, all one,

No *Attribute* is with it selfe alone.
Not like to severall *Lines* drawne to one *Point*,
For what doth meet, may separate, disjoynt.
But *this* a *Point*, from whence all *Lines* do flow,
Nought can diminish it, or make it grow.
Tis *its* owne *Center*, and *Circumference* round,
Yet neither has a *Limit*, or a *Bound*.
A *fixt Eternity*, and so will last,
All *present* is, nothing to come, or past.
A fixt *Perfection* nothing can add more,
All things is *It*, and *It* selfe doth adore.
My *Thoughts* then wondring at what they did see,
Found at the last* themselves the same to bee;
Yet was so small a *Branch*, perceive could not,
From whence they *Sprung*, or which waies were begot.

The glorious light of the mind, which turns out to be God's light, is self-involved as any animal: "A fixt *Perfection* nothing can add more / All things is *It*, and *It* selfe doth adore." The paradox of the one/many problem is charmingly enacted by the disagreement between the plural subject, "things," and singular verb, "is." The speaker then recognizes her Thoughts as diminutive instances of the great force she had perceived as external. Shifting its measures from thought to emotion, the poem next suggests that the Passions of paradise may exceed those of earth. The closure dismisses the calculations of astronomy, math, navigation, geometry, and natural philosophy as unequal to

---

All things come from God Almighty.

the breadth of the heaven. The immeasurable will always outnumber the measureable.

> Some say, all that we know of *Heaven* above,
> Is that we joye, and that we love.
> Who can tell that? for all we know,
> Those *Passions* we call *Joy*, and *Love* below,
> May, by *Excesse*, such other *Passions* grow,
> None in the World is capable to know.
> Just like our *Bodies*, though that they shall rise,
> And as St. *Paul* saies, see *God* with our *Eyes*;
> Yet may we in the *Change* such difference find,
> Both in our *Bodies*, and also in our *Mind*,
> As if that we were never of *Mankind*,
> And that these *Eyes* we see with now, were blind.
> Say we can measure all the *Planets* high,
> And number all the *Stars* be in the *Skie*;
> And *Circle* could we all the *World* about,
> And all th' *Effects* of *Nature* could finde out:
> Yet cannot all the *Wise*, and *Learned* tell,
> What's done in *Heaven*, or how we there shall dwell.

~~

"Those *Passions* . . . / May, by Excesse, such other *Passions* grow." When a poet is praised for her wide emotional range that amplitude includes the various shadings of joy, love, and grief. It does not include queasiness, disgust, and horror. The excesses of certain Cavendish poems, however, are likely to stir "such other *Passions*." Earlier I divided her verse into two kinds: those that shared the simplicity of George

Herbert and those that partook of Richard Crashaw's grotesque sensibility. I've concentrated on the first sort because I like them best and because critical opinion has fastened, unfairly, it seems to me, upon the Crashaw-like verses.

Richard Crashaw's poetry offers stupendous examples of ecstatic high seriousness that crashes unwittingly into banal low comedy. The disproportion between the work's intention and its affect are absurd. His excesses are models of camp. The textbook example, from his poem on the tears of Mary Magdalen, finds the pilgrim "followed by two faithful fountains, / Two walking baths, two weeping motions; / Portable and compendious oceans." Cavendish's discrepancies of intent and affect sometimes result in Crashaw-like campiness. The poem seems to have an emotive life of its own, quite beyond the author's control. Her conceits can be intensely discomfiting, yet she is naif enough to be unaware of the feelings she stirs. Keats said of the poetical character that "It lives in gusto, be it foul or fair." Cavendish's excesses are at times more foul than fair. Some of her poetry had me resorting to a vocabulary of teenaged squeamishness: Gross! Yucky!

Cavendish's temperament was pragmatic whereas Crashaw's was visionary; her exaggerations are fueled by realism rather than religion. Her sensibility, moreover, was tragic rather than ecstatic. As a result, she tends toward gory rather than silly extremes. Her macabre poems seize the facts of physicality, excavate their true, but truly unsavory implications, and push those implications to fantastic lengths that still retain elements of the realism necessary to horror. But even these poems reflect Cavendish's deep worldview, albeit in bizarre form. Their ghoulish tropes of embodiment violently enforce equity between humans and animals. From "flesh and blood," with its suggestions of divine transubstantiation, the human form is reduced to "meat." By dissolving the difference between flesh and meat, such poems enact the brutality of carnivorism. In one gruesome passage, human body parts are up for sale on "*shamble-row,*" the butcher's market, along with dead animals. ("Of a Travelling Thought") In "A Battle between King Oberon, and the Pygmees," she writes:

> Here *beasts* and *men*, both in ther *bloud* lay *masht,*
> As if that a *French Cook* had them minc'd, *so hasht,*
> Or with their *bloud* a *Gelly* boyle,
> To make a *Bouillion* of the *spoyle.*

While Cavendish's Herbert-like poems were anthropomorphic, her Crashaw-like poems are anthropophagous: They violate taboos concerning the eating of human flesh. Just as animals are personified in her "simple" poems, persons are animalized in her "grotesque" verse. The body's animality does not discount the possibility of divinity: It extends that possibility to beasts, an inclusion that refutes human assumptions of superiority.

I would suggest that horrific events in Cavendish's life forced her ideas into these ghoulish expressions. During the Civil War, Parliamentary troops disinterred and dismembered the bodies of Cavendish's mother and sister. Kathleen Jones writes that "the soldiers made game with the dead ladies' hair in their hats." When news of this defilement and of her brother's execution reached Cavendish, she was disconsolate. The ghastliness seems to have made its way, unmediated, into some of her poems.

Both Cavendish and Richard Crashaw were members of Queen Henrietta Maria's Oxford and Paris courts. Although her bashfulness no doubt prevented conversation, Cavendish might have read Crashaw's manuscripts in circulation. "Extravagant" is often used to describe them both. Richard Crashaw, however, is accorded eleven pages in the *Norton Anthology* (6th edition), while Cavendish is allowed two. What is "unique" in Crashaw is deviant in her. The best she can hope for is to be deemed eccentric, or outside the center. Historically, "eccentric" is what female poets get to be instead of "original." Yet it seems to me that eccentricity is to postmodernism what originality was to Romanticism: a foundational principle. Although Crashaw was ridiculed for his absurd conceits, his work eventually found its audience. Perhaps postmodernism will find new ways to revel in the excesses of Cavendish's outlandish passions.

The gusto that makes some poems unwholesome adds conviction to her best efforts. Her satire on pastoral romance is as good in its way as Sir Walter Raleigh's reply to Marlowe's "Passionate Shepherd."

A Description of Shepherds, and Shepherdesses

The *Shepherdesses* which great Flocks doe keep,
Are dabl'd high with dew, following their Sheep,
Milking their Ewes, their hands doe dirty make;
For being wet, dirt from their Duggs doe take.
The Sun doth scorch the skin, it yellow growes,
Their eyes are red, lips dry with wind that blowes.
Their Shepherds sit on mountains top, that's high,
Yet on their feeding sheep doe cast an eye;
Which to the mounts steep sides they hanging feed
On short moyst grasse, not suffer'd to beare feed;
Their feet though small, strong are their sinews string,
Which make them fast to rocks & mountains cling:
The while the *Shepherds* leggs hang dangling down,
And sets his breech upon the hills high crown.
Like to a tanned Hide, so was his skin,
No melting heat, or numming cold gets in,
And with a voyce that's harsh against his throat,
He strains to sing, yet knowes not any Note:
And yawning, lazie lyes upon his side,
Or strait upon his back, with armes spred wide;
Or snorting sleeps, and dreames of *Joan* their Maid,
Or of Hobgoblin wakes, as being afraid.
Motion in their dull braines doth plow, and sow,
Not Plant, and set, as skilfull Gardners doe.
Or takes his Knife new ground, that half was broke,
And whittles sticks to pin up his sheep-coat:
Or cuts some holes in straw, to Pipe thereon
Some tunes that pleaseth *Joan* his Love at home.
Thus rustick Clownes are pleas'd to spend their times,
And not as *Poets* faine, in *Sonnets, Rhimes,*

Making great *Kings* and *Princes* Pastures keep,
And beauteous *Ladies* driving flocks of sheep:
Dancing 'bout May-poles in a rustick sort,
When *Ladies* scorne to dance without a Court.
For they their Loves would hate, if they should come
With leather Jerkins, breeches made of Thrum,
And Buskings made of Freeze that's course, and strong,
With clouted Shooes, tyed with a leather thong.
Those that are nicely bred, fine cloaths still love,
A white hand sluttish seems in dirty Glove.

Cavendish's disdain for affectation is evident in this poem, which mocks the faux shepherds and shepherdesses of idealized courtly love. Kathleen Jones notes that Cavendish's fellow courtiers indulged in a fad for Platonic love, while she scorned such dissembling. Of course, her tendency to be out of countenance made her unpopular at court. In fact, "outness" seems to have been her salient trait. On the page, she is not only outspoken but, it seems to me, out of her epoch. Writers are shaped by inherent temperaments as much as by the climate of their age. Affinities spring up across centuries, in defiance of time. Margaret Cavendish has more in common with Whitman's hankering, gross, mystical nudity than with Milton's sonorous depths. Like Whitman, she is "one of the roughs, a kosmos." Like him, she could resist anything better than her own diversity, as her poems, letters, plays, fictions, and essays testify. "I love those best which I create myself," she wrote of her work in *Sociable Letters*.

But a "barbaric yawp" that issued from a woman's pen

could only seem vulgar. Imagine the reception that would greet a woman who wrote, "I dote on myself . . . there is that lot of me, and all so luscious." ("Song of Myself") Oddly enough, men poets have been praised for the very qualities that are maligned in Cavendish. The absence of rigorous formal education, counted as a debit for her, is no such thing for Burns, Blake, Clare, and Whitman. Although Christopher Smart, Blake, and Clare were "mad," their disorder has, if anything, stoked their legends. Cavendish, who was sane, has been slandered as mad and "handled with a Chain," in Dickinson's phrase. Even so sympathetic a reader as Kathleen Jones speculates that "paradoxes," along with "the sheer bulk of Margaret's work," have led to her neglect. Surely both factors would be construed as strengths in a man poet. In reference to her own verse, Anne Bradstreet wrote, "If what I do prove well, it won't advance, / They'll say it's stolen, or else it was by chance." Cavendish's single poem in the latest *Norton Anthology* is burdened with the following footnote: "The duchess clearly, *though perhaps not deliberately*, contrasts the world of women . . . with that of . . . Apollonian masculinity." (My italics.) It is hard to understand how a foundational belief that appears across an entire body of work can be regarded as a happy accident.

Cavendish hoped for a posterity in which her work would know "a glorious Resurrection . . . since Time brings strange and unusual things to pass!" It seems to me that she should take her place within a tradition of spontaneous composition and vitality: feral poets whose work Robert Lowell characterized as raw rather than cooked, and whose writing process Allen Ginsberg summarized as "first word, best word." Passages of her work show something of the shrewd earthiness of Chaucer; the sincerity of Christopher Smart; the forcefulness of Robert Burns; the innocence of Blake's songs; the heartfelt engagement of John Clare; the robust egotism of Whitman. An anthology of her best poetry and prose would give readers a place to begin. There is scholary interest in her work right now, so perhaps some enterprising publisher will issue such an "olio" or collection.

After I'd confessed my strange and unusual passion to the reading group, someone said, "Isn't it amazing that she can change you despite the distance of so much time?"

"Yes, and I can change her," I said, too quickly. "By changing the reception of her work." Would that it were so. In a letter "To Poets" Cavendish writes "I have no Eloquent Orator to plead for me, as to perswade a Severe Judge, nor Flattery to bribe a Corrupt one; which makes me afraid, I shall lose my Suit of Praise . . . But if the Judge be learned in the Lawes of Poetry, and honesty from Bribes of Envy; I shall not need to feare." She still has no Eloquent Orator; her writing is its own best defense. Although I am thrown out of countenance by her travails, she seems to have maintained her private equipoise. "The Worlds dispraises cannot make me a mourning garment," she noted. "My mind's too big." Her mind—that insatiable, unordinary place.

1998

Her Moment of Brocade:
The Reconstruction of Emily Dickinson

The way Hope builds his House
It is not with a sill—
Nor Rafter—has Mars—
But only Pinnacle—

1481, VARIANT VERSION

THE FOLLOWING BIT OF APOCRYPHAL GOSSIP MADE the rounds of writers' conferences last summer: Two well-known poets stand at a podium, both of them in their fifties. One waits to read her poems; the other to introduce her. The poet who'll read wears a circle skirt to which a large felt poodle is appliquéd. Her introducer, a short heavy woman, is dressed in paisley jodhpurs and a jeweled sweater. In the audience an up-and-coming man poet of a younger generation shifts restlessly in his chair. (The fashion report on him is never given.) Leaning toward the guy beside him, he whispers, "Debutantes from Mars." Hearing this story, I imagined a third figure flickering behind the lectern: a middle-aged woman in a long, button-front, kick-pleated white shift resembling a nightgown. If the audience could see this spectre, they'd recognize the template

of the female poet as alien invader: Emily Dickinson.
Would a poet of her genius and gender receive more re-
spectful attention today than the two women of my anecdote? Moreover, might this snippet, with its emphasis on
couture, girlishness, otherness, illuminate the resistance to
a Dickinsonian tradition in American letters?

Of course, Dickinson is a canonical writer. Among
scholars and general readers, her eminence is taken for
granted. But who among contemporary poets has been
placed within a Dickinsonian context? Where are her heirs?
Essays and reviews of twentieth-century poets frequently
point to Whitman as influence or forebear. The Beat poets,
among others, are construed as his descendants. Yet it's
hard to think of any criticism that places a man poet
within a primarily Dickinsonian orbit, although she's often
mentioned in passing. (The problems for female poets are
different, and I'll come to them.) Perhaps the resistance to
a Dickinsonian linkage or lineage has its basis in patriarchal assumptions and cultural insecurities surrounding
gender. Americans tend to view poetry writing as an un-
manly or "feminine" vocation. That "feminine" has associations of weakness or unworthiness in the common mind
says a great deal about this culture's unspoken assumptions. In her perceptive book *Made in America: Science, Technology, and American Modernist Poets*, Lisa M. Steinman quotes
Williams in 1949 as saying, "We seldom think of ... poetic
structure, as we do of engineering: a field of action worthy
of masculine attack." One notices the martial language
with which he describes his ideal enterprise. It implies that
poetry, properly regarded, is a combative activity. This atti-

tude is with us still. How could the women of my opening anecdote, those flaky, fluttery others, endow literary kin with a seminal aura "worthy of masculine attack"? If literature is warfare, men need robust father figures to defend, shield, authorize, and sequester their enterprise. Although *female* poets are sometimes compared to Dickinson, the comparison serves to underscore eccentricity rather than brilliance.

I said that Dickinson's eminence is taken for granted. I must add that her status is also resented. As part of a recent symposium in the *Texas Review* called "Nominations for Oblivion," novelist Robert Bausch wrote:

> No imagination could possibly wish to construct so many silly rhymes with the *same* rhythmical pattern except one that has been stilted by some sort of oddly imposed and intractable virginity. The only reason people are forced to study Emily Dickinson in American universities is that she is female and in these days of socially relevant education teachers *have* to include a woman somewhere. Imagine how disappointed everybody's going to be when critics and scholars return to their senses and discover that Emily Dickinson's poetry is nothing less than something less than nothing at all. . . . It leaves me feeling as though I have been trampled by a McDonald's advertisement.

I'm glad that Bausch published the above sentiment because most Dickinson-bashing takes place in private conversations. Since the symposium is presented as "satire, intended for fun," one is asked to believe that Bausch's comment (I've quoted only a fraction of his spleen) has no meaning, subtext, or effect. Like the debutantes-from-Mars anecdote, Bausch's words hide damaging premises behind a pretense of wit and ask for our laughing complicity. Anyone who detects hostility in such "fun" is a spoilsport. It's not that we can't have Dickinson jokes, but we have to acknowledge that humor has latent meanings and that those meanings can be sexist, racist, or just plain dumb.

Bausch's mention of "intractable virginity" shows that his knowledge of Dickinson begins and ends in superficial stereotypes. Such mythology began to take shape within Dickinson's lifetime, and there's been an undue emphasis on her biography ever since. The legend no doubt helps explain why students, writers, and readers often speak of "Emily" as if they held frequent tête-à-têtes with her. Perhaps the spurious intimacy she evokes encourages this fatuous address. But the poetry and biography of Keats provide equally fertile ground for identification and empathy. And who ever thinks of him as John? Referring to writers by their first names signals familiarity, and we know what that breeds; it also undermines the writer's authority. Ultimately it's a reductive address, a means of conferring minion status upon one who would be Queen.

The Dickinson of popular mythology is an ingenuous sufferer whose lonely life of seclusion results from a mysterious unrequited love (hence her "intractable virginity"). She is a naive folk artist, lacking an ars poetica or tradition, which of itself consigns her to eccentricity. Her genius, when conceded, is said to be anomalous: She will have no literary heirs because her accomplishment is too wayward for assimilation. Recent studies of Dickinson work against some of these tired notions. One can't, however, dismantle clichés so firmly entrenched in the collective imagination by publishing scholarly books. And in trying to dismantle The Myth, scholarship has produced new, sometimes more fantastic legends. The recombinant Emily Dickinson emerges as nun; heretic; psychotic; anorexic; agoraphobe; even unwed mother. In trying to counteract a phallocentric bias, feminist readings have turned the simpering flower to Fury; the jilted spinster to thwarted lesbian. Even those who knew Emily Dickinson were often mystified or fooled. According to Austin, his sister posed in her letters to editor Thomas Higginson. And she must have stayed in character for their single face-to-face meeting, a coming-out party for the interplanetary ingenue, if we can believe Higginson's description of a whispery, intense "half-cracked poetess." Given all this, it's tempting to view the poet as an actress, her lyric "I" a form of dramatic monologue. Whitman's self-descriptive lines apply: She is large. She contains multitudes.

In fact, Dickinson's current standing has nothing to do with her education (which was rigorous and wideranging), her own influences (which were diverse), the absence of an aesthetics (available in her poetry and letters as surely as in those of Keats), her method (again comparable to Keats), or her writing (which is anomalous only in its extraordinary achievement). The historical Dickinson is irretrievable. We are left with our fantasies, which say as much about us as about her. In poem 526 she reminds us of our intractable subjectivity:

To hear an Oriole sing
May be a common thing—
Or only a divine.

It is not of the Bird
Who sings the same, unheard,
As unto Crowd—

The Fashion of the Ear
Attireth that it hear
In Dun, or fair—

So whether it be Rune,
Or whether it be none
Is of within.

The "Tune is in the Tree—"
The Skeptic—showeth me—
"No Sir! In Thee!"

The observer alters what's observed; a poet's reception depends upon "The Fashion of the Ear." The listener
(reader) determines whether poetry is magical script
("Rune"), failure (ruin), or "none." The last fate is reserved
for work that remains unread, consigned to absence. We,
the current audience, create and alter a poet's standing. The
Martha Graham Dance Company, in their recent produc-
tion of "Letter to the World," cast the glamorous Kathleen
Turner as Dickinson. Why do we insist upon her as Belle of
Amherst? Perhaps it's because a nubile woman who writes
poetry is a pretty concept. She may adore her older male

teachers and pose no threat. But what if she continues to develop as an artist, devoting the main portion of her life and energies to her writing? What happens to the female poet too mature to be called "promising," too well known to be "emerging"? There's a good chance she'll become an object of scorn, the butt of jokes like the one at the beginning of this essay. Little will be written about her work. Her poems may go out of print, as Marianne Moore's did during the seventies. Whenever older female poets read for my classes, students are surprised that women their mothers' age can write about ideas, including sexuality and politics, without trotting out tuna-casserole platitudes. Some of the young men seem amazed that such women can think at all! Their reports dwell upon the poet's matronly appearance that belies (to their minds) the shocking (to their minds) content of the poems. "I'd expected a much younger woman," they write. In contrast, men poets of comparable age are said to be "distinguished," as if they embodied the debonair charm of aging movie stars.

Of course, some brilliant men poets also suffer neglect. But so few women have been accorded major status that one must connect their sex and gender with their disenfranchisement. Most significant awards still go to men. Whether the recipients of the accolades are more deserving, more gifted, than their less fortunate *brothers* isn't the point. Their sisters aren't in the running at all. "What about Adrienne Rich, Rita Dove?" Lest we confuse tokenism with equity, consider the following facts: In 1988, the Literature Department of the American Academy of Arts and Letters includes approximately thirty poets, six

of them women. Seven *members* of the Academy are poets,
none of them women. The twelve-member board of Chan-
cellors of The Academy of American Poets includes two
women. Either there are very few significant female poets or
else such poets suffer from discrimination. One must
remind oneself that women are not a minority. On the contrary, women's writing is majority writing, both in the sense
of numbers and in coming of age. Yet the evidence suggests
that most people still want their great poets to be men.
Such a cultural climate affects the reception of Dickinson's
work as surely as that of contemporary poets. She worried
that her poetry would be seen as "the only Kangaroo
among the Beauty." "It afflicts me," she wrote Higginson.
And how do we see her? As a wonderful yet anomalous
presence, given to unexpected leaps, equipped with bizarre
pockets, comic as a cartoon, powerful as a boxer—great,
yes, but aberrant, other: kangarooish!

Ironically, it was patriarchy that afforded Dickinson
time to write and think. Male dominance as practiced in
Victorian Amherst became for her both enablement and
disablement, protection and prison. The word *patriarchy*
evokes extreme reactions, perhaps because people are un-
sure what's meant by the term. I offer a definition from my
contemporary *Webster's*: "social organization marked by the
supremacy of the father in the clan or the family in both
domestic and religious functions, the legal dependence of
wife or wives and children, and the reckoning of descent
and inheritance in the male line. b: a society so organized."
In nineteenth-century Amherst, females of Dickinson's
economic class were not expected to be self-supporting.

Her father's social standing and wealth saved her from the grim jobs available to women: factory work or the middle-class option of teaching school. There's little doubt that Edward Dickinson ruled supreme within his family, and his possessiveness is said to have discouraged his daughters' suitors. If so, this might have been a disguised blessing for Emily. In the 1800s, women married for financial security (which she already had), companionship (which she found in Austin and Lavinia), and children (although many women did not regard pregnancy as a desirable aspect of matrimony).

A little reading on the development of obstetrics convinces one—and it is an astounding knowledge—of the overwhelming dread with which women historically viewed childbirth. The silence and neglect surrounding this formidably central province of human experience encourages us to misunderstand any American women born before contraception became commonplace. We have forgotten that until recently childbirth was woman's heroic sphere. As such, it provided a more frequent and dependably excruciating trial than man's transcendent analogue of war. In Dickinson's day, birth control was limited and seldom practiced; anaesthetics (chloroform and laudanum) were unreliable and sometimes unavailable; doctors were just beginning to attend births, and their lack of experience and ignorance of bacteria made their presence more risk than boon. Judith Leavitt, in *Brought to Bed*, writes: "Women knew that if procreation did not kill them, it could maim them for life." Children aside, a married woman of Dickinson's social standing was expected to oversee the details of an elaborate

household and play hostess to her husband's business associates, tasks that would leave little time for the writing of
1,775 poems. All in all, the realities of marriage might have
seemed less attractive to Dickinson than the relationships
she inhabited through writing.

Of all the forms of male dominance, perhaps the most
evident to Dickinson was patrilinaeage, "the reckoning of
descent and inheritance in the male line." Her domineering
father accorded Austin, his son and heir, immense respect
as his birthright. Dickinson undoubtedly loved her brother.
Yet she might have felt some chagrin at hearing their father
declare Austin's letters "altogether before Shakespeare"
while her own great talents went unremarked. Indeed, Mr.
Dickinson was so taken by his son's letters that he wished
"to have them published to put in our library." Here's how
Emily Dickinson reacted to the family's designated genius
in 1853: "And Austin is a Poet, Austin writes a psalm. Out
of the way, Pegasus, Olympus enough 'to him,' and just say
to those 'nine muses' that we have done with them! Raised
a living muse ourselves, worth the whole nine of them. . . .
Now, Brother Pegasus, I'll tell you what it is—I've been in
the habit *myself* of writing some few things, and it rather
appears to me that you're getting away my patent, so you'd
better be somewhat careful. . . ." By 1866, her sense of
poetic mastery extended beyond the household competition. In a letter describing the March weather she wrote,
"Here is the 'light' the Stranger said 'was not on land or sea.'
Myself could arrest it but we'll not chagrin Him." The
quote is from Wordsworth's *Elegiac Stanzas*.

As a cultural norm, patrilineage is responsible for the

most destructive prejudice surrounding Emily Dickinson: the view that she is a curiosity of American literature. Patrilineage means all children must receive their father's surname as a means of creating identity, order, legacy, and connection. A child who receives a mother's name is a bastard. The pervasiveness of this view makes it difficult for us to imagine women as creators of dynasties—be they familial, financial, or literary. Since lineage must pass from father to son, Dickinson cannot offer legitimacy to her successors. Unable to envision her as progenitor, critics and scholars regard her work as too eccentric to exert broad influence. The same prejudices apply to Marianne Moore, Elizabeth Bishop, and all poets who are women. They are our perennial spinsters, deprived of issue and succession.

In fact, Dickinson is not without her descendants, but they are the heirs unapparent: favored sons who have been awarded steadier pedigrees or orphaned females sans genealogy. A. R. Ammons, for example, should be recognized as a scion of Dickinson. Ammons's pervasive use of the colon is analogous to the Dickinsonian dash; his subjects are hers; his abstract vocabulary draws upon her matrix—from sphere to difference. His process of writing is comparable, as is the sheer amount of poetry he has produced. Yet the comment accompanying his National Book Critics Circle Award in 1981 summarizes the way his work has been read: "He is a poet of the American Sublime . . . standing in the tradition of Wordsworth, Emerson, and Whitman." Apparently Dickinson is not part of "the American Sublime." Although Ammons studied with Josephine Miles, her possible influence upon his work is never mentioned. Being female, she is unable to confer legitimacy. Miles herself shows a Dickinsonian influence in the ontological questioning, colloquial ease, and abstract vocabulary of many poems.

Dickinson's influence makes itself felt in the stropped language of Robert Creeley; the linguistic sparks of Heather McHugh; the wickedly unconventional wit and existential fables of Phyllis Janowitz; the delight in formal experiment, passion for the natural world, and colloquial ease of May Swenson; the religious sensibility of Denise Levertov. The work of Charles Simic, with its spacious leaps, honed syntax, and decocted folklore is also kin. When I mentioned this consanguinity, Mr. Simic wrote, "Dickinson is the poet who means more and more to me as the years pass. . . . Her poems think as they unfold—that's my dream! My hope is to understand her great art before I die." When I jokingly suggested that his line stemmed from "the seldom-mentioned Serbian side" of her family, Simic offered the following genealogy: "I believe they were Russian. Came out of Dostoyevsky's rooming house for poor students. A family of anarchists who kept their children out of school. Taught them themselves. They read so much they all wore thick glasses by the time they were four years old. When they came to America they opened a delicatessen in Springfield, Massachusetts. Miss Emily used to go there on the q.t. for gherkins. She thought she was pregnant. She was! With theology, poetry, and philosophy." Simic's imagined history places the poet within a context of intelligent rebellion (anarchists, thick glasses) while affectionately crediting her creative fertility.

For myself, I continue to learn from Dickinson's genius with abstraction; the manyness rather than singleness of her imagery; the pronouns enlarged by slippery antecedents; the variety one can achieve in prosody. In this age of conservative formalism, when every other poem one reads is in the C major of blank verse, Dickinson reminds me of the countless tones and keys at my disposal. Her poems show the heady brilliance of successful experiment. They convince me of the value and possibility of delineating inner states so subtle as to be almost subconscious. The volume and quality of her accomplishment instill a faith that language is both unbounded and mine: an infinite resource, limited only by my limitations. Her life teaches American poets to keep their eyes on the luminous infinite sphere of language rather than on the bouncing ball of regular iambs or the gold ring of poe-biz acclaim. Her poems prove that one can embrace complication without forfeiting the reader's pleasure.

~~

Dickinson's fame began in 1890 with the publication of a slim selection of her verse. The public adored the book, which went into multiple printings. Mabel Loomis Todd (with the help of Thomas Higginson) took on the monumental task of editing and selection. Their attempts to normalize meter, rhyme, and punctuation, along with their choice of the more conventional poems, made Dickinson palatable at a time when her experiments would have met with bewilderment. Although her work found a popular audience, serious acclaim was slow to come. The *Atlantic Monthly* stated that "an eccentric, dreamy, half-educated recluse in an out-of-the-way New England village—or anywhere else—cannot with impunity set at defiance the laws of gravitation and grammar. . . . Oblivion lingers in the immediate neighborhood." The adjectives in that first sentence live on in Dickinson mythology, along with the tendency to anthologize her least ambitious work.

Given its high degree of indeterminacy and plurality, Dickinson's most complex poetry is best suited to a postmodernist age. New literary theories and contemporary science offer ways of constructing reality that help us appreciate poems previously consigned to the periphery. Yet in trying to represent Dickinson's essential canon, *The Norton Anthology of Poetry* (3rd edition) prizes the simple, the plain, the ecstatic, the erotic, the natural, and the macabre, all traits of a Romantic disposition. More cerebral, disjunctive, and ambiguous poems are excluded. Of course, many of the anthology chestnuts number among Dickinson's great works. But poem 449, for example, expresses conventional nineteenth-century sentiments in fairly conventional style. It comes as close to being a set piece as anything Dickinson ever wrote.

> I died for Beauty—but was scarce
> Adjusted in the Tomb
> When One who died for Truth, was lain
> In an adjoining Room—

He questioned softly "Why I failed?"
"For Beauty," I replied—
"And I—for Truth—Themself are One—
We Brethren, are," He said—

And so, as Kinsmen, met a Night—
We talked between the Rooms—
Until the Moss had reached our lips—
And covered up—our names—

This poem owes so much to Keats's Grecian Urn that I can never read it without envisioning him as the One interred beside the speaker. At least the poem contains a few Dickinsonian grace notes. The extra comma in line eight ("'... We Brethren, are,' He said—"); the coupling of singular and plural within one noun ("Themself" rather than the "Themselves" in line seven); and the hypotaxic syntax (three of the last six lines begin with "And") distinguish it, though marginally, from brand X Victorian verse. Poem 1078, another favorite of anthologists, voices its platitudes in unremarkable language.

The Bustle in a House
The Morning after Death
Is solemnest of industries
Enacted upon Earth—

The Sweeping up the Heart
And putting Love away
We shall not want to use again
Until Eternity.

The pun on morning, the deletion of function words in lines three and five, and the metrical stress that underscores and isolates each syllable of the final word, "Eternity" — such stylistic oddities are Dickinson's signature. But these devices appear throughout her work. This poem differs from hundreds of other Dickinson poems in three ways: It is plainer in style, simpler in syntax, and it draws upon one central metaphor (housewifery) rather than melding two or more images into one new emotional nexus. As a result, it's an easy poem to grasp on a first reading. In fact, many of Dickinson's anthology poems seem to be chosen for their clarity rather than their intellectual or stylistic richness. I suppose editors might make these selections with student readers in mind. Yet the same editors never omit *The Waste Land* in favor of "easier" Eliot poems. As for students— I've heard them say they thought Dickinson a bees-in-her-bonnet versifier with an elfin range, the Beatrix Potter of American Literature, until they read her complex, lesser known work. In valuing imagistic, nondiscursive poems over more linguistically myriad work we are diminishing one whose "splendors are Menagerie."

Perhaps it's true that only a few Dickinson poems feature smooth prosody, a central governing metaphor, and pronouns with clear antecedents. Those who judge poetry's value by these lights will prize poems in which the language is most normalized. If we limit Dickinson's canon to "well-crafted" verse and work that can be understood within the Romantic tradition, we overlook poems whose success rests upon breaches of syntax and plurality of subject. By reading Dickinson according to standards derived from other major poets and movements, we blind ourselves to what she, and she alone, accomplished with language. It's as if all other poems are trees and her poems are birds. Given arboreal expectations, we admire hers most when they sit on the ground. "I don't like the way it keeps flitting around," we complain.

Dickinson is primarily an ontological poet with a unique ability to forge inner landscapes from abstract, rather than concrete, language and to express ideas—states of being, if you will—without resorting to an objective correlative. Her most characteristic use of language reverses Williams's famous credo, "No ideas but in things," to "No things but in ideas." The reversal of synecdoche is another signature technique. "You will perceive that the whole stands for a part in this place—" she wrote at the age of twenty (Letter 29). In her poetry an abstract whole such as Difference or Circumference elicits particular and partial examples in the reader's mind.

Poem 1046, for example, uses a high proportion of abstract language to describe a terrifying state of suspended animation in which one is neither fully alive nor fully dead.

> I've dropped my Brain—My Soul is numb—
> The Veins that used to run
> Stop palsied—'tis Paralysis
> Done perfecter on stone
>
> Vitality is Carved and cool.
> My nerve in Marble lies—

A Breathing Woman
Yesterday—Endowed with Paradise.

Not dumb—I had a sort that moved—
A Sense that smote and stirred—
Instincts for Dance—a caper part—
An Aptitude for Bird—

Who wrought Carrara in me
And chiselled all my tune
Were it a Witchcraft—were it Death—
I've still a chance to strain

To Being, somewhere—Motion—Breath—
Though Centuries beyond,
And every limit a Decade—
I'll shiver, satisfied.

The speaker's inner being has ossified, although she was "A Breathing Woman / Yesterday—Endowed with Paradise." She was, however, "Not dumb—," and the figures used to describe her lost legacy, dance and birds, are among Dickinson's favored metaphors for poetry. The poem implies that the ability to smote and stir, the narrator's power, is linked to her disinheritance. For a woman to speak her mind is dangerous: "I think Carlo would please you—," Dickinson wrote to Higginson in Letter 271. "He is dumb and brave." Carlo was her dog. The persona's creative life is changed from active force to tombstone engraving: "Who wrought Carrara in me / And chiselled all my tune," she asks. If this petrifaction is a result of Witchcraft or Death, the speaker still may "strain / To Being, somewhere—Motion—Breath—/ Though Centuries beyond." The lines imply that there is a deadlier abnegation than that of mortality: the silencing of one's creative futurity. In the case of women, patrilineage leads to the loss of rightful endowment, an eternal silencing. If, however, the speaker's ossification is due to those lesser forces—Witchcraft or Death—she plans to sprint through the Centuries until she finds that Utopian "somewhere—," a world in which she will be allowed to sing.

Poem 326 ("I cannot dance upon my Toes—") finds the narrator transforming such disinheritance into private enablement. Her poetry, she implies, is freakish because "No Man instructed me—." Indeed, if she had "Ballet knowledge" she could "blanch a Troupe—/ Or lay a Prima, mad." Here Dickinson describes the professional, published poet as engaged in an outlandish performance that passes for dance. Such poeticians hop "to Audiences—like Birds, / One Claw upon the Air," more grasping than graceful. Rather than engaging in such ignominious public display, her Art plays to the audience of herself, a gathering "full as Opera."

Whether she's protesting her pure, unpublished state or feeling obscurity as a deadening force, such poems underscore Dickinson's ambivalence toward fame. I think she liked to imagine herself as a renowned writer. "I play at Riches—to appease / The Clamoring for Gold—" she wrote. (801) As long as she was able to envision herself as a powerful literary presence, she could live with her effacement. The act of imagining herself to be both woman and acknowledged sovereign writer, a Queen, keeps her from the "Sin" of becoming "that easy Thing / an independent Man—." She is comforted to know that should she "in the long—uneven term" be declared a winner, she'll be fitter for her experience of Want. Poem 486 undermines the act of publication by means of puns: "I was the slightest in the House—" (publishing house); "I never spoke—unless addressed—" recalls Dickinson's habit of enclosing poems in letters to friends. "I could not bear to live—aloud—/ The Racket shamed me so—," she says, and the Racket refers as much to the life of a public poet as to any audible sound. Although the poem equates obscurity with integrity, in the last stanza the speaker realizes that because of her awkward ethics she might have no posthumous literary existence: "—I had often thought / How noteless—I could die—."

On the other hand, the voice of poem 612 is far less content with her small lot and furious to think that suicide would lead to hereafter rather than to an appealing obliteration of consciousness.

> It would have starved a Gnat—
> To live so small as I—
> And yet I was a living Child—
> With Food's necessity
>
> Upon me—like a Claw—
> I could no more remove
> Than I could coax a Leech away—
> Or make a Dragon—move—

Nor like the Gnat—had I—
The privilege to fly
And seek a Dinner for myself—
How mightier He—than I

Nor like Himself—the Art
Upon the Window Pane
To gad my little Being out—
And not begin—again—

Here, as in other poems, Dickinson defines subtle states by saying what they are *not*, possibly because no word exists for the emotional realm she's creating. She describes what she can't do as a means of evoking her backgrounded achievement (as in poem 486) or her entrapment (as in poem 612). The speaker of "It would have starved a Gnat—" can't remove the Claw of need; she can neither fly away to independence nor kill herself. Such negative locutions might well be influenced by gender. Women are defined in terms of what they are not (not man, not central; the other, the peripheral, the distaff) and constructed according to what they lack rather than what they have. The female self is seen as the negative space that allows positive pattern to emerge. Dickinson created a language embedded with this gendered attrition, a world in which what-is-not is something in itself. The voice of poem 646 uses negative definition to imagine a fuller life than the one currently known. In this poem, once again, the speaker and her work are stymied, without the power to live or the power to die.

I think to Live—may be a Bliss
To those who dare to try—
Beyond my limit to conceive—
My lip—to testify—

I think the Heart I former wore
Could widen—till to me
The Other, like the little Bank
Appear—unto the Sea—

I think the Days—could every one
In Ordination stand—
And Majesty—be easier—
Than an inferior kind—

No numb alarm—lest Difference come—
No Goblin—on the Bloom—
No start in Apprehension's Ear,
No Bankruptcy—no Doom—

But Certainties of Sun—
Midsummer—in the Mind—
A steadfast South—upon the Soul—
Her Polar time—behind—

The Vision—pondered long—
So plausible becomes
That I esteem the fiction—real—
The Real—fictitious seems—

How bountiful the Dream—
What Plenty—it would be
Had all my Life but been Mistake
Just rectified—in Thee

In stanza two, the speaker's self (the Heart of being) widens to oceanic size, a feat that necessarily removes her from a tangential position. When placed beside this expanded self, the not-me or Other takes on a new scale: ratioed as "the little Bank" is to the Sea. The speaker's wishful vision includes days that stand "In Ordination," a time when Majesty is easier to achieve than inferiority. To ordain is to canonize, in both literary and religious senses. In Dickinson's day, as now, the highest religious and political offices were held by men. For those whose religion is literature, the poet must be priest and prophet. It's difficult to envision a woman in this sphere when actual religions restrict her, at best, to the role of nun, sybil, or handmaiden to men of the cloth. Thus, the role of poet/priest is seldom accorded a female writer, as it is an Emerson, Thoreau, or Whitman. In this poem, the speaker imagines an impossible utopia or "Bliss" in which her life, her "Days," would be officially invested (ordained) with literary or religious authority. This condition is so hard to describe (because it has never existed) that in stanza four Dickinson resorts to negative definition. She creates the ideal, enfranchised state by saying all it is not. The fullest realization of life is achieved only when one manages to be unafraid of "Difference," possibly because, as stanza two suggests, the Difference has been eradicated: One is no longer in a position of perennial gendered otherness. Instead of "Bankruptcy," the fully alive woman enjoys "Certainties of Sun—" (Son). Her world of negative definition is replaced by the sure singular faith experienced by Sons, the birthright of those who are culturally central, rather than "Polar." The last two stanzas find the poet utterly convinced by the fantasy she's concocted.

In poem after poem Dickinson defies notions of otherness by reminding us that all components are mutually dependent and equally important to the whole. The second stanza of 1754 asks us to consider the unseen depths that support the ocean:

> The Caspian has its realms of sand,
> Its other realm of sea.
> Without the sterile perquisite,
> No Caspian could be.

The sandy ocean floor is Other to the ocean's dominant One. Its position, like woman's, is that of "sterile perquisite" or unfruitful privilege. Yet without such a hidden pedestal the sea's visible aspect could not exist.

~~

In poem 430, which I will analyze in depth, syntactical deletion, compression, and blurred pronouns create a degree of profusion extreme even for Dickinson.

It would never be Common—more—I said—
Difference—had begun—
Many a bitterness—had been—
But that old sort—was done—

Or—if it sometime—showed—as 'twill
Upon the Downiest—Morn—
Such bliss—had I—for all the years—
'Twould give an Easier—pain—

I'd so much joy—I told it—Red
Upon my simple Cheek—
I felt it publish—in my Eye—
'Twas needless—any speak—

I walked—as wings—my body bore—
The feet—I former used—
Unnecessary—now to me—
As boots—would be—to Birds—

I put my pleasure all abroad—
I dealt a word of Gold
To every Creature—that I met—
And Dowered—all the World—

When—suddenly—my Riches shrank—
A Goblin—drank my Dew—
My Palaces—dropped tenantless—
Myself—was beggared—too—

I clutched at sounds—
I groped at shapes—
I touched the tops of Films—
I felt the Wilderness roll back
Along my Golden lines—

The Sackcloth—hangs upon the nail—
The Frock I used to wear—
But where my moment of Brocade—
My—drop—of India?

Almost every line can be reconstructed in several ways, allowing for many variant meanings and a high level of reader involvement. Of course, all literary texts require imagination and reconstruction from a reader. In Dickinson this process is exaggerated as the reader's decisions create one of many possible narratives. If asked to describe the poem's meaning in the simplest terms, we might say it tells a story of gain followed by loss. But what the speaker has won and forfeited is not revealed. The poem's first word, that expansive It, enforces multiple interpretations by refusing to be pinned to a definite antecedent. Rather than creating an annoying vagueness, as might be expected, Dickinson's unspecified catalysts allow for a greater degree of reader engagement. One notices, too, that this poem does not settle on a single image to describe the inner domain, the way housekeeping represents grief in "The Bustle in a House."

Dickinson's signature dashes and her technique of capitalization imbue abstractions with concrete presence, satisifying our preference for physicality without sacrificing conceptual thought. We linger on *Common* (line one) because of the capital *C:* our minds give the abstract word a solidity equal to its typographic weight. In stanza two, line four, "'Twould give an Easier—pain—," the adjective *Easier* precedes the pause of the dash, momentarily taking the syntactical place of the direct object. Since the object of a sentence is frequently a noun, and nouns are often concrete words, *Easier* borrows a nounlike substance before our eyes move on to the syntactically normal direct object, *pain.* The potential melodrama of the latter word is undercut by the absence of capitalization, and the lowercase *p* throws *Easier* into high relief.

Quantum physics, the representative science of our age, offers not one but many ways in which the world might be constructed. One popular theory holds that reality is created by the observer. That is, phenomena such as the moon or trees do not exist until they are observed. This belief is akin to idealism in philosophy, which holds that the world is nothing but mind, and to reception theory in literary criticism, which stresses that readers create a text by connecting and interpreting a series of "gaps" between words and phrases. In an early letter (32), Dickinson replaced the entire salutation with a dash, explaining "That is'nt [*sic*] an *empty* blank where I began—it is so full of affection that you cant see any—that's all." Dickinson's dashes underscore the high proportion of such resonant gaps in her poetry.

In *Physics and Philosophy,* Heisenberg says that the elementary particles "form a world of potentialities or possibilities rather than one of things or facts. . . . The probability wave . . . means a tendency for something. It's a quantitative version of the old concept of *potentia* in Aristotle's philosophy. It introduces something standing in the middle between the idea of an event and the actual event, a strange kind of physical reality just in the middle between possibility and reality." Dickinson's dashes are a linguistic analogue of probability waves. Moreover, many of her poems are marked with tiny crosses directing us to alternate word choices in the margins. Scholars cannot determine which of these possible words she finally privileged since various drafts make various selections, and other options are never ruled out. One must allow the poem to be a palimpsest of multiple inscriptions or participate in the composition by choosing the best word.

One of the more outrageous claims made by some physicists is that reality consists of a steadily increasing number of parallel universes. To quote Nick Herbert's *Quantum Reality*, "For any situation in which several different outcomes are possible (flipping a coin, for instance) some physicists believe that *all outcomes actually occur*." Just as a flipped coin can show both heads and tails in Heisenberg's world, in the kingdom of Dickinson contradictory events occur simultaneously. Her poetry affords such pleasure in part because it allows us to have many cakes and eat them all. In real life, taking one path usually means forsaking all others. A Dickinson poem, in contrast, allows us to experience many outcomes, some of them conflicting. "I dwell in Possibility—" she wrote. Her poems prolong the intoxicating moment before choice when all options are potentially ours. The loss implicit in any decision is permanently forestalled.

The first line of 430, for example, can be reconstructed in the following ways:

> It [my life] would never be Common [ordinary, taken for granted]—[what's] more—I said—

> It [my purpose] would never be Common [known to all, as in common knowledge or held in common]—[it would be] more—I said—

> It [your love for me] would never be Common [something that occurs frequently]—[so give me] more—I said—

All of these narrative catalysts can be extended throughout the poem. And as we read on, additional narratives spring up to accommodate the connotations of new words, syntax, and context. The poem becomes more myriad with each line, as possible meanings mutate and increase. Hence my reading of 430 doesn't pretend to be the one "right" interpretation or the meaning Dickinson intended. Rather, I offer it as an approach that allows us to appreciate the text's expansive quality.

It's possible to read 430 as a poem in which a woman confronts literary effacement. There are two revelatory moments: the first an experience of empowerment, the second of divestment, as the speaker realizes that lineage and legitimacy must pass from father to son, that she is a Commoner rather than a Queen with a Queen's power to bequeath succession. The narrative progresses from the speaker's recognition of her gift and her ensuing euphoria to her attempts to "dower" or bequeath her poetic legacy. The temerity of this action leads to her sudden downfall and an awareness of her "beggared" state. The languages of royalty, textiles, botany, spatial abstraction, chemistry, publishing, and the writer's trade create a bouquet of meaning different from the one that would be achieved by extending a single metaphor throughout. "My Lexicon—was my only companion—" Dickinson wrote in letter 261. She used *Webster's* 1846 edition. Her testimony suggests its powerful influence on her poems, and I have used that dictionary as my source for all the definitions that follow.

As the poem begins, the speaker has just become aware of her extraordinary poetic gift. She speaks confidently, in the first flush of accomplishment.

> It would never be Common—more—I said—
> Difference—had begun—
> Many a bitterness—had been—
> But that old sort—was done--

This is the moment of triumph all artists know upon achieving work that pleases the inner critic: It [my poetry] would never be Common [plebian as opposed to royal]— [any] more—I said—/ [My awareness of] Difference— [from other writers] had begun—. Difference entails Otherness; the speaker recognizes herself as alien, "from Mars," if you will. This line also implies that Difference in the sense of argument had begun. The speaker's quarrel is with her peers and with those writers who preceded, indeed overshadowed, her. Another reconstruction is: It [my poetry] would never be Common—[any] more—/ [*because*] Difference—had begun—. Hence, the reason for my newly royal status *is* this Difference, this otherness, this argument. Many a bitterness—had been—[as a result of my Difference] / But that old sort—[of bitterness] was done—[once I saw my Difference as a strength].

> Or—if it sometime—showed—as 'twill
> Upon the Downiest—Morn—
> Such bliss—had I—for all the years—
> 'Twould give an Easier—pain—

The indeterminate *it* in the first line harks back to "bitterness" (stanza one) as the closest antecedent. But since we've already defined *It* as the speaker's poetry, that meaning must be allowed as well. The last word in line one, *'twill,* can be read as a pun, a figure of speech seldom found in Romantic literature but occurring frequently in the metaphysical poets and Shakespeare, where Dickinson might have schooled her usage. Readers first recognize TWILL as an archaic contraction of "it will." But in Dickinson's dictionary TWILL also is a verb meaning "to weave in ribs or ridges; to quill." Given her tendency to abbreviate, the bitterness that showed "as twill" could be an acrimonious "twilling"—the act of weaving or quilling. Of the verb QUILL, her dictionary notes "In the United States, this word is generally pronounced *twill.*" For Dickinson, then, *twill* and *quill* were interchangeable homonyms. As an avid amateur botanist, she might have been intrigued to find that a QUILL was "a piece of small reed or other hollow plant, on which weavers wind the thread which forms the woof of cloth." But its foremost meaning was "the large strong feather of a goose or other large fowl; used much for writing pens." Dickinson's dictionary quotes Dryden as exemplar: "'To carry a good quill,' to write well." Given all this, the bitterness that showed "as 'twill" could be a resentment made evident by the quill of her pen.

The vanquished bitterness sometimes reappeared "Upon the Downiest—Morn—." We first hear UPON as meaning "on the occasion of" the most soothing dawn, but the preposition also suggests "being on the top," a meaning that introduces the poem's spatial metaphor. When empowered, the speaker views the imminent day from on high; her vantage point is akin to a bird's free-wheeling prospect or a queen's enthroned pinnacle. She's on top of things, in the contemporary sense. A DOWN was "an elevation of sand," making "the Downiest—Morn—" a lofty yet tenuous palisades. If, however, DOWN is read as "the pubescence of plants, a fine hairy substance," and a means "by which seeds are conveyed to a distance by the wind," "Downiest—Morn—" connotes the dawning of reproductive power, when the poem is capable of inseminating literary heirs over a distance of years. *Webster's* 1846 also defined DOWN as "the pappus or little crown of certain seeds of plants." "Little crown" is a charmingly Dickinsonian descriptor for the pappus, which tops the plant's ovary and helps with the dispersal of its fruit. With this inference, "the Downiest—Morn—" could be a queen's coronation day when her lineage is assured.

Either a bitterness or the "twill" of her writing might show "Upon the Downiest—Morn—." The most obvious reconstruction is this: Or—if it [the old bitterness] some-time—showed [permitted itself to be seen]—as 'twill [as it will]—/ Upon [on the occasion of] the Downiest [most soothing]—Morn—/ Such bliss—had I—for [in spite of] all the years—/ 'Twould [the bitterness would] give an Easier—pain—. However, the lines take on another dimen-sion when read as follows: Or—if it [my poetry] some-time—showed [proved itself]—as 'twill [twill/quill, the weaving/writing of raised lines] / Upon [resting on top of] the Downiest—[most generative] Morn—/ Such bliss—had I—[enough] for all the years—/ 'Twould [the bliss would] give an Easier—pain [than the bitterness I'd had before]. In this reading, the speaker's poetry becomes a crown for the Crown: an exalted or "raised" fabric veiling her downy coronation day.

> I'd so much joy—I told it—Red
> Upon my simple Cheek—
> I felt it publish—in my Eye—
> 'Twas needless—any speak—

The punning Red/read and the verb *publish* work as slant allusions to writing; *Upon* appears again, building spa-tial hierarchies with the image of the blushing surface of the skin. UPON also can be heard as "on the occasion of" the speaker's brazenness or "simple Cheek." Although Dickinson's dictionary did not specify "cheek" as impu-dence, this meaning entered British English around 1820, and she no doubt had encountered the usage. Her lexicon first defined SIMPLE as "Single; consisting of one thing; uncompounded, unmingled, uncombined with any thing else." In these terms, Dickinson's spinsterhood was "simple." *Webster's* also noted that "*A simple body*, in *chemistry*, is one that has not been decomposed, or separated into two or more bodies." If marriage constitutes a single or "simple" identity's separation into two, to wed is to decompose. A poem, moreover, is "a simple body" in that it is "composed." The botanical meaning of SIMPLE was "undivided . . . only one on a PETIOLE." PETIOLE, "the foot stalk of a leaf," derives from the Latin diminutive for foot and suggests the small measures Dickinson favored.

These definitions imply the following renderings: I'd so much joy—[that] I [had] told it [my poetry]—Red [I am read]—/ Upon [by means of] my simple [single, unmarried] Cheek [audacity]—/ I felt it [my poetry] publish—[therefore] in my Eye—[view] / 'Twas needless—any [other] speak [on my behalf]—. Or alternately, I'd so much joy—[that] I [had] told it [my poetry]—Red [read]—/ Upon [by means of] my simple [composed or written] Cheek [impudence]—/ I felt it [my poetry] publish—in my Eye [in my single "I," within myself] / [therefore] 'Twas needless—[that] any [of my poetry] speak [aloud or publicly]—.

The poem at midpoint finds the narrator held aloft by her new powers; her body of work levitates. When contrasted to the "Difference" of this poetry, her "former" meters seem absurdly large and cumbersome.

I walked—as wings—my body bore—
The feet—I former used—
Unnecessary—now to me—
As boots—would be—to Birds—

Of wing, *Webster's* notes: "In *gardening*, a side shoot. . . . In *botany*, the side petal of a papilionaceous coral; also, an appendage of seeds." (Papilionaceous: "resembling the butterfly.") Dickinson's nickname for herself was Daisy, and the poem's persona, with her wings of seeds, now assumes a botanical aspect. Once again, her raised status depends upon her ability to disseminate her creative legacy. Most broadly, a wing was "any side-piece—," and this denotation locates puissance in periphery: Her wings are built on the circumference of central structures, and therein lies their value. In a fleet, wings were "the ships on the extremities, when ranged in a line . . . —" Thus, the speaker's "wings" are her lines. And the poem's martial trope begins if we hear wing as "the flank or extreme body or part of an army . . . the longer sides of horn-works, crown-works, & c.—" A crown-work, for its part, was "an out-work running into the field, consisting of two demi-bastions at the extremes, and an entire bastion in the middle, with curtains." *Wings*, then, were the "demi-bastions" of a fortification. The speaker is bolstered by the "crown-works" of her "never . . . Common" poems.

On first reading "I walked—as wings—my body bore—," we hear the word bore as "supported." However, its primary definition was "To perforate or penetrate a

solid body, and make a round hole. . . . To penetrate or
break through by turning or labor." The stanza's opening
lines can be reconstructed as follows: I walked—as [the
way] wings [walk]—[which is to say I flew]. My body [of
work] bore [perforated] / The [poetic] feet—I former
used—/ [which are] Unnecessary—now to me / As
boots—would be—to Birds—." The speaker's new prosody "bores" through the "old sort" of meter, leaving it riddled with round absences. To BORE also was "to pierce the
earth with scooping irons, which, when drawn out, bring
with them samples of the different stratums, through
which they pass. This is a method of discovering veins of
ore and coal without opening a mine." In like fashion, her
new measures drill through her "former" feet to discover
"a word of Gold."

> I put my pleasure all abroad—
> I dealt a word of Gold
> To every Creature—that I met—
> And Dowered—all the World—

Thus far, Dickinson has stressed the value of what is
"never . . . Common" but royal and exotic. Now her winged
speaker becomes a social butterfly or queen bee, flitting
"abroad" and endowing the World with portions of her es-
tate. By putting forth the "pleasure" of her writing, she
makes a public assertion of her talent. "Bullion is better
than minted things, for it has no alloy," she wrote (Letter
889). The first meaning of DEAL ("To divide, to part; to
separate") countervenes the "simple," whole, unalloyed

state she preferred over "minted things." To DEAL, moreover, was "To traffick; to trade; to negotiate." Just as precious metals are combined with less valuable ones for commercial use, the speaker's "dealt" word of Gold "decomposes" into a mercantile alloy. Her metallic words are dealt like blows to "every Creature," and the denotations of that noun—"an animal of any kind; a beast—... A human being, in contempt.... A dependent; a person who is subject to the will or influence of another...."—reify her linguistic imperialism.

The stanza's last line ("And Dowered—all the World—") finds the persona bequeathing her lines/lineage to all posterity. The noun DOWER referred to "That portion of the lands or tenements of a man, which his widow enjoys during her life, after the death of her husband." A dowery also is a sum required of postulants by some religious communities. By dowering the world, the persona enacts two roles forbidden women under patriarchy: She bequeaths her poems (synonomous with her name and lineage) to her literary heirs, and she offers her work as religious dues, a dowry to secure her status as poet/priest. "When a little Girl," Dickinson wrote, "I remember hearing that remarkable passage and preferring the 'Power,' not knowing at the time that 'Kingdom' and 'Glory' were included." (Letter 330)

> When—suddenly—my Riches shrank—
> A Goblin—drank my Dew—
> My Palaces—dropped tenantless—
> Myself—was beggared—too—

The narrator's sudden divestment is the predictable outcome of her temerity. Her formerly wide prospect shrinks like unsized cloth; the amorphous Creatures she hoped to endow clarify into monsters: "A Goblin—drank my Dew—". The portion of fame the speaker justifiably expects, her due, is consumed by the Goblin posterity. Her resources, which once encompassed a vast sphere ("all the World"), are reduced to tiny globes of DEW: "The water or moisture collected or deposited on or near the surface of the earth, during the night, by the escape of the heat which held the water in solution." Formerly "held in solution," expansively "abroad," her shrunken "Riches" now are deposited in banks of earth.

"My Palaces—dropped tenantless—" she notes, and one can envision those sovereign residences raining down in tiny dew-shaped pieces. Such watery bullets are unable to drill or "bore," enabling deletions in their targets. To DROP ("to descend suddenly") also suggests the speaker's Palaces, her semantic architecture, as descendant rather than progenitor. ("For the Voice is the Palace of all of us . . ." [Letter 438].) She who wished to endow the World is patronized instead: My Palaces [writing]—dropped [descended to me from on high] tenantless [without a legal occupant]. And since DROP meant "to utter slightly; briefly or casually," the speaker's "dropped" Voice/Palace is something of a diminished soliloquy. If we hear DROP as "To die, . . . to be neglected and come to nothing," her verbal Palaces perish without issue. The last line ("Myself—was beggared—too—) goes out of its way to equate disenfranchisement of work with impoverishment of being. Now that the persona is "beggared," her inner life (My self) and the eternal life of her work (My Palaces) depend on the largesse of others.

The poem is composed entirely of quatrains until its penultimate stanza, which has one extra line. As the speaker's patterned, hierarchical spheres dissolve into entropic Wilderness, the breaking of stanzaic form enacts her loss of control.

> I clutched at sounds —
> I groped at shapes —
> I touched the tops of Films —
> I felt the Wilderness roll back
> Along my Golden lines —

The syntax of the first two lines is simple and declarative. The protagonist's voice takes on optimum directness, as if she can't afford more complex formulations. This is the only stanza with no midline dashes since hesitant caesuras would brake the urgency. I noted earlier that Dickinson's abstractions frequently have a concrete quality. In this extremity, her persona views abstract sounds and shapes as physical solids able to support her. She who relied upon the marvelous "twill" of her poems, a cloth of gold suspending her above "the Downiest — Morn," now finds herself supported by "the tops of Films," a substance flimsy as down. FILM had only one definition in Dickinson's lexicon: "A thick skin; a pellicle, as on the eye." Earlier, the speaker had said of her work: "I felt it publish — in my Eye —"; now she gropes blindly, divested of her self-reliant vision. (In fact, Dickinson suffered from an eye problem serious enough to call for prolonged treatment in Boston.)

Since to ROLL was "to move, as waves or billows, with alternate swells and depression," a rolling Wilderness has an undulating contour. A composite of high and low, it rebuts the poem's firm spatial hierarchies. In fact, the motion of this vortex is frighteningly hard to predict. Are its revolutions a way to "inwrap, to bind or involve in a bandage," and in doing so film the Eye with gauzy fibers? Is this Wilderness the Common, old sort of bitterness returning, closing over the Golden lines of poetry like a rolltop desk? Or is it coiling backward in accordance with the speaker's directions (Along her Golden lines)? Rather than settling such questions, Dickinson's syntax and vocabulary allow us to locate agency in either Wilderness or speaker. One can imagine the Wilderness as an immense "roller," pressing the metrical wrinkles from the line, or as a percussive snare whose "rolling" obliterates the poem's rhythm altogether. (ROLL: "To beat a drum with strokes so rapid that they can scarcely be distinguished by the ear.") I felt the Wilderness roll [drum] back [in response] / Along [over the length of] my Golden lines—. The enabling holes the speaker drilled in meter return in this monstrous whirling topography capable of extinguishing her language entirely.

The twill of her poetry is spun from long fibers of flax known as LINES. But the word also meant "a rank or row of soldiers, or the disposition of an army drawn up with an extended front." Both protection and succession are implied by the heraldic aspect of LINES, "used in armories to divide the shield into different parts, and to compose different figures." Most importantly, LINE referred to "a series or succession of progeny or relations, descending from a common progenitor." Thus the Wilderness, in rolling back along the speaker's "Golden lines," effaces her literary issue.

By the last stanza, the narrator's linguistic cloth of gold has been woven into a garment of mourning and placed on high, in the honorific realm where she had flown.

> The Sackcloth—hangs upon the nail—
> The Frock I used to wear—
> But where my moment of Brocade—
> My—drop—of India?

In stanza five, the narrator tried to "dower" all the World with poems, as if they were the dues paid by a religious postulant. However, rather than being canonized, she now finds herself defrocked. "My—drop—of India" most obviously refers to the speaker's lost imperial domain, while "moment of Brocade" signals her forfeited instant of ordination. That Brocade had connotations of legacy, firmness, and solitude to Dickinson is clear from her letters. To Samuel Bowles (Letter 277) she wrote of "your memory that can stand alone, like the best Brocade." And in letter 368, to Thomas Higginson, she said, "—But truth like Ancestor's Brocades can stand alone—." Since George Eliot was one of Dickinson's enthusiasms, the heraldic notion of Brocade as a coat of arms might have been suggested by a passage from *The Mill on the Floss*: "Mrs. Glegg . . . had inherited from her grandmother . . . a brocaded gown that would stand up empty, like a suit of armour." Heraldry, however, is based on patrilineage; hence the narrator's attempt to forge heraldic "lines" of her own has proved an impossible task.

Dickinson uses the verb *to drop* in the sixth stanza ("My Palaces—dropped tenantless—") to show a grand verbal structure descending sans descendants. At the poem's conclusion, we hear her persona wondering what has become of her literary heirs. MOMENT ("importance in influence or effect; consequence; weight or value") suggests this reconstruction: But where my moment [influence] of Brocade [language]—/ [which was] My—drop ["a small portion of any fluid . . . which is pendent, as if about to fall"]—of India [ink]?" DROP had another, ghastlier denotation: "the part of a gallows which sustains the criminal before he is executed, and which is suddenly dropped." The platform of her "never . . . Common" poetry was such a trapdoor: But where my moment [importance] of Brocade [word of Gold]—/ [which was also] My—drop [death sentence]—of India [ink]? And since DROP was "a diamond hanging from the ear . . . something hanging in the form of a drop," the poem's last line oscillates between words as gems and words as noose. Dickinson's ophthalmological troubles, moreover, suggest drops used to lubricate the eye. Where is the drop that fostered my linguistic vision? she asks. Under INDIA, *Webster's* 1846 included INDIA RUBBER: "the *caoutchouc,* a substance of extraordinary elasticity, called also *elastic gum* or *resin.*" The narrator's "—drop—of India" could be the stretch embedded in her poems, the elastic syntax that yields flexible substance. Having lost her "moment of Brocade," the narrator herself is in a pliant state of indeterminacy: neither high nor low, royal nor common. Yet her relinquishment of fame might signal her ordination as poet rather than poetician.

The Newtonian definitions of MOMENT probably were available to Dickinson, who was educated in the science of her day. These meanings speak to the poem's large tropes of center and periphery, public and private spheres. Scientifically speaking, a MOMENT is the tendency to produce motion, especially about a point or axis. When applied to "moment of Brocade" we see the gorgeous raised patterns of the narrator's poetry creating a stir on the periphery of a literary center. MOMENT is also the product of quantity and the distance to a particular axis or point, as in moment of a couple, moment of a force, moment of inertia, or "moment of Brocade." In Dickinson's poem, "moment" results when her genius (force) is multiplied by her distance from a literary axis. Thus in the last lines, the speaker, having gone public, has lost the problem of genius times distance that resulted in the "product" of her poems. But she is unable to lose or "drop" her imperial longing: "But where [is] my moment [product] of Brocade [poems]—/ [And where] My—drop [relinquishment]—of India [the endowed sphere I briefly entered]?

Cristanne Miller writes, "In poetry, meaning may lie as much in the interaction of semantic content and form as in a message that can be isolated from the poem. The more a poem calls attention to its formal elements by various foregrounding techniques, the more the reader is likely to learn about its meaning from them. If we assume as a norm language that calls no attention to its formal properties by deviating from the conventions of standard communication (that is, an utterance intended solely to communicate a message), then Dickinson's poetry is richly deviant." (*Emily Dickinson, A Poet's Grammar*) BROCADE, a "silk stuff, variegated with gold and silver, or raised and enriched with flowers, foliage, and other ornaments," was such a "deviant" textile when compared with "Sackcloth." But where my moment [important deviance] of Brocade [foregrounded "Difference"]—? the speaker wonders.

A *Poet's Grammar* provides a fascinating analysis of Dickinson's syntactical strategies. The book also will interest all who enjoy thinking about the formal aspects of language since Miller's tools and methods can be applied with profit to any poet's work. While considering the distance between biographical mythology and Miller's brilliant formalist approach, I was tempted to call this essay "A Poet's Glamour." In the middle ages, those who had "grammar" or knowledge seemed to possess magical occult powers. Eventually the Scots substituted an *l*, making "glamour" the etymological daughter of "grammar." In like fashion, Dickinson's glamour is the corrupt form of her grammar. Her poetry has been diluted and her readers deluded by fanciful images of the poet—from debutante to dragon lady. It's time we turned our attention to her grammar in the ancient sense: that enchanting, learned language she inexplicably magicked from hymns, trash, canon, culture, and self.

I think Emily Dickinson believed herself to be a great

poet. She needed that faith in order to make poetry central to her life. By choosing to be a recluse and refusing publication, she protected herself from the world's opinion of her talent, which might have destroyed her as an artist. Helen Hunt Jackson, a highly successful poet herself, pressed Dickinson to publish and could have helped her had Dickinson shown any interest. But it was as if she intuited (perhaps from her correspondence with Higginson) that publication would diminish her. Indeed, had she read the scathing *Atlantic* review of her debut, it would have been much harder to regard herself as Queen of language. Only full enfranchisment, the recognition of her stature as a mature female genius, would suffice. "Queen" appears in nineteen of her poems; "princess" in none.

Although Dickinson went to great lengths to protect her gift, at times the world's disregard must have impinged. Like 430 ("It would never be Common—more—I said—"), the following poem, 458, can be read as a female writer's awakening to disenfranchisement. In this case, the persona addresses either her own reflection or an imagined literary daughter. The speaker may be regarding herself and considering the same question posed in another poem: "What would the Dower be / Had I the Art to stun myself / With Bolts of Melody!" (505) As a woman, however, she is incapable of endowing herself or her descendants with any illuminating lineage. As in 430, the speaker's slant vision, her culturally defined otherness, is recognized as the source of both her creative power and her historical effacement. Having said this, I must add that I offer such suggestions only as an invitation. I hope readers will stitch shimmering absences and orchestrate bountiful options to arrive at their own versions of the poem.

Like Eyes that looked on Wastes—
Incredulous of Ought
But Blank—and steady Wilderness—
Diversified by Night—

Just Infinites of Nought—
As far as it could see—
So looked the face I looked upon—
So looked itself—on Me—

I offered it no Help—
Because the Cause was Mine—
The Misery a Compact
As hopeless—as divine—

Neither—would be absolved—
Neither would be a Queen
Without the Other—Therefore—
We perish—tho' We reign—

1989

IV

Praxis

Seed Ink

To Organize a Waterfall

ACH TIME I CONTEMPLATED AN ESSAY ON MY OWN poetics, I began a hesitation waltz in my head. The refrain went like this: Why write about your own work? Who would be interested? Why not leave commentary to the critics rather than expose yourself through explication? To explain yourself is vain (in both senses of the word) and unseemly. When I wasn't tripping over personal misgivings, I was hampered by the obstacles others might raise. Some might say no poet could be "objective" about her own work. And I'd agree, adding only that no one else can be objective about it either. Since everyone's stance is tainted by unspoken assumptions (about aesthetics, gender, culture, you name it), objectivity doesn't exist. God alone might be an objective critic—if God existed. While warding off this or that imagined charge, I began to wonder how the essay could avoid defensiveness. Every explanation is in some sense a defense, after all. What would prevent me from slithering into self-indulgent writing that says *how infinitely interesting I am* behind everything it says. I saw myself sneaking under Kmart laurels of my own making: a halo on a stick growing from the back of my head as in old comic books. It put a pause in the waltz.

The turning point came while I was preparing to teach a course structured around the work of living poets. The plan was for the poets to give a public reading and visit my class to talk with students. I asked the visitors to help me by naming a couple of writers from any previous generation who had been important to them. The authors they cited would be part of the assigned reading. In this way, I could provide a broader historical context that had an element of serendipity; it would be the past as suggested by the chance passions of my peers. I also asked the poets to name a few contemporary writers whose work had affected them. The idea was not to pin them to specific influences, but to place their work within the quirky nexus of other writers they'd read and admired. The poets agreed to send me any statements they'd published about poetics. As their answers arrived, I was pleasantly amazed at the names named and the intentions explained. The absolute unpredictability of the opinions made me realize the value of asking poets to speak up. No critic could have foreseen the admirations and quiet strategies informing the work. Yet the invisible hopes of the poems became apparent once I knew where to look. I've come to feel that too few contemporary poets are leaving any record of their aesthetic concerns.

Poets often shy away from commenting on their work because such statements are reductive. They're to the poems what Tang is to orange juice. Yes. Still, Tang can be a handy thing to have when camping in the wilderness. There's a prejudice that says people should understand the poem on their own: It isn't polite to point. My response is, "We need all the help we can get." As readers, we see what we want to see, what we've been trained to see, and what we've seen before. This is how human perception functions: Habit never rests. But the limitations of perception mean that the original, the subtle, the previously untried will be misunderstood or invisible. The poet's intentions, though everywhere in the work, are sometimes like those sounds too high to be heard. Who knows what readers might find if they knew where to look, how to listen?

Some poets are afraid that analysis will smother the exploratory impulse that makes them write. I find I can't write about future work for that reason. The feeling that this isn't quite it, we can do better, leads us to try again. In an essay commissioned by *Scientific American*, John H. Holland says, "Improvements come from trying new, risky things until something better is found. Because many of the risky things fail, exploration involves a degradation of performance compared to what might be achieved with no exploration. It is a classic problem for all systems that adapt and learn. To what degree should the present be mortgaged for the future? The 'hopeful monster,' awkward in itself but embodying changes that make possible future adaptations, is one of the more striking images of early genetics."

Although some poets feel comfortable saying nothing about their work, others can't say enough. These more vocal people have a way of finding each other and forming factions. Until recently, the teaching of literature relied heavily on labels to organize the past. Names (Confessional, New York School) are usually a critical convenience

that imposes order by suggesting what is worth reading
and how we should read it. Labels save us the effort of sift-
ing through all that's written and deciding the quality for
ourselves. The desire for order, for mastery over the messy
plenitude of texts, leads to a canon. Since no one can read
everything, it's argued that the canon serves a useful function. If that sentence read "canons" I could agree. As it is, I
find myself yearning for adventurous readers, willing to
take the gems and junk their chance progress affords.

I think most critics would agree that poets are "the irri-
table race." Given a mixed review, a poet usually fastens
with a vengeance on a critic's one misgiving. The most generous interpretation is this: Poetry books often receive only
one or two reviews. If one of those reviews is unfavorable,
it has a proportionally greater impact on the writer. Imagine how it feels to work for years on a volume, and then receive one lukewarm appraisal in the *Remnant Review*. It's an
uncomfortable position for both the poet and the critic.
I've learned that my reading of others' work often has little
connection to their intentions. This doesn't mean that my
response is wrong, and it doesn't make the author's views
less right. Poets, like their poems, are "hopeful monsters."
Perhaps our reactions would be more mature if our books
were more widely reviewed. There's an enforced passivity in
our collective stance, as though we were Cinderellas waiting for our prince-like explicators to come. One response
to the shortage of princes is for more poets and readers to
shoulder the burden of commentary themselves. But those
poets who decide to review often find they've called atten-

tion to others and made themselves unpopular in the process. Their own work is as misunderstood or invisible as ever. Predictably, the good-citizen reviewer begins to feel slightly martyred. Maybe the solution is for poets to write about their own poetry occasionally, as a means of saying what needs to be said.

In this essay, I address the specific as a means of addressing the general. My future poems are likely to resemble my earlier work in unforeseen ways and to grow in ways I can't predict: always and more and more. As A. R. Ammons has noted, "About the only thing we can look to to break up our standard patterns . . . is an accident or a mistake. . . . A mistake is obviously a point where originality can begin." The quirk, the oddity, the extreme, the line where the language tilts can be a poem's most valuable facet. They are the linguistic equivalents of genetic "point mutations": variants produced by small changes in an organism's chromosomes. Of course, this idea (like most ideas) is dangerous in that it can be used to condone careless or self-indulgent writing. Some mutations are harmful, after all. For every "mistake" that lets originality creep in, there must be a thousand that repeat errors of the past. The writer's intensity, passion, standards, and commitment must be at the highest pitch. One needs a rigorous self-criticism in order to distinguish slackness from accidental insights.

This essay is a way to welcome you into a microclimate I've made from my life and mind to date, from a language that is more than mine. I'd like to fit you out with the right

address you the reader

gear for the trip through the interior, give a password, point out the cascades, the sun kinks, the hem and brink: to call your attention.

—~

I have a hard time saying a poem is "about" this or that subject because the poems are never so pat. Every poem has a certain reticence or reserve that has nothing to do with its surface density: It isn't eager to divest itself of its meaning. And my poems are always about several things; they have ostensible and embedded subjects, occupations and pre-occupations. But I will try to say what certain poems are "about" with the understanding that they're about more than I can say. Lest my comments make it seem as if I had everything plotted and under control as I wrote, I should say this wasn't the case. "I prepare meticulously and then play with freedom," Wanda Landowska wrote. "Preparation is organizing the intuition. Even the best improvisation is that which is well-prepared."

Ideally, I'd like the titles of my books to suggest the more sequestered concerns and dynamics of the work. I'd prefer that there be no "title poem" in the volume so people aren't tempted to single that poem out for undue importance. (But only in *Palladium* have I been able to avoid a title poem.) I chose *Powers Of Congress* as a title for my third book because it suggests merging and transformation through government, discourse, assemblage, and sexuality. It implies both hierarchy ("powers" indicating dominance) and a disintegration of hierarchy by means of "congress."

The book has no sections or part openings, and this undivided structure enacts the enmeshed union and removal of boundaries implicit in the title. One poem triggers another, so that the overall design has more in common with waterfalls than with compartmentalized plots. The book's formal progress on the largest scale can be likened to a "cascade experiment," a term stolen from science. I often lift scientific language for my own wayward purposes. That isn't to say I play fast and loose with denoted meanings. I'm as true to the intentions of science as my knowledge allows. But my appropriations from science are entwined with other discourses, other ideas, so that a term such as "cascade experiment" comes to stand for more than the laboratory event it is. Scientifically speaking, a cascade experiment is a kind of domino effect in which each event incites the next. The first poem in *Powers Of Congress* is both trip wire and torrent in small. Its form is based on the continuous chain of a cascade. Logic has this quality, I think: It's an extremely connected form of thought, in which each successive statement depends on the truth of other, previous ones.

Cascade Experiment

Because faith creates its verification,
and reaching you will be no harder than believing
in a planet's caul of plasma,
or interacting with a comet
in its perihelion passage, no harder
than considering what sparking of the vacuum, cosmological
impromptu flung me here, a paraphrase, perhaps,

for some denser, more difficult being,
a subsidiary instance, easier to grasp
than the span I foreshadow, of which I am a variable,
my stance is passional toward the universe and you.

Because faith in facts can help create those facts,
the way electrons exist only when they're measured,
or shy people stand alone at parties,
attract no one, then go home to feel more shy,
I begin by supposing our attrition's no quicker
than a star's, that like electrons
vanishing on one side
of a wall and appearing on the other
without leaving any holes or being
somewhere in between, the soul's decoupling
is an oscillation so inward nothing outward
as the eye can see it.
The childhood catechisms all had heaven,
an excitation of mist.
Grown, I thought a vacancy awaited me.
Now I find myself discarding and enlarging
both these views, an infidel of amplitude.

Because truths we don't suspect have a hard time
making themselves felt, as when thirteen species
of whiptail lizards composed entirely of females
stay undiscovered due to bias
against such things existing,
we have to meet the universe halfway.
Nothing will unfold for us unless we move toward what
looks to us like nothing: faith is a cascade.

The sky's high solid is anything
but, the sun going under hasn't
budged, and if death divests the self
it's the sole event in nature
that's exactly what it seems.

Because believing a thing's true
can bring about that truth,
and you might be the shy one, lizard or electron,
known only through advances
presuming your existence, let my glance be passional
toward the universe and you.

God

The poem's cause-and-effect movement goes like this:
It states an assumption of causality ("Because faith creates
its verification"). That statement sets off a chain of
amendments, clauses, augmentations that pour down the
page before coming to rest in the effect ("my stance is passional toward the universe and you").

I want to talk about the content of this poem because
its concerns are important to my work in general. I'd have
no interest in writing a poem that described, in linear and
logical fashion, a scientist working on a cascade experiment. That topic, in and of itself, is not one that engages
me profoundly. Gleanings from philosophy and science
must be transformed before they become part of a poem.
It certainly isn't a question of paraphrasing, prettying up,
or watering down specific information. For me, the process
is one of time and thought: I need to let new ideas permeate my view of things so that the poem, rather than

describing or being "about" a whiptail lizard, becomes an exploration of mind. The mind in question can't be totally confused (as happens if knowledge or experience is unassimilated) and it can't be rigidly focused on a thesis (as happens when one fails to account for the plethora of conflicting evidence). When I arrive in a state somewhere between these two extremes I feel ready to write. "Cascade Experiment" has scientific inclusions (electrons, species of whiptail lizards), but these are examples, cases in point. They illuminate the poem's real investments: the way our present beliefs affect or distort our future knowledge; the unreliability of human perception; the old-fashioned question of whether consciousness might in any way continue after death.

Faith, in my poetry, means not only religious belief, but all the suppositions and convictions that allow us to live in the world. Much of the information brought to us by science strains our capacity to imagine, let alone believe. The poem seizes on such facts and says, if I can believe these extraordinary things, maybe I can believe in "you." For me, the "you" addressed throughout is the ultimate power or First Cause: that which ignites the cascade of being, evolutionary on the grandest scale. "God" is the common abbreviation. I'll use that word with the understanding that I don't mean a personal, theistic God. Some readers might think of "you" as a mortal instance of the divine. That's okay by me. If one reaches this "you," one is enlightened or fulfilled.

"[R]eaching you will be no harder than believing / in a planet's caul of plasma, / or interacting with a comet / in its perihelion passage." Believing that a planet is wrapped in plasma isn't very hard, even though we've seen neither the planet nor the wrapping. We accept this as another fact brought to us by science. But interacting with a comet! It seems to me that if "reaching you" is no harder than this, it's already one of the hardest things imaginable. Although the tone is insouciant, the analogues suggested are anything but a breeze. Epiphany isn't easy. I find the idea of "interacting with a comet" somewhat comic. "Interacting" has the sound of pop psychology, as if the fiery orb were expected to talk back. And the task is not simply to cross paths with said star, but to meet it during the perihelion passage, the point at which it's closest to the sun. Difficult as this interstellar square dance sounds, it has been done. Our high-tech proxies, modules, are capable of crossing a comet's path at a targeted moment. In fact, no matter how unlikely or impossible the poem's examples sound, they are all verified by science. The first stanza goes on to suggest ugh. that "reaching you" will be no harder than considering the panoply of chance sparkings that led to one's own appearance here. It tentatively defines the human self as a *Reader's Digest* edition of God or the watered-down version of a more complex whole.

The proposal that ignites stanza two, "faith in facts can help create those facts," is slightly different in meaning from the poem's opening assertion. Facts are "objectively" true information. However, the poem does away with the notion of objectivity by asserting that our prior beliefs affect our present facts. In the spirit of Heisenberg's principle (the act of observing changes what's observed), the poem implies that our preconceptions—the questions asked, the assumptions held before the search—affect what will be found. The behavior and properties of electrons sound like theology as written by the Brothers Grimm: Electrons exist only when they're measured (and why would we have tried to measure them without a prior belief in their existence?); they can vanish from one side of a wall and appear on the other "without leaving any holes or being / somewhere in between." Science discovered these facts fairly recently. Previously it didn't know where to look, what to look for, what to look with. Given the history of our ignorance, it seems intellectually immodest to insist, for instance, that consciousness ceases after death. Perhaps, the poem suggests, our perceptions and instruments aren't sophisticated enough to measure what occurs. The tumbling, hypotactic structure halts toward the end of stanza two, giving the weight of pause to the last five lines, which take the form of three relatively short sentences. They describe the state of the speaker's belief. Her belief is the sort of place in which electrons exist after they vanish and before they reappear. She finds herself "discarding and enlarging" both the orthodox religious views ("an excitation of mist") and the "vacancy" of atheism. How do you enlarge upon something you've discarded? How do the electrons go through a wall "without leaving any holes or being / somewhere in between"? A fact can be a paradox.

"Because truths we don't suspect have a hard time / making themselves felt" begins stanza three, ringing a slight change in the poem's catalytic premise. Whereas the first causal lines considered the power of existing beliefs to

Feminism hidden in
secluded language

change what exists, this line sees things from the viewpoint of the hidden facts, waiting to be found. Scientists recently discovered "thirteen species / of whiptail lizards composed entirely of females." Although the lizards have existed for eons, nobody noticed that they were all female because of a prevailing belief that lizards come in two sexes. That the lizards are female is significant. The feminist strategies of my work are embedded because I believe linguistic structures are most powerful when least evident. If we are aware of racist language, for instance, we either fight it or accept it (and are thereby in league with its assumptions). If people notice an idea, they can argue against it, thus undermining it. But a more secluded assumption won't be disabled. It will be absorbed and work its stowaway changes. The covert traces of language operate on the subconscious to affect our views. I have tried to turn this linguistic tendency against itself: Whereas concealed meanings usually enforce the status quo, I use recondite structures to say subversive things. Few readers have noticed the preoccupation with gender in my work because it's eclipsed by the poems' starring subjects. The unnoticed female lizards suggest that many "facts" about females are obscured or influenced by our existing notions. At least that is the submerged pertinence of those lines.

I don't mean to say that the poem's overt meanings exist in order to provide a smoke screen for its actual absorptions. The poem's open devotions are as important as its closeted endowments. Overtly the lizards support the possibility of consciousness continuing beyond death: If we failed to notice that thirteen species of lizards were all female, we might have failed to notice some unexpected aspect of consciousness. Of course, the concept of an afterlife isn't relevant to science (and of little interest to most philosophy) because both disciplines have produced such strong proofs against immortality in any guise. The proposition that consciousness might (in some shape) persist after death is almost insupportable. Given this, I was pleased to arrive at one slim argument in its favor. "Cascade Experiment" builds toward this moment of possibility, realized at the end of stanza three: "if death divests the self / it's the sole event in nature / that's exactly what it seems." After reaching this apogee, the poem ends with the brief coda of the last stanza.

The causative and formative elements of belief have played a part in my poetry for some time. Three examples from *Palladium* come to mind: the pilgrims of "603 West Liberty St." who "believe this // because they believe that"; "The Wreckage Entrepreneur" who is able to salvage valuable things because of a faith that those things are there to be found; and the scientist of "Peripheral Vision" who notes that "the God of triangles would be / three-sided: we see what we want / to see."

A "law of nature" is supposed to be an objective truth. In our courts, laws are a means of clarification based on custom and precedents. But my poetry argues that "our laws block less / Visible more spectral evidence." Those lines are from "The Fractal Lanes," one of several poems in *Powers Of Congress* that consider (among other things) the architecture of belief.

The Fractal Lanes

Being menial, how can we let vastnesses strike through
Our fastened nerves, or see—being the ordered smallnesses
We are—the whole spill, squeeze, and boiling without
Losing heart, mind, or being
Insinuated—hugged or struck into the unwanted
Northless utmosts, the Southless balconies between
Gables of dust, rotundas of sun? Can it be our comfort's

Derived from our dumbness? It's good to know there are infinite
Exponents within the arrays we've made, that our laws block less
Visible more spectral evidence. Maybe a little
Equity—currently scarved in subterfuge—some
Linchpin—circumspect, magnetic—is yet to be
Opened and made cogent. Practice makes
Pattern. Repeat a thing till the *again*
Sculpts presence. It's some world when

The power leavening each cell's so variously
Hushed that we can't see or hear it. The thrill's in thinking it
Exists as latent prism: the red, yellow, and blue

Rays within a spun concolorous white wheel, the phrases
Interwoven down the left side of some poems, which might stay
Ghostly and unknown till pointed out. Though we base the stars'
Hermetic chemistry upon the light they hurl,
The earth's so close our measures blur. We go by lakes

And rumblings from the core. To think the ground we glide on then
Reside in holds more oxygen than the air! It makes our dying
Meager, too evident for credit—that unreckoned—breadth.

Readers usually fail to see acrostic lines. To insert words that remain invisible seems a perverse strategy. However, this formal device enacts the idea under discussion: the notion that we see what we've been trained to notice or what we've seen before. Surely there are infinite patterns, meanings, and people rendered invisible by our unintentional disregard. We fail to see them (or some aspect of them) either because we're unaccustomed to their presence or because we've been taught to "read" existence in a certain limiting fashion. "The Fractal Lanes" has self-referential lines that call attention to its own acrostic and to those in other poems. It calls such reclusive components a "latent prism." If this strategy works, the reader, having already noticed the rhymes, meter, etc. in preceding poems while remaining oblivious to the acrostic dimension, will grasp the larger point about perception, marginality, and invisibility. Once an acrostic is pointed out it seems terribly obvious, and one wonders how one failed to see it before.

In my poems, the acrostic runs down the left-hand side: a spindle weaving a distaff thread, a subversive hinge. I say "subversive" because I like an acrostic to unhinge some of the poem's certainties. "The Fractal Lanes," for instance, is an exploratory prayer, with a prayer's high seriousness. The acrostic adds an element of wit (to pray is human, to play is divine), undermining pretentiousness: Only after you've noticed it can you see the poem's silly puns. This tactic, of enlarging or reversing the central content with a fell (and falling) stroke, is one way acrostics work in my poems.

"Lanes" are narrow roads or tracks, while "Fractal" (from the Latin *fractus,* meaning "irregular" or "fragmented") is a term coined by the mathematician Benoit Mandelbrot. The order of "Lanes" next to the smash of "Fractal" gives the title an oxymoronic twist. (The title also takes on a bit more meaning after you read the acrostic.) Fractals describe certain structures of nature previously thought to be amorphous or chaotic. There are two types of fractals, random and geometric. The geometric type is self-similar. "A self-similar mechanism is, formally speaking, a kind of cascade, with each state creating details smaller than those of the preceding stages."* "Practice makes / pattern. Repeat a thing till the *again* / Sculpts presence," the poem says, describing both the process of perception and self-similar fractals. Formally, "The Fractal Lanes" contains a nesting of design within design. It could be talking about fractals when it praises the "infinite / Exponents within the arrays we've made." A tree's foliage, the lungs' interior, and galactic clusters are examples of fractal forms previously regarded as too chaotic to map. Now scientists are able to find a deep logic in those circumspect structures and in phenomena such as the sun's oscillations or the surface of a coral reef: They have become irregular instances with enough regularity to plot. Of course, the sun's behavior and the coral's structure haven't "become" or changed. Rather our "objective truths" have enlarged to accommodate new understanding.

---

*The essays in Section II (pp. 41–82) contain fuller discussions of fractal form's relation to poetics.

The penultimate poem in *Powers Of Congress*, "Behavior-ial Geography," notes that "the first explorers charted all / they hoped to find," and ends by discarding such "objec-tive" measures as maps:

> All views are seasoned
> subjectivities, beds
> carved by freshets,
> warps of the heart.
> Ecstasy has its reasons.

The last poem in the book, "Art Thou The Thing I Wanted," makes a similar point. Here are the concluding stanzas:

> . . . Like others,
> I mistake whatever is
> for what is natural.

> You know the commonplaces. How people think
> women are good
> at detail work when that's the only work
> they're given. Or how
> the city's invisible

> engines jiggled our coffee
> till we believed quivering a constant
> property of liquid.
> Everything happens to me, I think,
> as anything reminds me of you: the real estate

most local, most removed.
As on the remains of prairie
the curving earth becomes a plinth—
from which we rise, towers
of blood and ignorance.

The title of this poem is a first line from Emily Dickinson (1282: "Art thou the thing I wanted? / Begone—my Tooth has grown—"). A couple of old saws (women are good; women are good at detail work) are dismantled in double-edged ways. The lineation suggests that detail work is of supreme importance, "the only work," before it suggests a reason for the false assumption concerning women's aptitude: Detail work is the only work they're given. The next example, about the persistent jiggling of urban coffee, also speaks to the theme of romantic love that numbers among the poem's concerns. It implies that the rigors of unrequited love encourage lovers to believe "quivering a constant / property of liquid." "Everything happens to me, I think," says the speaker, noting the mind's tendency to make itself the center of the action. The last image stresses the deceptive nature of our sensory perceptions. The earth is round, but it doesn't look that way from where we stand: "on the remains of prairie / the curving earth becomes a plinth—." The dash that ends the line is a tribute to Dickinson's influence. I also liked it as a mimetic gesture: A dash looks like a plinth, so it's a little illustration. With "Art Thou The Thing I Wanted," *Powers Of Congress* ends on a less hopeful note than it began. In the concluding lines, humans rise from the false "plinth" of the prairie, imagining themselves as towers. "Towers" is amended by "of blood and ignorance," undercutting the heroic stature. "Blood" points to our animal nature, while "ignorance" describes the mind's vaunted ability to reason.

Speaking of reason, poets tend to shy away from abstractions (and ideas) because they seem dry and generalized. The first thing writers learn is to prize the specific, which has come to be synonomous with the concrete. Vivid, sensual description is useful as a place to start because it prevents students from confusing poetry with the abstract gush of greeting cards. And most of us have heard the numbing white noise of technical discourses composed largely of abstractions. But as I analyzed the poetry I love most, I realized that its beauty greatly depended on the poets' ways with abstract language. "A clover blossom's a province" is the first line of "Mechanics," by A. R. Ammons. It might have become something like "A clover blossom's a reddish cotton rag," the title "Flower Arteries," if Ammons had "gone in fear of abstraction." (Pound, who gave that advice, also called Imagism "the grammar school of poetry.") Of course, Rainer Maria Rilke's poems are built almost solely of abstractions: "And if I cried, who'd listen to me in those angelic / orders?" The poems in *Duino Elegies* not only make abstraction beautiful, they are made beautiful by their abstractions. "Abstractions seem magical because they can exist independent of matter—and also because they can do things that matter itself cannot do," writes K. C. Cole in *Sympathetic Vibrations, Reflections on Physics as a Way of Life*. Dickinson's enchanting, vast, and at times terrifying cosmos relies upon repeated conceptualizations—"Circumference," "Difference," "Amplitude," "Experiment," and so on—which she makes particularly her own through varying contexts.

Schooled by the poetry I love, I began trying to give life, urgency, and a kind of body to abstract language. The poem "Toward Clairvoyance," from my first book, *Dance Script With Electric Ballerina,* was an early move in this direction. It grew from the Dickinson line that is its epigraph: "Dust is the only Secret—" (153). The final poem in *Dance Script,* "Diminuendo," takes its first line directly from a very early, very slight Dickinson poem (2!), which begins "There is another sky." The book's title poem owes something to both Whitman's "I Sing the Body Electric" and Dickinson's "I cannot dance upon my Toes . . ." (326). In *Palladium,* "603 West Liberty St." has as epigraph Dickinson's famous paradox "Captivity is Consciousness. / So's Liberty" (384). Over the years, I became intrigued by her echoing abstract vocabulary. What gave her particular lexicon its magnitude? Two things seem clear: The recurring words must be gorgeously capacious. And they must be important to the poet's largest views of the way things are.

The concrete and the abstract are more closely linked than we allow. K. C. Cole points out that "Even a galaxy of stars is largely an abstraction, in the sense that the individual stars are continually replaced by new ones." Of course, what we call a star is actually light that left home billions of years ago: an intangible ghost of itself. The word *palladium* is both an abstraction (meaning "safeguard or security") and a concrete term (meaning a dance hall or theater, among other things). I was attracted to the word's sound when I chanced across it, and its meanings spoke to my absorptions. Since my informal survey showed that most people didn't know one definition of palladium, let alone the six I had in mind, I reluctantly decided to preface each section of my second book with epigraphs that spoke to a particular denotation or connotation of the word. This solution struck me as unimaginative, but at least readers wouldn't be told what they already knew. If the poems in each section had defined a meaning of palladium, I would have found the project too obvious. But "palladium" pointed to the slant truths of the poems. The word retrieved submerged concerns that readers might not find without prompting.

The six meanings used as part openings arc backward and forward through the book, glossing the poems in their section, those in other sections, and those in my other books. In part one, *palladium* is defined as a metallic element "used in alloys (as with silver) for electrical apparatus and jewelry. Symbol Pd." The elemental has connotations of perfection. It raises the question of transience by being in itself a form of *forever.* An element stands alone yet is capable of being "alloyed" with others, an aspect that points to the theme of estrangement versus engagement. The symbol for palladium (the element) is the same as the abbreviation for *paid.* The poems "Night Gold" and "Traveling Light" (among others) deal with guilt and debts: They are in part about owing, giving back, paying your dues.

A quote from an old watch manual also prefaces part

one: "The balance spring is usually of palladium." And a sentence from *Metallic Materials* says, "The single largest use for palladium is as a catalyst." The moment of balance and the moment of catalytic change have been important to my work for some time. The poem "Dance Script With Electric Ballerina" was a metaphor for change and stasis. "Equilibrium / is so soothing—while any strain is a reminder / of the pain that leads to grace" the dancer said. And I've mentioned the catalytic, triggering metaphor of "Cascade Experiment," from *Powers Of Congress*.

Each line of *Palladium* contains words comparable to counterpoint in music. The poems have a polyphonic texture, in which "the music derives its expressive power and interest from the interplay of the several lines" (Joseph Machlis, *The Enjoyment of Music*). In a fugue or a canon, the first voice enters alone to establish the theme. It is answered by a second voice that plays the theme while the first voice weaves a counterpoint around it. A third voice comes in with the theme, the first and second voices weave, and so on. When all of the voices have stated the theme, the exposition section ends. The composer then improvises with countersubjects and inversions. The fugue is not an exact analogue to the poem, of course. But it affords another way to think about structure.

I decided to start *Palladium* with "Babies" since an infant is a beginning, a catalyst. "Babies" also are what lovers sometimes become to each other. The poem is attentive to consciousness and conscience: language, growth, truth, maturity, and perfection are its business.

Babies

born gorgeous with nerves, with brains
the pink of silver polish or
jellyfish wafting ornately
through the body below.
An invertebrate cooing
on the mother
tongue shushes and lulls them into thinking
all is well. As they grow they learn

salvage: tear-out
guides to happiness say apologies can outshine
lies, guilt be lickspittled from their lives, bad
glycerined to good. Like a child's first school pencils
in their formal brilliance
and sharp new smells, they lie

as lovers. Maybe one cries
the wrong name and the night skinning
them pleasantly alive
leaps away in shards.
Then it's time for restitution:
a tin of homebaked,
holding gingham safety, fetal
as the light through mason jars of beets and brine,
or jewelry, clasping and unclasping
aisles of fluorescence from great department stores,
a distracting plenitude, and tempting.

Still, the beloved may stay bitter as an ear
the tongue pressed

into, unwanted.
And the word *end:* spiney, finally-formed,
indents them and is
understood. They learn

the hard way as hurts
accrue, and the brain is cratered as a rock
by rain that fell ages past
on unprotected mud. An insult keeps
despite apologies. And when it vaporizes at last,
its space fills with grains that harden
to a fossil shaped exactly
like the insult.
They grow up when they know that

sometimes
only a gesture responsive as a heart-
shaped parachute above a jump
a life depends on
to be perfect
the first time will ever do.

The first stanza describes a state of perfection: the gorgeous innocence and physical lushness of the untried body. The power of the mind is evoked with the image of a brain "pink as silver polish." Palladium, the element, is "silver-white." But the simile is more than an excuse to work in the title's connotations. I chose the image because it accurately described the color of the brain (grayish pink), while implying that the mind, like silver polish, could confer shine. The line in its entirety reads "the pink of silver polish or."

There's a pun on *ore*, the raw state of an element. Moreover, breaking on this function word gives the line a tipsy, unbalanced quality. It's less resolved than a line that forms a complete syntactical phrase. The brain is then compared to a jellyfish whose long streamers of nerves run down through the body. If you picture a jellyfish you'll see an invertebrate in parachute form. The poem's opening imagery is of gooey, soft, incipient things: The brain, the baby, the jellyfish are amorphous in quality. This is the primal state— the mush and blur before boundaries and orders are imposed. The objects harden as the poem progresses.

Palladium is a synonym for a safeguard, and that definition prefaces the poems in section two. Casting ahead to the second epigraph, the "babies" are motivated by a desire for sanctuary: They want to create a haven on earth. The first lines of stanza two continue the polishing motif: Language is seen as a means of shining away lies, guilt, and evil. The world has become a harder place, and the imagery reflects this obdurate, sharply delineated state: The new lovers, lying tensely in bed, are compared to "a child's first school pencils." And since we write with them, "pencils" continues the countersubject of language, as does the punning line break, "they lie // . . . ."

The lovers betray each other with language and try to fix the damage with objects (which speak without words). In contrast to the cushioned muck of the beginning, by stanza three the night is a sharp thing that skins them alive and breaks into piercing shards. The objects chosen as a means of restitution are the sorts of gifts one gives oneself as comfort or gives another to beg pardon. The first, "a tin of homebaked," signals the wish to regress to the cozy safety of childhood. It holds "gingham safety, fetal / as the light through mason jars of beets and brine." Murky, reddish, bloody, the fetuses of biology labs lurk in this image, evoking a little horror or a floating preconscious peace. The second offering is the traditional gift of jewelry. This fix-all is the opposite of homebaked: You can't make a gem yourself. You select gems from the welter of culturally condoned perfection. Like most things that aspire to the ideal, jewels are highly formal—a hard surface of tiny, precise planes.

The fourth stanza contains the moment of enlightenment or maturity when the "babies" learn that some events are irrevocable. Language can cause a havoc beyond its own power to mend. The first three lines are an image of sexual and linguistic penetration: the tongue pressing into the ear. The intrusion (of words or tongue) is "unwanted" by the recipient, just as the earlier lies and name calling were unwanted corruptions of the tongue entering the defenseless ear. Hearing and smell are the most vulnerable senses: We can close our eyes and mouths, withhold our touch, but we have no means of shutting off our ears or nose. As a result, they're constantly bombarded by stimuli—not all of them pleasant. Language itself, the word *end*, is embodied as a "spiny" thing that "indents" the mind. Both the first and fourth stanzas end on the words "They learn" to underscore the process of growth through a punishing language of experience.

"They learn // the hard way" the line continues into the penultimate stanza, where hardness takes a final literal turn: The brain, once "unprotected mud," is now a rock.

The damage done by language, the "insult," resists the reconstructive language of apology. Even when words succeed in vaporizing the insult, the emotional space it occupied remains. This wound gradually hardens "to a fossil shaped exactly / like the insult." Language, while too weak to banish its own havoc, seems powerfully immortal here. Its half-life extends beyond our efforts of effacement, beyond our lives or reach.

The babies "grow up when they know that // sometimes." "Sometimes," the first line of the final stanza, can also be linked to the lines that follow it: "sometimes / only a gesture responsive as a heart- / ...." This syntactic doubling initiates the twisty construction that ends the poem. In this final sentence, language seems to have a will of its own. Its progress is wily, duplicitous: It refuses to be subdued into an orderly, simple form. The lifesaving heart-shaped parachute recalls the jellyfish of the first stanza and the world before the forms of language. It is the perfect gesture, rather than the perfect word, that can afford us with a sanctuary or "parachute." Here the notion of perfection is seen in a more positive light than is usual in my poems. But it's frightening to think that refuge depends upon a perfect anything. I resent (and perhaps the poem resents) the necessity of such perfection. The last line contains the word "first," thus placing the final emphasis on beginnings. This seemed right for "Babies," the first poem in the book.

While *Palladium* leaned heavily upon one word, *Powers Of Congress* develops a lexicon of recurring words and images. When certain words reappeared in several poems, I realized they'd become a force in my imagination. I then used them more consciously. Instead of openly defining the leitmotif as I had in *Palladium*, I wanted to let the meaning of the words accrue and change through their presence in the poems. I think of the repeating words as superclusters and clusters. (In astronomy, a *cluster* is a group of galaxies; an association of such clusters is a *supercluster.*) A supercluster word—charged, vibrating, mutable—creates itself anew within the poems: Its definition is available only by reading it within the context of the work. It differs from a symbol in that its meanings are more multiple and literal than archetypal. The clusters are the smaller units of the supercluster. For instance, I consider the word *cascade* a supercluster. The cluster words or components of CASCADE include: the spill, waterfall, blitz, flood, accident, slip, pivot, fountain, anima. The supercluster words recur throughout my work, while the clusters appear less often. Oddly enough, I don't find all of the supercluster words interesting on their own. The eccentricities they gain in association with the cluster words enrich them.

Here are a few other superclusters, followed by some of their clusters in parentheses: CORE (matrix, marrow, fulcrum, center, cortex, plexus, province, cargo); ELECTRIC (electrons, lighthouse, watts); CONGRESS (chemistry, union, fusion); CRYSTAL (frost, snowflake, solitaire, winter, arctic, jewel, gem, diamond, Lucite, prism, sugar, hygienic); ROSES (womb, romance, velvet); FIRES (forge, bombs, shot, bed); HALO (skein, link, snare, cymbal, wheel, lathe, nimbus, spool, hoop, curl, chain, perihelion, fan, plate, ring, rosary, coronet, radial, spring, lariat); POWER (marble, granite, engine, brass, bronze); PALLADIUM (bonds, plate, silver, gold, swaddling, casing, swathing, iron, shield, lock, bolt, lane, chapels, cathedrals); DANCE (waltz, tulle, ballerina); SILK (selvage, shift, fabrication, synthetic, skin, cellulite); EXPANSION (plenty, amplitude, flux, fractal, dilations, breadth, sea, liquid, experiment); LINE (beam, band, lane, exponent, pins, channel).

The list is partial so that readers might discover other galaxies on their own. I certainly didn't compile this lexicon and then write poems to fit the bill. The concepts of cluster and supercluster, as well as the particular words and images, evolved over many years as I was propelled, sometimes sluggishly, sometimes feverishly, by the demands and momentum of the poems.

Before concluding, I'd like to say a few words about what might be the most controversial poem in *Powers Of Congress:* "Point Of Purchase." I worry that it will be seen as a gimmicky effort or cute trick. Yet the poem's form describes (and argues with) my aesthetic in oblique fashion. I think of it as a fourteen-page contrapuntal structure. Counterpoint means "point against point" or "note against note." Thus it is a rather argumentative form of music. Unlike "Babies," which absorbed its counterthemes into a single texture, the counterpoint of "Point Of Purchase" takes the form of marginal, handwritten comments. These discrete opinions and anecdotes oppose the typeset text.

The central part of the poem is a dramatic monologue spoken by a pool-playing artist. This typset speaker has a fast-moving, funny voice, but she is so opinionated as to be obnoxious. When I wrote her part and showed it to friends, I found they wanted to argue with her. I decided to let this dissent into the poem by means of marginal comments representing the divergent responses of imaginary readers. I hoped this would prevent the poem's actual readers from feeling obliterated, excluded, or bludgeoned by the text. I asked four friends to inscribe the comments I composed so that the marginal speaker/readers could be distinguished by their various handwriting.

In polyphonic music, the opposing melody is called a mirror. The narrative infrastructure of "Point Of Purchase" is dense with echoes. The typeset speaker is an unreliable narrator in the tradition of literature's madwomen and ranters: figures such as Crazy Jane or the Wife of Bath, who make both wise and dubious claims. This speaker, nicknamed "The Magic Marker," is a fanatic painter and pool player. She tells of receiving a grant to visit Easter Island and being influenced by a culture with a communal notion of property, as evidenced by a practice known as "steal trading." Some twelve pages later, she describes another fellowship to the fictional artist colony "Stormport": After her fellowship ended, she stayed on, living in the woods on nuts and berries. She also stole into the studios of the other painters every night and changed their work-in-progress. The marginal comments turn the speaker's own tactics of appropriation against her. In a doubling gesture, her own opinions, authority, words are revised by the poem's readers. The four fictional readers stand for the actual readers who will revise, paint out, or trash her words as they read them. The chorus of scribbles also underscores the speaker's false witness by pointing up the holes in her argument. Having said this, I must add that the marginal commentators are themselves unreliable narrators. Thus, there is no firm purchase available in the poem. Although actual readers might find their opinions expressed somewhere, they'll have a hard time finding any solid ground or single prevailing view.

The marginal readers include a Marxist-poststructuralist critic, fond of quoting from documents such as "Politics of the Fiction Workshop." To her mind, the poem is full of economic subtexts (beginning with the title). The precise, small hand belongs to a critic who believes language should disappear (rather than "call attention to itself") so that author and reader can commune without linguistic distractions. He wants to forget that he's reading a book. I believe this attitude represents the prevailing assumption of poetry criticism in America. It opposes the view that all language is a manipulative construct with the notion of the ideal poem as a transparent pipeline of emotion. This critic also favors sexist metaphors, which catcall forth feminist critical theory. The wildest script is that of a naive reader who says, "I can really relate to it," and begins to recount her sister's story in the margins. Her sister is a double of the typeset speaker, creating a mirror narrative on the poem's outskirts. The Palmer method exclamations are those of a pragmatic, impatient person who might read Stephen King novels most of the time. (The poem must have been an assignment.) This reader heeds the advice of the conventional critic and abandons the poem before the end. Thus, the imaginary readers influence and argue with one another as well as with the poem's speaker.

Everyone has had the experience of reading a library book that's littered with the comments of previous readers. The written comments are often annoying but always enticing: You can't help reading them. They upstage the printed word. It's equally true that the content of such marginalia is usually boring or banal. Formally, "Point Of Purchase" is modeled on the debased library book—with a difference. Like those used books, I wanted the poem to show evidence of the human hand. But I also wanted the readers' comments to be enriching rather than redundant. Another formal analogue is suggested by the poem's epigraph: "Sermons on unbelief ever did attract me" (Dickinson). "Point Of Purchase" is a disheveled, heretical sermon.

The first friends who read the poem sought out historical precedents in Coleridge's glosses of "The Ancient Mariner" and Nabokov's *Pale Fire*. But the poem is not meant to be read within the context of either work. The actual influences were contemporary critical theory and Emily Dickinson. The fair copies of many Dickinson poems are marked with little crosses indicating alternate word choices in the margins. A perusal of the variorum edition shows that she never made a firm decision in many cases. Instead, readers must make the decision of which word to select, thus participating in the poem's composition. My enjoyment of Dickinson's marginal options made me wish to include a similar element of choice and chance in "Point Of Purchase." The poem changes according to how much weight a reader gives each of the marginal voices. Its structure is indeterminate, which brings me to the influence of critical theory. "Point Of Purchase" speaks to Marxist-poststructuralist, reader response, reception, and feminist ideologies as well as to those rugged individualists who disavow all ideologies.

On a lighter note, "Point Of Purchase" can be read as a parody of how poetry is composed at this moment in America: it is a formalized display of the process by which a new poem is inscribed with the critical comments of one's friends and teachers. Lately, the MFA workshop has become a scapegoat for all the ills of contemporary literature. I disagree with that too-convenient placement of blame. The process the poem mimics is not limited to workshops. All over the country, poets inscribe one anothers' efforts. Poems bearing handwritten descants are returned to authors who revise their lines into white-framed perfections. (At least that's the goal.) It's likely that poets have always done this to some degree: What we call "Homer" was a workshop that extended over centuries; Dickinson revised to please Susan Gilbert; Pound pruned Eliot. Rather than absorbing or effacing dissenting voices, "Point Of Purchase" retains traces of the comments it elicited and invents new responses: The poem comes disarmed with its own critique, ready for assembly (or disassembly) in the reader's head.

I realize that "Point Of Purchase" is not an easy read. The marginalia are distracting. Although the analogy to polyphonic music is far from exact, I chose it because the subjects and countersubjects of a fugue present difficulties akin to the poem's multiple voices. I sometimes have to listen to a fugue twenty times before I can distingish and follow all the episodes. Without such an effort of attention, the counterpoint is a maddening blitz of dizzy notes. But if I make the effort, pattern unfolds and rewards are given. In like fashion, "Point Of Purchase" needs to be read many times. Anyone who makes that investment is in a better position to judge its worth than I.

Tomorrow I begin teaching the course in Living Poets mentioned at the beginning of this essay. A friend called who works in the store that carries the required books. He said one of my prospective students had asked why I wasn't teaching the work of a well-known poet I'll call Halcyon Angeltongue. This student had heard Hal Angeltongs read before. In fact Angeltogs was the only poet the student had heard. He had decided that Angeltoes was great, and he wanted the class to verify that impression. The human wish to have one's present beliefs confirmed makes teaching a difficult undertaking. Reassurance is doubtlessly one of the powers of poetry: We read it and are grateful that another being felt as we feel. But poetry also exists to jostle cozy notions and wake us up to what we've never known. Those dimensions entice and hold me. I want a poetry that scores the waterfall, language, into parabolic heresies: a canon for infidels of every tradition.

1990

V

Penchants

A Canon for Infidels

Three Poets in Pursuit of America

James Schevill, Kenneth A. McClane, Phyllis Janowitz

I T'S EASY TO THINK OF THREE OR FOUR VOLUMES OF fiction or poetry published in the past few years with "American" in the titles. The adjective has become a kind of a buzzword for an author's desire to say inclusive things about the United States. In *The American Fantasies: Collected Poems 1945–1981* (Swallow Press Books), James Schevill takes the pursuit of Life, Liberty, and Happiness as his theme. In doing so, he captures many qualities— exuberance, naiveté, generosity, toughness—associated with America. Foreign writers seem to lack our self-obsession: *The English Fantasies* has an improbable sound, entertaining though such a book might be. Perhaps our shorter literary heritage encourages self-consciousness, or perhaps this country's disparity makes us long for unity, if only on paper.

Whitman wrote, "I am the poet of the commonsense and of the demonstrable," and the same could be said for James Schevill. Many of his titles have the plainness of headlines or the narrative quality of captions: "New York Subway Rush Hour," "Boy Watching a Lightbulb," "Death in a Country Town," "Mississippi Sheriff at the Klan

Initiation." His art is a continuation of the realistic characterizations and conscientious moralism of Frost and E. A. Robinson. While he shares with these poets a fondness for colloquial speech rendered through dramatic monologues, the absence of regionalist or formalist ties enables Schevill to explore a wider spectrum of language. The inventive wildness of his humor distinguishes it from the sly ironies of Frost. Although the latter showed more insight into female psychology and avoided stereotypes more adroitly, there is a warmer, happier sensibility at work in Schevill's poetry.

Since many of these poems are narratives, they lead to the question of how narrative poetry must differ from prose. If the answer is that poetry may be less linear, that it may manage richer connotation in a shorter space through density of language or rhythm, some of these poems fail to make the transformation. The strong didactic strain in American poetry shows in lines that slip into the rhetoric of sermons or good prose. The strength of moral poetry lies in its ability to win us over through engaged and generous empathy, its quality of fellow feeling. Problems arise if the morals surface in the poems like pills in jelly.

In fact, both the major flaw and the major glory of the work are meshed in its content. Schevill aspires to the democratic poetry Whitman envisioned. However, the book's worldview is based upon a traditional interpretation of history and the established canon of literary sovereignty. It takes less imaginative energy to reinforce the existing notions than to research and suggest alternatives. This might explain why many of the poems concerning historical or literary figures fail to awaken interest: They offer no fresh perspective, and a versified survey won't do. The first definition of "canonize" is "to declare officially to be a saint." Just so, these poems whitewash people who were reputedly more difficult to admire when alive. In their determined praising, they become conventional panegyrics. We hear the voices of Jefferson, Melville, Poe, Hemingway, Faulkner, Williams, Stevens, Eliot, Roethke, Whistler, Charles Ives, and so on, but pay the price in silence from Abigail Adams, Susan B. Anthony, Sojourner Truth, Margaret Fuller, Edith Wharton, Frederick Douglass, George Washington Carver, Emma Goldman, and Mary Cassatt, to name but a few of the fruitful possibilities. The exclusion of women in numbers (there are a few tokens) disappoints not because books should represent a random sampling of the population or be "politically correct." Rather, such an omission, in a book that strives to embody an American identity, implies that women's contribution and presence are negligible, or that the writer is incapable of inventing their voices. In these *American Fantasies,* men have the power of identity, history, action, and effect. When women appear, however, they are often idealized or simplified into archetypes or stereotypes: Thus, we have "The Moon and the Beautiful Woman" and "No-Name Woman"; we have the dumb broad asking "Mister Pollock, / HOW do you KNOW when you've finish-dead / a pic-ture?" and receiving a sexual analogy in reply; we have the "eighteen years of feminine fragility / in prim white office dress / and tortoise shell glasses" who gets her comeuppance from a construction worker; and we have Sarah Louise Burkett, the "old maid" who rescues a parakeet. In addition, many of the poems in the voices of well-known writers repeat what these writers said more effectively themselves, as if Schevill were imitating, rather than extending a style.

When Schevill invents characters instead of relying upon existing types or well-known personae, the poems shine with wit, intelligence, and craft. He is at his best "where imagination reveals its proud presence / Transforming the commonplace into points of brilliance" ("Wallace Stevens at Ease with Marble Cake"), or when he follows Dickinson's advice to "Tell all the Truth but tell it slant—." The strongest poems evoke wonder at the rich strata of American speech and unpredictable shifts of character. The colorful narratives allow one to read the book with the ease and pleasure of good prose fiction. Schevill introduces us to "The Suicide Runner," a jock who chews up drinking glasses with the disclaimer, "'Course I didn't eat / The real big pieces of glass or the long stems. / That's looking for trouble"; Hog, the blues guitarist, who says of a performance, "That night I sing my Hog-elegy to any / Crazy thunder-power shining in the spotlights"; the scientist who surveys the protozoa, noting "Before and beyond / The blasting age of atoms, they reproduce their world / Of miniature beauty, conquest, by radiant fission."

Sight, especially "obsessive American sight," is a recurring theme for this poet, who writes "the jumping thing is to see." In poem after poem, one senses the moral imperative of bearing witness. Schevill has a gift for noticing unexpected details: He looks at subjects usually excluded from poetry, although they carry considerable weight in our lives. In doing so, he appropriates unusual registers of diction: "Learn American language—balance of payments, / Deficit spending, bull markets, net and gross figures" ("The Money Man"). "Wrecking for the Freeway" (which contains the epigraph "A highway is a true index of our culture") manages to use the methods and language of highway construction as metaphor: "A Johnson Float Finisher smoothes the surface / That everyone may finish and float." In Schevill's best work, one recognizes the workings of a humane and generous intelligence. Thus, the spectacle of T-shirted citizens on the fourth of July leads to the following conclusion: "When I retreat from laughter / Into my isolated search for community again, / I'll think of our desire for poetry, / How we don't know what to do with it despite Whitman, / And so we try to display it on our chests." When his fancy catches fire, the poems are illuminated with a devilish energy. Consider the lunatic imagination behind a ten-part poem based on the notion that "A Buddhist exiled in the United States, dies suddenly and finds himself reincarnated as a car." Here is the first stanza, in which the transformation takes place:

Slowly, I feel myself. Eyes squint at me
Through a long window. Across the glass is lettered
FURY. My skin is growing hard, my bones hammered longer.
My veins flow in glistening wires, tubes.
The curious, glittering people glide in
To touch me. My face is etched with polished lines,

A metal beehive. Singular words sound against
My antique English, *throttle, mileage, accelerator*
Suddenly, my heart explodes, sparks of energy
Shoot through my bowels. I hum, flow out
To hard streets. I glide on rubber circles.
Children call to me, smile, speak my title.
I know who I am . . . Across my rear puffing fumes
Curve the letters. F-U-R-Y- . . .

"The Buddhist Car" seems an appropriate emblem for
the United States, given our passion for the automobile,
fixation on self-knowledge, and childlike search for answers. The poem can be read as an attempt to locate the
sublime in an object that is absurdly kitsch, and yet by
virtue of its prevalence and formal appeal, as good a vehicle as any other for divine yearnings. This car is cursed with
self-awareness and a family who rides in it. "I sense their
fear of quicksand loneliness / Their need to honor the
American verb to do," says the Fury, playing on the meaning of hoopla, making a big to-do. As the group journeys
across the country, the trip is recounted from the car's
point of view in a tone one could hope to encounter only
in a Plymouth with spiritual leanings: part Zen, part popular mechanics.

Schevill deserves to be more widely read. Other poets
could learn from his willingness to explore the many registers of American speech. From the first poem, "Always We
Walk through Unknown People," to the last, "Masks in
1980 for Age 60," *The American Fantasies* lets us listen to the

strangers around us; their stories afford a feast of foibles and splendors.

~~

It seems fitting that Kenneth A. McClane's selected poems should be dedicated to Gwendolyn Brooks. Like Brooks, McClane writes with fiery compassion, as if empowered by the strength of his belief. *A Tree Beyond Telling: Poems Selected and New* (The Black Scholar Press), collecting five volumes of his poetry, charts the growth of his style and the maturation of his subject. In McClane, the lyric and narrative forms of the black urban tradition are coupled with an Emersonian reverence for nature. At its best, this results in a haunting amalgam of the two strains: There is the immediacy of an Ammons composition combined with the improvisational flux of black jazz. The poems are not meticulously "crafted"; it's more as if they resulted from the play of strong emotions upon a prepared and linguistically gifted mind. As in Ammons's work, we get a sense of the process of thought, as well as thought's conclusions.

McClane seeks transcendence in our ability to witness, survive, and love, despite the world's brutality. The urgency of black religious oratory flows through lines that have the ring of prophecy, the rhetoric of Biblical injunctions: "and god is in the moon, heart and dusk / of our turning: it is a new relevance / collect yourself—there is / much to do." ("No One May Rest") Images of the natural world— trees, birds, rivers—serve as vehicles for a hardwon faith.

Although many poems affirm existence, there is no easy yea-saying in the poet's stance. "The Black Intellectual" (dedicated to W. E. B. Du Bois) begins with a meditation on oppression:

> We have shored up so much
> to keep from rioting. To keep it down
> we move in and out of our skins
> in some grotesque obeisance, some wretching of our forms
> as if we were addled neon signs.

McClane then speaks of students who want to know "how earth / shares so little," and finds himself giving in to an uncharacteristic, but riveting, despair:

> And now I see nothing in their stunted lives
> but death; I see nothing in their hopeless
> celebration but blood; I see nothing but the ceaseless waste
> of dark bodies, piling up as they ask . . .

The naked desperation of this voice invites comparisons to James Wright. McClane's diction is often more complex, however. His lyrics have a way of singing in a simple idiom until a Latinate, abstract word suddenly looms large, all the more noticeable for its context. This gesture attains a casual elegance: "everything / is a presupposition like fruit-fly, camps of / meadowlark / and sunflower." The syntax is often challenging, and McClane's skill matches his daring: "Though much seems to be broken / as we pass / nothing is diminutive, tottering: with love / whatever imaginings we yield to / (be they in warm spring or seen at the mouth of cities) / climb with the gravest surety of angels." ("Family")

The poems' central figures are taken from the rich symbology of the black oral and written tradition. The title's "tree beyond telling" is at once a grim reminder of hanging trees and a reference to the life-engendering, systemic properties of language. Paul Laurence Dunbar's "The Haunted Oak" foreshadows McClane's "tree on which our cross hangs," while Langston Hughes's "Jazzonia" with its cry, "Oh, silver tree!" provides a brighter prefiguration. Ever since Dunbar struggled to cast off the minstrel-show diction of his dialect poems, black poets have fought to embody their own experience in their own language. At this point, there is so much to recover, so much to explore, that words must begin to seem inadequate: The poet writes despite the knowledge that the subject is "beyond telling." "To Hear the River," a tribute and reply to Hughes's "The Negro Speaks of Rivers," adapts the repetitive chant of the earlier poem. The river becomes a symbol for the ongoing legacy of blackness, the necessity of facing "What is lost / and possible." "At the Bridge with Rufus," a direct address to Baldwin's character from *Another Country*, shows the river calling "like some ill-fashioned gravity," dangerous because "it moves us past what we know." McClane interprets Rufus's self-destruction as an act that shows us "not how to live but how mighty the cost." Whether he writes of the poor, of women, or of a child, we are assured that the subject will be treated with tenderness and respect. He has the courage to face inequity and yet maintain that no matter "how difficult the singing . . . the inlet, a natural tuning fork, / will not let the slightest voice suffer silent."

~~

"The form of a rite must be beautiful, exhibiting, for example, balance, closure and aptness to that which it is the form of," wrote Auden. *Visiting Rites* (Princeton University Press), Phyllis Janowitz's second book and a nominee for the National Book Critics Circle Award, is full of well-wrought poetry that admirably fulfills Auden's dictum. Although Janowitz favors neat quatrains, tercets, and couplets, her formal elegance is never attained through sacrifice of the content: The tightly structured lines reflect the constraints of the world they describe.

Visiting Rites expands upon the themes of isolation and identity explored in the poet's first volume, *Rites of Strangers* (selected by Elizabeth Bishop for the Associated Writing Programs Award), to include poems about rituals of aging, communion, and our attempts to escape confining cultural roles. In this work, Janowitz articulates the "lives of the obscure" that Virginia Woolf longed to see represented more fully in literature. Rather than creating heroic fantasies or blue-sky utopias for her female characters, Janowitz confronts the despair felt by many who are defined as other in a patriarchal culture. The women in these poems desperately need to improve their connection to the outside world. However, the book implies that improvement of their status is not possible unless the external world is changed, along with their perception of it and of themselves. In the meantime, as people with no access to the larger world of power, they bring their frustration to bear upon their own limited lives. Thus, we have the indomitable "Mrs. Lucky," an old woman whose curiosity about the world drives her to take "courses in the language / of children, penguin socialization / and creative writing"; "Letitia and Prue," an odd couple who spend their claustrophobic lives unpacking heirlooms, reading in bed, and pickling; "Stubby Janina" who watches her weight, reclines on a BarcaLounger, and wonders whether to define herself as mother, daughter, or old woman, "possibilities / indifferent as roses." The limitations of traditional male roles are treated with equal discernment. Several poems recount the yearnings of men who "wear their simple birthrights like / shiny gold watches on long gold chains." There is Herman, a beleaguered father who leaves "with a passionless kiss and returns / with a daily paper, circles of sweat // ringing his armpits." Gregory, "the Solo Electron," asks, "Are there // no islands for a recluse? . . . // . . . no monasteries for a heretic?" In "Cells," the poet's father, a retired policeman, is dying in the prison of his hospital room, "hooked / to a machine lit up like something / you drop quarters into." After the hospital visit, the poet, on a train, sees a billboard with the graffiti "*Rosie, I Love You,*" which leads to the superb conclusion:

> The word love, read in a jolt of wheels.
> Astonishing. Ineludible. Like a blissful
> couple, joined at the chest, thighs,
> knees, kissing in the doorway
> you're trying to exit through.

The concision and imaginative power of this work recalls Plath, as do some of the themes. Her "disquieting muses" resonate in the guardian angels of "Music of Stars and Wheels," Janowitz's poem on the rite of christening. However, whereas Plath's demons sometimes seemed to hover over herself exclusively, Janowitz realizes that everyone's birthright amounts to the toy truck "that will break an axle, . . . / . . . sharp edges sticking / up for the children to rip their hearts on." Instead of feeling that she has been uniquely selected for extinction, Mrs. Lucky, the feisty grandmother, reminds herself that "It is not to me, alone, the little / angels cry, *Come to dust Come to dust* / The sun has ten billion years to go." For the most part, Janowitz's imagery is free of Plath's recurring figures and prominent color symbology. The stylistic difference between the two is characterized in Plath's remark that she could never get a toothbrush into a poem. While no one would argue that her poems are weaker for the absence of a Water Pik, the comment indicates that there were aspects of life so mundane they resisted her best efforts at transformation. On the other hand, Janowitz has forsaken mythological imagery to focus upon aspects of the quotidian world and popular culture as signifiers. In several of her poems, personae surrounded by tape decks and self-cleaning ovens speak of Mario Andretti, Mick Jagger, Gucci, Pucci, John Wayne, and Elvis Presley. They feast upon No-Cal and Cheerios, read *People* magazine and the *National Enquirer*, amuse themselves with bingo and encounter groups. They live in Newark and shop at Sears. Of course, when such personae rage against the dying of the light, the source of radiance is likely to be a flashlight or traffic signal. Mrs. Lucky, for example, rails against the dying spotlight that shines upon the "rococo grimaces, sequins / and pearls of despair—baubles / suitable for someone younger," and in a desperate striptease, peels off her costume of sexual attraction. This woman, who pretends that dying is "something / to look forward to" while secretly embracing life, is an antithesis to Plath's "Lady Lazarus," who invites death and becomes a passive witness to her own "unwrapping" or resurrection ("The peanut-crunching crowd / Shoves in to see / Them unwrap me hand and foot—/ The big strip-tease").

Janowitz's poems are something more than protests against mortality, however. The female personae realize that their bodies have been responsible for the status or bondage they've known, whether as mothers or goddesses. The gesture of stripping away the sentimentalized versions of motherhood and marriage recurs throughout the book: Gone are the *Good Housekeeping* visions of *Kinder, Kirche, Küche.* The Gerber babies have been replaced by furious infants in long lace gowns, illustrations by Tenniel for a grown-up Alice's journey through the looking glass. Letitia imagines "a baby, / a toothless red mouth and a howl. / Newborn it will look like a pig. / She will allow no illusions." The choice is between a limited domestic sphere, for which the baby is emblematic, and freedom of movement or autonomy, which she envisions as "driving a subway / through measureless caverns / while moonlighting at

Dunkin' / Donuts." Because each possibility involves a diminishment, "Whatever she does will be wrong."

In another poem, Letitia plays hide-and-seek with shifting images of self that surface in her mirror. Reading it, one remembers how women have regarded mirrors as weaponry capable of conferring victory upon the fairest or terrorizing through glimpses of aging or rebellious doubles. In Plath's "Mirror," for example, the looking glass becomes the "eye of a little god," and the poem ends on a fearful note as an old woman rises in it "like a terrible fish." Letitia's mirror-rite reads like a parodic version of Plath's poem and of Mary Coleridge's "The Other Side of the Mirror," in which a horrific, silent face appears, causing the poet to "whisper, 'I am she!'" In Janowitz's poem, apparitions of Millard Fillmore, Victoria Regina, and George Washington surface like fusty reminders of the limitations history places on women's self-interpretation. Amid images of "threadbare drawing rooms" and ivory hands passing cups, Letitia asks, "Is she never to be rid of this persona, /... / browsing on meringue glaces and sugary tea?" Whereas Plath and Mary Coleridge were terrified by their shifting identities, Janowitz's tone is more playful than gothic. Indeed, her persona calmly refers to these rites of passage as "daily occurrences." Such nonchalance offers hope that although millions of women are still in transition, the process of self-definition is becoming less threatening.

The book's final section asks what part our own volition plays in determining our fate. The poem "Jitters," with a characteristic sense of the absurd, finds the poet suffering a moment of metaphysical angst in a parking lot:

Last night I dreamed my spirit-guide,
a young man in a T-shirt labeled
CIRCUMSTANCE, was pilfering, downstairs
in my residence, a few pitiful knick-
knacks with the aid of a plastic sack.
So! I am the victim of Circumstance!

No. I will not accept this excuse
offered from me to me, a white
narcissus in a grubby hand. Do I not
possess the silver key that slides
into the ignition slot? Who turns
the wheel? Who starts? Who stops?

Here, as in Schevill's "Buddhist Car," the automobile serves as a metaphor for the American obsession with self-realization. However, in Janowitz's poem the car, instead of serving as narrator, becomes a means of establishing identity and controlling one's destiny. With self-mocking humor, the speaker practices deep-breathing techniques (learned from a spurious yogi who resembles Peter Sellers) while leaning against her "declining vehicle." Yet, even as she tries to find the "still, null center" of herself, "around which insects whirr," one gets the feeling that Janowitz is more fascinated by the insects than the stillness. Rather than being a seeker of spiritual transcendence or a creator of mytho-demonic personalities, this poet is an expert on the "little lives / designed to chase intoxicating blooms." She is a student of survivors and of those who ask more of life, despite the slim chances of

receiving the desired plenitude. Her plucky, compassionate poems imply their points subtly, without predictabil-
ity or polemics. In *Visiting Rites,* Janowitz has written one of
the few recent poetry books that does justice to our helplessness and our resilience.

1985

The State of the Art

Amy Clampitt, Michael Collier, Aleda Shirley,
Allison Funk, Maurya Simon, John Dickson

NYONE WHO READS WIDELY IN CONTEMPORARY
poetry must notice the preponderance of certain
subjects and stylistic devices. Of course, the broadest
human concerns appear in the work of any era; it's likely
that poets will always write about their relatives, for example. However, meditative poems about *photographs* of
relatives form a genre of our time, as do the countless biographical poems about canonical figures and the ubiqui-
tous expatriate travel poems. (How many contemporary
poems are set in Italy as compared to, say, New Jersey?) As
our poetry narrows in expression, one suspects that ours is
an age of imitation rather than experimentation. Has the
medieval conception of the artist as replicator returned, so
that skillful execution is valued above originality? Or are
readers supposed to say, "Although yours is the fourteenth
meditation on a photograph I've read this week, you've
brought your own sensibility to bear in such a way as to
render the subject unique"? The tricky part is that such
a transformation is entirely possible. It is possible to write
fresh poems on stale themes, but in doing so the poet
must work against our skepticism as well as against the

hackneyed aspects of genre. Each of the poets under review is, to some extent, engaged in such a labor for our attention. In addition to the topics already cited, I'll risk a few generalizations on the store-brand poem of our day: *memory* and *desire* are the favorite abstractions. The prevalent tone is elegiac. Birds and angels are (still) the common emblems of transcendence; women are (still) depicted as angels or monsters; the experience of men is (still) assumed to be universal. To quote Amy Clampitt, "Are all these rigors fixed?"

What's fixed and what's fluid is a central concern of Clampitt's third volume, *Archaic Figure.* She is fascinated by the past's presence in the present, and an epigraph from Virginia Woolf specifically directs us to "the ancient consciousness of women." Despite this good intention, the old notions concerning women are reinforced as much as challenged. As in her other books, the poetry is heavily descriptive, meditative, and determinedly focused on high culture. Here Clampitt's interests include mythology and the remnants of classicism in present-day Greece. Time is her subject: this historical moment in America in comparison to other times; the eternal realm of the classical; the limited time frame of the mortal; and the timeless flux of nature. Must it be true that nothing ever changes? The more capacious poems raise this question.

Several poems try hard to demythologize classical romance, as when the poet, on a bus trip through Greece, finds a past of "sardine-tin litter dripped on / by unmythic fig and laurel." Yet the style of the poems is itself decorous, ornamental, and premodern. Although suited to certain effects, this baroque style is not sharp enough to scrape the gilt from an acrolith. And the observations of a tourist, however intelligent, cannot portray the complexities of a nation's past. With their accumulation of trivial details, some of the diaristic travel poems read like minute-by-minute accounts of her journey. "Trudge, trudge," as she says. Reading them is like watching slides of a neighbor's vacation. One wishes for a more selective vision. This is also a didactic poetry, and some of the lessons get pretty tired. In "Seriphos Unvisited" we are told that "Progress, a century and more of it, has gotten / us nowhere"; "there's no true novelty"; and finally, the "Nereids of consequence have passed us by." Still, Clampitt has a speculative, judicious mind. After the rock slides of description, her better poems widen and illuminate. The sense of closure can be so disciplined and surprising that one feels rewarded for the hardships of the journey. "Dodona: Asked of the Oracle," which ends the first section, includes a faintly subversive subtext ("strutting cocks / no threat, merely ridiculous") and a siren depicted as "male, ancient / mindless." The opening poem's exhumed statue of a headless girl and the mindless male form reticent bookends to "Hellas."

In Part Two, the headless (and harmless) girl is ousted by a women who is all monstrous head: Medusa. Given its long use, classical mythology is surely the most deadly terrain for a poet. The farther Clampitt gets from the literal Greek bones of the thing, the more likely that the myth will ignite into a fresh telling. In one of the more successful poems ("The Nereids of Seriphos"), we learn how mythology endured in nineteenth-century Greece; that the

Nereids (water sprites) were perhaps whirlwinds; and how a "well-off farmer's wife, / witheringly millinered" was nineteenth-century America's best approximation of a Gorgon. This poem quotes extensively from other books: The supposition, a troubling one, is that prose broken into lines becomes poetry.

In fact, Amy Clampitt writes text-reflexive poetry: work that arises from and entirely depends upon one's knowledge of another text. Such poetry presumes that we share the same library, values, and worldview. There's a certain complacency to this assumption, as there is to some of the book's language. Grasmere, for instance, is portrayed as "so tea-cozy cozy, so snugly / lush." And there's a bedrock naiveté and ethnocentrism at work when men wearing the fez can be termed "peaked-cap seaweed" and the word "Asian" is followed by "inscrutable." Of the text-reflexive, biographical poems, the George Eliot sequence is most engrossing. In considering Eliot's gender, class, and genius, Clampitt arrives at original connections. The Wordsworth poems, essentially pyschological studies, depict Dorothy as pillow to "the lying-in of genius." In doing so, they bolster the cliché that male creativity gives birth to culture (intellect), while female creativity gives birth to children (nature, nurture). These poems are like polished gossip: there's a certain pleasure, but one feels finally that more understanding would be gained by returning to Dorothy's journals and William's poems.

Clampitt is not a poet of emotional depth: Her most common note is contentment. The range of feeling is limited by her diction, which has two registers: lofty and loftier. The latter effect is reserved for ironic, faintly arch euphemisms ("what we quaintly call // Our Time"). This tone is as close as the poems get to wit, although the language is sometimes unintentionally funny. *Archaic Figure* is riddled with poetic diction and periphrasis, that bane of eighteenth-century poetics. The absurd textbook examples of the latter trope—"the finny tribe" for fish; "household feathery people" for chickens—are rivaled by Clampitt's periphrasis for women: "the sex whose periodic / blossom hangs its ungathered garland / from the horned clockwork of the moon." And when she says "this / elbowed, unsheltering, / obtrusively / concatenated fiefdom," she means "the world." Clampitt's predictable syntactical strategy is to pile clause upon clause until all references vanish in a haze of compound adjectives. Those adjectives ("one human barrel, / chalk-stripe-tailored, curly-brilliantined, / Lech Walesa-mustachioed, jovial") turn the music turgid, as do the many "of" constructions, such as "the warped treadmill / of antiquity."

When Amy Clampitt's first book appeared, American poetry was mired in the doldrums of the plain style. There was a certain renegade chutzpah to her excesses; she was an anomaly. However, her new work has the air of self-parody, of mannerisms run amuck. A love for language is still evident, as is her powerful ability to see and describe. When these strengths are coupled with restraint, her work can be quite eloquent. "The Waterfall" is such a luminous poem, addressing, as it does, the congruencies that underlie our tenuous hold on consciousness:

The veining
in this hand, these
eyeballs, the circuitous
and scintillating

leap within the brain—
the synapse,
the waterfall, the black-
thread mane of fern

beside it—all, all
suspend, here:
everywhere, existences
hang by a hair

In his first book, *The Clasp and Other Poems*, Michael Collier visits some of the same countries as Amy Clampitt, yet they would never be mistaken for fellow travelers. Despite the place names of the titles ("In Khabarovsk," "Bruges"), one feels that Collier's poems could be located anywhere: The real country of visitation exists inside his head. He is a poet of personal rather than literary or cultural history. His poetry, more elegiac than descriptive, prefers the turns of memory to turns in literal landscapes. The word *clasp* with its connotations of handshake and hug, underscores Collier's attempt to embrace experience. There is the cold clasp of his ancestors' dental instruments; the serpent-shaped necklace clasp of the title poem—a symbol for the id's primal drives; the hand clasped to the comforting otherness of animals.

In fact, the most compassionate poems in the book are those that focus upon animals. Collier convincingly portrays the mistrust other creatures feel for the intrusiveness of human touch and the artless affection that cloaks our need for their assurance. The sympathetic intelligence of "What Heals" shows how one's perspective changes what is seen. After his sister tells him that horses are stupid because they see things four times larger than they are, Collier notes:

> My niece turned calmly from her horse.
> The huge blankets that had stilled the animal
> draped the fence, and my niece's hands,
> which had stroked its head all night,
> darkened the sun as she waved.

When he turns outward, Collier portrays the inner life more vividly than when he speaks subjectively, relying upon abstractions such as love and desire. The vagueness of his aphorisms ("Sometimes / we have nothing but the wrong words / for desire") coupled with the wistful tone makes one wonder, "What do poets want?" The difficulty of deciding what, exactly, is yearned for reduces desire's inclusion to a romantic posture. Too often the word is thrown like seasoning into poems when greed, avarice, or lust might be more accurate (and refreshing) choices. Collier writes of drivers who see birds in the air and "wonder what it is that brings desire / so effortlessly to view?" Influenced, perhaps, by the radiant closures of "Ode to Autumn" and "Sunday Morning," poets seeking emblems for transcendence often reach for birds. As a result, we now have scores of poems in which birds rise to a forgettable immanence. It gets hard to make it new, and Collier's poems of this ilk remain vague and unconvincing. In "Night Waltz" the premise is that while we sleep the "broken possessions of our lives / begin to stir." A *Nutcracker* scenario of dancing furniture follows. Yet this too-adorable fiction is almost redeemed by an ending that invites us "to imagine an ascension / into the next world, where suffering / is rewarded with glue, oil, / and electricity." Another poem begins, "I worry for the broccoli's sake / that it works too hard in this bad weather, / is too anxious to please me." The ultrasensitive pose is hard to swallow. But again, the unexpected ending, with its talk of disfigurement and justice, mitigates the preciousness. There are also several photograph poems. For Collier, photos serve to imply the mutability of memory, trigger specific recollections, and testify to the transience of affection.

This is a masculist poetry in that it focuses upon paternal relationships and men's struggle to be brothers, despite a conditioning that tells them to be warriors. All this is well and good. However, Collier's universal-seeming "you" or "we" can exclude women through its highly specific, male viewpoint. Williams wrote, "When I say 'I,' I mean also 'you.'" When Collier says "we" or "you," I'd like to think he also means me. Substituting "he" or "I" for a falsely generic pronoun often solves the problem. In "Sand

Figure" the universal "you" is envisioned as a man sculpted in sand by a woman. The poem's conclusion, "you'd have to convince / the woman that it is her you love, / and not what she's created / and not yourself," transforms the sand figure into a metaphor for male narcissism, women's manipulation of men, and men's of women. Despite its fallacious address, this poem shows a willingness to implicate the self and bear a certain degree of moral culpability. *The Clasp* offers a number of such thoughtful poems.

~~

Aleda Shirley's *Chinese Architecture* is constructed of equal parts tenderness and speculation. Like Collier, she is a poet of inner voyages, memory, and desire. In fact, the epigraph from Proust at the beginning of her book might have prefaced five of the six books under discussion: "the countries which we long for occupy . . . a far larger place in our actual life than the country in which we happen to be." A number of emblems recur: rivers, planes, mirrors. But these figures are so subtly integrated that they permeate one's consciousness gradually. In fact, the entire book works its miracles by accretion, so that the sum is finally greater than the parts.

Shirley is intrigued by notions of the ideal: perfect love and the perfection of classical form. In the opening poem perfection cracks when the planet is discovered to bulge at the equator. This poem also introduces the theme of merging and individuation: the idea that "an edge / is never a simple or a sudden thing." In the title poem we learn "the

pailou is a symbolic gateway / that defines / the entrance
to an ideal space." Shirley's thought processes mimic the or-
nate yet balanced quality of such structures. Many of the
poems are themselves a sort of Chinese architecture; they
create ideal spaces one enters through a pailou of words.
The body in its expression of romantic physical love forms
another such haven, as does the mind with its ability to
hold the past. In "Finding the Room" the poet's memories
are stored "in places / of fitting size. I kept / my father's
planes and my first glimpse / of the sea in a meadow / of
white grass." The lovely concluding anecdote describes the
room (both literal and figurative) needed to express the
heart.

> You told me a pearl
> was hidden under my tongue and, as evening emerged
> from the trees in its many shapes,
> I removed the pearl
> and thought of how, in Japanese prints,
> a girl pulls from her mouth the hair
> she's stuffed there
> to mute the sound of pleasure or pain.

The passage of time is important to Shirley, but her scale,
in contrast to Clampitt's, is lifesized; her inner clock marks
off seasons rather than epochs. The sense of time is more
folkloric than historical, and this utopian indeterminacy
can be irritating. In one poem the archetypal portrayal of
woman and man had me envisioning a pair from a Vermeer
painting until a red convertible entered the picture. There

aren't many women in these poems. The few included wait at home while men go forth and return with exotic gifts from the world of experience.

All of the first books by women reviewed here contain an inordinate number of love poems. Shirley's are often exquisitely sensual first-person lyrics to a particular male "you." In fact, she is primarily a love poet, and as such her work is remarkably touching. Her thought is most intoxicating when most complex, but in her less successful poems the logic can be hard to follow. The wide leaps of her fairly free associations don't always land her on solid ground. At times, too, the lines are disappointingly prosaic. To leaven the flatness, Shirley sometimes resorts to the poetic diction of our age. Rather than the old froufrou of "cerulean" or "darkling," we now have the lace edging of "star," "moon," "silver," "candles," "desire," and so on. Oddly enough, poems in the "plain" style are most apt to overuse these pretty simplicities. In Shirley's weaker poems pomegranate seeds become "garnets," or the speaker becomes so ethereal that mourning doves "fly right through" her. Her aphorisms on "desire" sound very much like Michael Collier's, and italics are used to give plain words a false portentousness. At its worst, this poetry is simply sappy. One recognizes the stuff of romance novels or pop songs ("there is a sense / of thunder outside each time you walk / through the door").

Only Shirley's speculative mind can save the day. The first question to appear in the book ("Remember?") seems fitting in a poetry of recollection. But Shirley has more eloquent queries: "If I reached inside your skull, would I touch / a globe with a world drawn on it?" "What if I scooped up the air around me and demanded / a dress the color of dusk?" Fittingly, the book's last question is, "Was that you, / saying goodbye, or simply the trees in the wind?" However, Shirley is not all sweetness and light, all trees and wind. "Talking in Bed" describes an attempt to tell a lover about a childhood experience in the Philippines. In its understated way this poem says a lot about ugliness, cruelty, fear, revulsion, and power. It concludes, "That was all / I was trying to tell you: that I had trouble / sleeping and the sky, in Manila, was green." Despite such modest disclaimers, Shirley's poems "stun us by degrees," to borrow Dickinson's phrase. Her questions in themselves are illuminating answers.

The word *conversion*, a verbal palimpsest, is denotated for four-and-a-half inches in my unabridged. Given its richness, I was disappointed to find so many familiar transformations—winter to spring, youth to age, love to hate—in Allison Funk's debut volume *Forms of Conversion.* If these progressions are to seem time honored rather than time worn, new resources of style, ambition, feeling, or mind must be brought to bear. Funk manages such a feat in the book's opening poem, "The Lake," a lucid Shakespearean sonnet that recalls a childhood summer when a favorite cousin drowned. The poem is rich with mutability: Life changes to death, the speaker changes from girl to woman, the lake itself changes into a stunned repository of death.

It is an elegant and poignant poem. Traditional forms are not Funk's preferred format, however. Most frequently she writes elegiac, understated (or underwritten, as the case may be) free verse lyrics. There are poems here called "Elegy" and "Desire."

The title poem is a thoughtful meditation on the nature of change. In some forms of conversion—miles to kilometers or stone to pounds—what is being measured (distance and weight) stays the same. On the other hand, in chemical changes a substance is irrevocably altered. The poem uses these two types of metamorphosis—one a change in language, the other a change in being—as analogues for the conversions of love and religion. "Forms of Conversion" expresses complex thoughts in plain language; it embodies the kind of scope I longed to find more often in the book.

In Part Two, "Mirrors," Funk's meditations on a stereoscopic photo of her grandparents lead her to conclude, "I must invent them myself." Poems in the voices of her ancestors follow. These monologues are curiously passionless; in fact, the grandmother's voice sounds like her husband's and both of them sound like the first-person narrator of all the other poems. Funk hasn't the technical skills—fictional, imaginative, or what have you—needed to create character. In the book's third section, "Crossing," she visits Israel and writes a couple of mythological poems. Here is the voice of Isis:

> In the market I ask the men
> if they've seen you.

> They do not look up from the tables.
> They do not turn from their work.
> When again I ask they offer me
> one word only, *widow.*

Like Shirley, Funk tries to empower words by italicizing them. To my mind, there's no difference—of tone, diction, rhythm, or music—between the voice of Isis (above) and the lyric "I" of the following:

> A man is no different
> than a woman in this:
> the body changes to accommodate loss.
> But let me tell you, my love,
> the story of mute Zechariah,
> who recovered his voice
> when a son was born to him at last.

One wonders whether "mute Zechariah" would have found his tongue had the child been a daughter. Funk, however, is untroubled by such questions. Two of the love poems in the last section depict women, stereotypically, as angel or monster. (Funk's dichotomies are "whore" and "idolized wife.") In "The Ghost of Elinor Wylie" we learn that Wylie "haunts writers at night, / inquiring 'Am I beautiful?'" The poem's speaker shares Wylie's valuation of beauty as a means of self-affirmation: "And because no dream can answer / this doubt, I implore the whirlpool of a man at night / to erase the sad boundaries of the self." It's 1987. Are there no other options? Though Funk's lyrics are not as morbid as Wylie's, they strike the same note of graceful suffering. Incidentally, Wylie's ghost appeared to me years ago at the MacDowell Colony. She asked, not "Am I beautiful?" but "Are my books read?"

~~

"As to the stories of breeze / and moonlight, they all deal / with such obvious things." So says Tsao Hsueh-Chin in the opening epigraph to Maurya Simon's *The Enchanted Room*, a first book that delves beneath the skin of the quotidian in search of latent magic. The title is a metaphor for the heart, the body, childhood, and memory—which Simon, like Aleda Shirley, envisions as architectural space. The book has considerable reach, beginning slowly and gathering strength toward the end. Along the way there are folkloric tales; love lyrics; dramatic monologues; historical narratives; and symbolist, oneiric poems. In Simon's world, a door is usually something other than the aluminum-screened variety. The poems occasionally strike a surreal note, although the intention is not to unhinge reality but to reveal its mystical underpinnings.

Least interesting are the mock-folkloric poems located within a generic rather than particular past. Images of peasant girls, horses, coriander, children "fat as new potatoes," and women plucking chickens signal that we are in this homespun never-neverland. "We have all been there at least once," Simon alleges; only in contemporary poetry, says the reader. The poems anchored more firmly in the real are strong: the story of a woman married to a soldier affected by Agent Orange; or "Volga Tale, 1944," a chillingly lyrical evocation of privation and murder. "Blue Movies," which shows old men waiting to get inside a theater, speaks to our longing and loneliness, and a poem in the voice of the Tooth Fairy succeeds despite the cuteness of its premise. One learns how she was conceived, how she operates, and finally, what use she makes of the teeth. ("I implant them in the mouths / of prophets, so their words forever / remain small, pure, unfinished.") In the last section, Simon writes of a child's moral indignation and loss of innocence; an adolescent's sexual awakening; a woman's examinination of conscience in regard to the Vietnam War. These are moving, thoughtful poems—reason to own the book in themselves.

Another section explores the sensibility of India. In writing about foreign countries, the question is how to get beyond decorative or stereotypical description. How can a poet convey something as complex as a nation's consciousness after a week's (or a year's) visit? We have trouble enough forming interpretations of our own country. Simon's best work avoids superficiality; it lets us know India more deeply. Here she describes an Indian wedding:

> Her belly pushing open the door,
> my sister carries her pride, wedges
> it through the shuffling corridor
> as petty bureaucrats peer over paper hedges
> on dismal wooden desks, the hand-me-down
> relics from the British Raj:
> brass embossers, rubber stamps, pious frowns.

A witty syllabic poem ("Conversation in Madras") implies the difference between an American and an Indian political consciousness. The stanzas' second lines, each composed of a seven-syllable word, give a sense of this cultural friction: "Kalianasundarum," "polyunsaturated," "unconstitutionally," "plenipotentiary," "subequatorially," "anthropomorphically," and "unsophisticatedly." These formal poems are free of the poeticisms that sugarcoat much of the free verse.

Simon's gospel, simply put, is that everything—animate or inanimate—is potentially treasure. This is as good a message as most; however, the cloyingly fey diction of some poems can turn a giant wonder into a munchkin of fancy. There's a lot of moon and candlelight here: "cobwebs / of starlight / enshrouding the passion vines." At its worst, the language slips into a diminutive, whimsical register: "The wind's little brother visits the air"; "Marbled pebbles swoosh and hiss / their little prophecies." One expects unicorns and rainbows at any minute.

But taken as a whole, this is an impressive first collection. Simon tries to see through things, as if they were composed of light rather than matter. And her vision leads the reader into a world rendered luminous, its radiance sharply, almost painfully defined.

~~

In contrast to the five preceding authors, John Dickson is a poet of all that is mundane, American, and human. He also is a damn good storyteller who makes such common stuff uncommonly engrossing. *Waving at Trains,* his second book,

is both funny and sad. The warm comedy laced with strong
characterizations makes for a good read. The best poems
have some of Robert Frost's canny clarity and Richard
Wilbur's wit, although in place of the latter's urbanity, one
finds a tough-minded common sense. Dickson mourns
people's inability to reach one another, and he rails at death
as if it were his own discovery. His broadest subjects—
failures of love and communication, loss, the passage of
time—are the age-old stuff of poetry, yet his selective
vision makes the familiar fresh.

Dickson also has an intrepid streak. As a result, some
unexpected areas of experience find their way into his
work. He is the first poet, to my knowledge, to write about
a gallbladder operation. And he is mature enough to be
amused at human foibles and egocentricity—his own included. "The Night the Dorfmans Met," a hyperbolic account of lust at first sight, concludes with a torrential
piano performance as objective correlative for "all sounds
of Joseph Dorfman speaking." Most of these poems are
free verse, and some are enlivened by inventive, analogous
structures; there are ghost stories, science fiction, a fugue.
One love story is told in contrary motion, from end to beginning. The book is especially rich in people: McNealy
who "fell in sewers looking up at the stars," and Harvey
"already partly dead with one bad eye" who jumped from a
bridge. Here is the latter poem's empathetic closure:

> Why couldn't a band of friends he never knew he had
> have crooned to the river some gentle choral chorus,
> hummed some Harvey requiem in voices like

paper sailboats sailing across the water
until he finally rose again, his flesh gone gray
with death . . . until he rose and let them lift him up
and carry him through the old familiar streets
and far away?

Not all of the endings are so resonant. Too many fall
flat when they matter-of-factly state the obvious, leaving
the reader with nothing to do. Toward the middle, the
book widens to include "the idiotic acts of history," *history*
being the story of decimations. Several poems address confining gender roles. "The Dashing Figure" recounts the
adventures of Uncle George, a workaholic who rushes "to
his uncertain future / like a man with his hair on fire." And
"Reunion of the Third Platoon" strips away the masks of
bravado to show the price men pay for the follies and glories of war. Although he is quite perceptive when writing
of the trappings of male roles, Dickson's imagination goes
on automatic pilot when he turns to women. The dichotomy of angel or monster rears its weary head, as
women become "half floosie, half madonna" in one poem
or "half schoolgirl, half bawd" in another. Someone
should have told Dickson that single women are no longer
called "aging bachelor girls" and that they no longer wear
girdles. At least three poems play shamelessly on the dreary
stereotype of the "Old Maid" [*sic*]. Here is the beginning
of "Miss Green:"

Be not dismayed, Old Maid,
that the Invisible Man hides in your room

or is playing kneesies with you on the bus.
Why he could have any dreamy little
gooey little harlequin romantic . . .

The tone here is both mean and supercilious. "Options" tries to sympathize with limited choices and winds up sounding patronizing since all of its possibilities define women according to their relationships with men: "birdsie little ladies with their / lavender dry armpit lives" (the spinster stereotype); mistress; unhappy housewife; siren. "Why did the women with their plunging necklines / keep glaring their equality, daring you to look?" he asks, in an otherwise lovely poem. Only someone vastly indifferent to or ignorant of women's history could confuse plunging necklines with the struggle for equal rights.

In a poet this self-aware and generous the blindspots are all the more disappointing. Still, the delightful moments outnumber the offensive ones. "On Living Too Close to the Music School," with its description of "sound-drenched neighbors," whose heads "sway like daffy metronomes"; the dancing fools of "The Aragon Ballroom"; the jealous neediness of an adult viewing the babies in "Maternity Ward"—such work makes Dickson an exceptionally entertaining writer. *Waving at Trains* is both an ambitious book of poetry and a real page-turner.

1987

Main Things

A. R. Ammons, Pattiann Rogers, Susan Ludvigson,
Lisel Mueller, Robert Morgan, Carolyn Kizer

> Leaving it to you to prove and define it,
> Expecting the main things from you.
>
> WALT WHITMAN, "POETS TO COME"

EVERY POET OF SUBSTANCE FORCES US TO EDUCATE ourselves anew. For those who haven't made the effort yet in regard to A. R. Ammons, the expanded *Selected Poems* offers the best introduction to the glories of his work. From the first, he has been fascinated by duality: the relationships between choice/chance; one/many; microcosm/macrocosm; center/periphery; motion/stasis. His obsession with polarities stems from a wish to break down such oppositions and reveal the underlying unity of forms. In Ammons's mind, art involves motion rather than classical stasis. As a result, his poems are more like kinetic sculptures than well-wrought urns. Nature fascinates because it (unlike art) is constantly in flux. "Honor a going thing, goldfinch, corporation, tree, / morality," he writes. He delights in fractal forms that fall somewhere between order and chaos, between the Euclidean cracks. Knowledge is that which consigns itself to "approximation, order to

the vehicle / of change, and fumbles blind in blunt innocence / toward divine, terrible love." This is a poetry of
ideas, yet ideas are important only insofar as they help us
live our lives. In human terms, the one/many dichotomy
speaks to the need for autonomy versus the need for ab-
sorption into the shared experience.

Perhaps Ammons is most famous as nature's scribe and
prophet, one in whom river weeds and gulches confide. He
is also a seer in the etymological sense of "one who sees."
His poems illuminate the marginal: the plants growing on
rocks that "people never see / because nothing should grow
on rocks." Like the plants, the self in his poems is a slight
presence arguing against or adjusting to its impending abnegation. In fact, the language's intentions are ontological
rather than geological. Far from being a cold clinician of
the soul, Ammons is a keeper of peripheral flames; his
stance is one of modesty before the universe and tenderness
before humanity. In the magnificent early poem "Still," the
speaker sets out to find "the lowly" as "a handy focus and
reminder" of his own significance.

> I found a beggar:
> he had stumps for legs: nobody was paying
> him any attention: everybody went on by:
>   I nestled in and found his life:
> there, love shook his body like a devastation:
> I said
>   though I have looked everywhere
>   I can find nothing lowly
>   in the universe:

"Hymn," another important early poem, recalls Whitman in its chanting parallel structure and pantheistic search for a force that exists "past the blackset noctilucent clouds" or with "the microvilli sporangia." Like Whitman, Ammons is fond of cataloging the specimens that comprise the One. Yet the poet of transcendental affirmations is also the poet who asserts "I see no / god in the holly" and who sternly locates the "surrendered self" among "unwelcoming forms."

Formally, this is an experimental poetry. Although the poems are often analogous to prayers or fables, the smaller structural elements are miraculously inventive. Ammons's subjects are reflected in the formation of his lines. Seldom end-stopped, often enjambed with prepositions or articles, they enact the infinite adjustments of balance that comprise equilibrium. The registers of diction within a single stanza can range from oracular to scatological, pastoral to technical. The poems sometimes begin with a thesis ("You cannot come to unity and remain material") and proceed to argue it out of existence. Ammons's signature colon, the most democratic punctuation, builds equivalence on both sides. Its indeterminate pauses are to his poetry what dashes are to Dickinson's.

In fact, Ammons insistently recalls Dickinson. His dazzling turns of abstraction ("parabolas of bliss," the soul as "an area of poise") are hauntingly Dickinsonian, as is his volatile grammar. Both poets favor a compressed, reflexive syntax that requires readers to participate in the process of composition by filling in grammatical deletions. And this process of reconstruction accounts for the interwoven

difficulties and pleasures of the poems. The complexity is
not there for its own sake, but because the states elucidated
are intricate. It takes a formidable poet to give them voice.
Ammons's distinctive vocabulary embraces such Dickinsonian terms as *circumference, arc,* and *difference,* in addition to
his own lexicon of *sphere, salience, periphery, motion,* and so on.
And as with Dickinson, you have to read a lot of him in
order to say you've read him at all. His canon forms an ongoing, multifarious sequence. In fact, my one complaint
about the expanded *Selected Poems* concerns its exclusions. I
miss "Grace Abounding" and "Uh, Philosophy" from the
early years. Although the book includes work from three
volumes published since 1977, such important and beautiful poems as "Poverty," "Zero and Then Some," and "Lo-
calizing" are omitted. But I am quibbling. Through these
119 pages, one feels the pressure of an inexhaustible intelligence keeping language on the stretch. The resultant poetry
opens intoxicating vistas in the heart and mind, coming as
it does "from the self not mine but ours."

In his latest collection, *Sumerian Vistas,* Ammons, like the
god Janus, gazes backward to antiquity and forward to
mortality, seeking "plateaus of staying and view." One of
the book's subjects is inscription: the origins, permanence,
and transience of writing. Poetry and epitaphs are seen as
efforts to fix time, while nature is read as a script of motion, a text of regeneration. Although the book's title
might lead one to expect archeological finds, Sumeria is invoked as a metaphor of inception. It was there that writing
first developed, and antiquity serves as a backdrop for explorations of beginning and closure, of generative cycles.

The first fifty pages are devoted to "The Ridge Farm," a discursive sequence covering a wide aesthetic terrain. A ridge, after all, is a *line* where two upward-sloping surfaces meet. The poem investigates the relationship between fluency and form, the paradoxical holding to "the rigid line of the free and easy" within free verse. The ridge (like the poetic line) was there 500 years ago, and it "provides a / measure." The ridge also stands for the relationship between self and other. Those living on the raised land can't see it. What they can see is the nonself of the opposite hillside, an otherness to the East. And since it is an exaltation of landscape, the ridge becomes a metaphor for the divine. Indeed, some of the poem's loveliest lines examine the properties of holiness. The sacred may be recognized by its quality of concern, but it is also "something we could / miss altogether even while it / sustained us through." The holy and profane are united, as when "the waste in a woods gives / off the best heat and brightest / illumination." Nature consoles because it has designs without having designs on us. In fact, Ammons goes to nature precisely because it lets him "miss anything personal in / the roar of sunset." In contrast to human cruelty, which frightens since it is "like one's own mercilessness," nature's cruelty is mitigated by its impersonality. Lest all this seem ponderous, I must mention that Ammons has a wicked, self-mocking humor. "I love nature especially if there's / a hospital nearby and macadam or / glass in between," he admits.

Of all our poets, Ammons is perhaps most committed to an aesthetic of inclusion. He is concerned with "how to exclude the central," "how to get out into the looser /

peripheries." In his view, "the truth is commodious, abundant: we / must make a room so sufficient it will / include till nothing will be left / over for walls." Given his capacious vision and suspicion of hierarchies, I found myself wondering why "man" appeared generically in the poems. One current limitation of our language is its assignation of otherness or periphery to woman. Although the generic "man" or "he" pretends to encompass everyone, when we read those words we envision a male. To substitute "woman" for the universal "man" (or create a new inclusive usage) would be to question bedrock assumptions of marginality. "I am . . . maternal as well as paternal," said Whitman. Sympathetic, brilliant, generous—Ammons might, if he chose, prove and define this "main thing," to which Whitman gave a passing nod.

The Sumerians carved their religious poetry on clay tablets. Part Two, "Tombstones," is a meditation upon those tablets we raise against transience. The vista of this long poem is enormous in scope: A human life is compared to a mayfly's and to "a pulse in one of earth's orbits" that "beats once in four hundred thousand years." The motions of wind are contrasted to "the stone's slow swirl" that "keeps the name." "Nothing" is a tangible presence since "grooves of absence" tell the names on tombstones. Perhaps, Ammons suggests, fine things—wind, light—last longest. If love is such a fine evanescence, we dishonor it by trying to name it "on the hard waters of inscription." It follows that blowing dust might be the best memorial, reassuring us "that what is gone is / going on." In a bold move, the cosmos itself is conceived as "love's memorial:"

a vast, complex tombstone. After all, Ammons notes, "ninety percent / of the universe is dead stars, / but look how the light still / plays flumes down / millennial ranges."

The last sixty-one pages of *Sumerian Vistas* contain many superb poems. "The Hubbub" posits mundane actions and Zen-like stillness as respites from "divinity's loftier stations"; "Telling Moves" offers insights into aging and our rebellions against the inevitable; "Recoveries" illuminates cosmic dissolutions and formations; "Some Any" casually persuades us of love and thought's abundance; and the book's final poem, "Citified," opposes the hazards of isolation to those of community. In "Autonomy" and "Power Plays," Ammons explores romantic love with sensitivity and wisdom. Here is the latter poem in its entirety:

Power Plays

I know that splendor's your
arms, your hands,
not spools and drifts of stars:

your hair, falling, gives in
the way desire builds defenseless:
you soothe my twists; unwinding,

they wind into your calm:
don't be afraid: deference
controls me: I can

win or lose you and find
the bone in your arm
still too fine to bear.

"The Dwelling," another luminous verse, argues that "the heart's cravings" should flare bright into what is near at hand, earthly. Through Ammons's poems we are consoled into just such celebrations. Reading them, one feels assured "that here the plainest / majesty gave us what it could."

—~

"I believe a grass leaf is no less than the journeywork of / the stars." So Whitman sings, so Ammons sings, and in her moving lyrics, so Pattiann Rogers sings. *The Tattooed Lady in the Garden*, her second book, assimilates Ammons and Whitman even as it makes their great topics her own. Like Ammons, Rogers combines a religious vocabulary with the diction of a naturalist. In her poems "the short-snouted / Silver twig weevil" and "the fetal araneus" lie down with angels and atoms. Rogers also shares Ammons's need to enter the sensibility of "what is lowly." She wonders why the horned lizard wants to live when "The only drink it will ever know / Is in the body of a bug." A mystical Thou-art-That conviction causes her to witness nature as a means of witnessing the self. In the gospel according to Rogers, the Fall from grace is a fall from oneness into many forms.

While much of the wit in our poetry is seasoned with irony, the humor of this book is refreshingly benign. We see an old man's identification with nature go one step beyond pantheism into madness when he believes he *is* a plant. "How can the actual white-haired, five-inch stems / Of the hoary puccoon be expected to bear the weight / Of a witness such as this?" Rogers asks. A delightful quintet of friends turns up, speaking words as sweetly outrageous as those of Ammons's talking mountains. These characters are to Rogers what the personified landscape is to Ammons: a way to explore the nature of reality without didacticism.

The repetition of cellular structures is mirrored within the form of Rogers's work. I can think of no other contemporary poet who uses repeating phrases so artfully. The poems are braided with sinuous <u>repetends</u>, balancing the pleasure of fulfilled expectations with the surprise of variation. Cataloging and polysyndeton (repetition of conjunctions) are also used to great rhythmic effect. Expansive rather than compressive, the lines tend to be long, lyrical, and end-stopped.

The book contains the most glorious metaphysical sex poems I've seen in some time. They are metaphysical not because they recall the seventeenth century's elaborate conceits, but because they wish to rise above the quotidian and encompass the procreative wealth of the natural world. "Love Song" questions human primacy: "You're no better / Than the determined boar snorgling and rooting," the speaker tells her lover. "But it's all right. Don't you know / This is precisely what I seek." "The Possible Salvation of Continuous Motion," an adaptation of a letter written by one E. Lotter (1872–1930), retains an old-fashioned quality of tenderness without slipping into manners-and-customs quaintness. The poem is a convincing and elegant depiction of transgression, guilt, and desire. "The Delight of Being Lost," a wish for anonymous sex, avoids tawdriness in favor of pure sensuality. I hesitate to excerpt Rogers's poems since they depend so much on a cumulative context. Nevertheless, here is the opening of "Trinity":

> I wish something slow and gentle and good
> Would happen to me, a patient and prolonged
> Kind of happiness coming in the same way evening
> Comes to a wide-branched sycamore standing
> In an empty field . . .

Nature, sex, and death, the three main forces of Rogers's work, are the possible agents of something that is "slow and gentle and good." The poem imagines a transfiguration through the first two powers before concluding "Death / Might be that way if one knew how to wait for it, / If death came easily and slowly, / If death were good." This poem, like several others in the book, has the inevitable rightness of great rather than good poetry.

Other topics include time, generative cycles, and the making of art. Rogers's poems are unfailingly fresh in premise and execution. She is capable of imagining herself into "the sole intention present" in a bog turtle, and by doing so, illuminating our vulnerability. And "The Possible Suffering of a God during Creation" supposes a deity who hasn't had time yet "To elicit from his creation its invention / Of his own solace." Rather than settle for fashionable postures, Rogers questions assumptions: We must consider this possibility, she says, coming up with the ingenious. She is aware that the questions one asks partially determine the answers. So Heisenberg's principle (the observer changes what is observed) means "nature exposed to our method of questioning" is nature colored a human tint by that questioning. Given Rogers's mindfulness, I was disappointed to find that the god of these poems is always "he." This easy locution reinforces the idea that power, indeed the ultimate power, must be male. One wonders why god needs gender at all. In light of the poems' pantheistic bent, why shouldn't god be of indeterminate sex—an "it"? Or both male and female?

But this is my sole complaint about a spellbinding collection. *The Tattooed Lady in the Garden* contains poems you'll want to read to friends for the solace and joy they offer. Through its greatness of heart and intellect, this book should establish Rogers as an important poet of her generation. That's the main thing.

~~

Whereas Ammons and Rogers find sustenance in nature, in her third book, *The Beautiful Noon of No Shadow,* Susan Ludvigson must find a way to live in the stark light of a faithless world, in the "absence of angels." The poems take place in a high noon of unremitting clarity; the lens is wide open, the shutter fast: Fear and failure advance in sharp relief. By this light, religion and love are unreliable sanctuaries; mortality, the only certainty. An epigraph from William Stafford underscores the sober outlook: "Even pain you can take, in waves: / Call the interval happiness." The book is not grim; rather it is a field guide to the process of maturation and the prospect of bereavement.

Among other things, we learn that there is a use for grief: It is the way the dying know they will be missed. More dreamscapes than landscapes, many poems investigate the mind's ability to collapse time and distance. The book's last section focuses on familial legacies, the literal and figurative gifts we exchange.

Ludvigson reveals emotional treasons and treasures by recording rather than transforming reality. Although the language is occasionally figurative, the poems do not rely upon metaphor for their effects: Inner dramas are presented through as few linguistic filters as possible. Several poems mention film in one of its guises. In "The Sudden Approach of Trees" the point of view shifts as in a cross-cut, and one gets the sense that the trees are rushing toward the car rather than the reverse. Like a cinema-verité director, Ludvigson observes and participates in the poems. Her handheld camera records the ironies of time and subtly questions religion: Children play in the Germans' pillboxes while a Japanese movie crew builds a sand model of a Gaudi cathedral in order to film the tide washing it away ("Sunday in Normandy").

The poems tend toward dimeter, even monometer, and in their minimalism look like filmstrips laid on paper. The syntax is lucid; the tone quiet. But transparent language can be surprisingly hazardous. A plain style can reduce rather than unveil a complex topic. And since the poem's surface offers minimum resistance, readers are tempted to presume comprehension before further thought reveals murkiness. Documentaries, especially documentaries of the heart, can seem arbitrary without the discipline of a structure. Given all this, it's not surprising that two of the book's finest poems are in terza rima. The speaker of "Point of Disappearance" witnesses a young man's suicide attempt and recalls her own adolescence when "Death was an alternative to everyone else's mild // acceptance of the world's devouring / loneliness." A triumph of empathy and technique, this poem captures the fierce self-consciousness of adolescence in its conclusion:

> But now, I read, even more of the young are leaping
>
> from bridges, lying on tracks, their gift
> to themselves mere absence
> of all that emotion. I see my son lift
>
> his head to examine his awkward presence
> in a hall of mirrors. He locates
> on a shimmering surface his point of disappearance.

The interweaving rhyme scheme reinforces the linkage of stranger, self, son. The volume's final poem, "From the Beginning," eloquently portrays "The baby we'll always be," equally frightened by loneliness and connection, coming to terms with the knowledge that "nobody's saved, / as far as we can tell." Ludvigson defines the self in extremity: disfigured by loss and betrayal. As palliatives she offers "love, / in all its guises" and "the will / to believe." One might add the bright terrain of her poems to the list.

Reading Lisel Mueller's fourth book, *Second Language*, is a bit like gazing at a lake or a tree. At first you think nothing new here: another wave, another leaf. But if you bring your full attention to bear, you're amazed at the implication and activity of an apparently simple surface. Like so many plain-style poems, these equate invisibility of craft with authenticity. The important difference here is that one does not feel manipulated by a disingenuous sincerity. There is no see-how-sensitive-I-am posing, no subtext of self-congratulation. Instead, the sensibility couples kindness with intelligence.

Mueller favors short, imagistic free verse lyrics or longer meditations in numbered sections. The sense of closure is one of the keenest pleasures of the poems. Even if the previous lines didn't make me want to jump and shout, I was usually won over by the aptness of the endings. Although the book's five sections share overriding concerns, the first part focuses upon an autobiographical past. In a moving elegy to her father, "Voyager," the poet holds a negative up to the light and contemplates its ghoulish reversal. The poem's reticent closure is typical of her delicacy:

> How can you see, your glasses
> are whitewashed and there are holes
> where your teeth used to be
>
> Nevertheless you smile at me
> across an enormous distance
> as you have so many times
> to let me know you have arrived

This poem, like others in the book, establishes values without succumbing to didacticism: Engagement is prized and distance mourned as the ultimate hardship. In Mueller's view, memory is the great moral necessity, begetting self-knowledge and culpability. It is also an ungovernable force that "raises landmarks, / unbidden, out of place / and time." In fact, memory is to Mueller what nature is to Ammons and Rogers, what love and the will to believe are to Ludvigson. In its guise of garden "where . . . / nothing ever changes," remembrance affords the only immortality we will ever know. However, other poems imply that the Eden of recollection is neither permanent nor infinitely expandable. When one becomes comfortable in a new language, for example, the old tongue, old home, takes on a quality of strangeness akin to forgetfulness. Memories, moreoever, are generative: Broadcast like seed, they may fall on someone who in turn recalls "a forgotten childhood scene." In its obsessive aspect, reminiscence can be a prison. But it also allows us to crack the code of absence: A widow listens until familiar sounds "turn into messages in the new language" her husband "has been forced to learn." "All night she works on the code, / almost happy . . . / . . . while the food in its china caskets / dries out on the kitchen table."

The tongue we learn after death is but one of many second languages in this book. Nature has a script, although we are poor translators: Blackbirds compose themselves "in the ancient pen-strokes," the "unreadable signature." Looking at milkweed pods, Mueller thinks this is "what we would say to each other / if we could find the heart."

"Letter to California," an argument for landscape's effect on semantics, reveals the multiplicity of English. To one speaker it's "strictureless," to another it's "a low-keyed continuous struggle." Music and sex are dialects, as is confabulation, the language we invent, like Scheherazade, to save our lives.

Several poems explore the aberrant: identical twins who point to the double within us all; the Cassandra figure of a psychic; a disco queen turned gospel preacher; the otherworldly daughters mothers worry about; the abused child who "will not betray her keeper." Far from being a random assemblage of freaks, these lives reveal the discrepancy between facade and inner life. Mueller is especially attentive to the masks women forge to get by in our culture. "Southpaw" celebrates difference, the self as "a mermaid with two left arms," while "Face-Lift" asks facetiously if the operation also removed memories "like the soiled / part of a roller towel." A poem about a suicide observes "her mind was not like her house / with its open door, its yard full of flowers." Home, for Mueller, is more state of mind than geographical locale. In answer to the question "How can one teach 'Spring and Fall: To a Young Child' in the Hawaiian Islands?" Mueller argues that the mind's climate supercedes the actual weather: For the bereaved a tropical paradise can become "bare ruin'd choirs." Several poems seek intention in nature, even as they recognize "childish superstition" in the impulse of the search. Unlike Ludvigson, Mueller finds the will to believe a self-protective hoax: It saves us from having to admit to "the broken connection, / that the world resists meaning / not to tease us, but because / there is no meaning / except the one we invent."

The last poems examine self-definition and free will: To what degree are we formed by others' expectations of us? "What Is Left to Say" describes maturity as a "new frugality," a time when the self "stops trying to please / by learning everyone's dialect." In *Second Language* Mueller attains such a calm majority.

~

At the Edge of the Orchard Country, Robert Morgan's fourth book, should secure the wide readership he deserves. There are two types of poems here: short meditations and longer narratives focusing on character. Although most are beautifully crafted free verse, "Chant Royal," which takes its name from its form, triumphantly fulfills the challenge of rhyming sixty lines on five sounds and ending each stanza with a refrain. Morgan's genius for imagery is such that ordinary things become new without any contrivance. And no poet writing today has a better ear. The poems' muscular music is in accord with the physical world they embrace. Nouns and adjectives like "prisms" or "drab" are recycled into verbs. This sinewy language is one of the book's splendors. The closures are unfailingly balanced: One comes to expect a little thrill at the end as the poem widens to collect its disparate pieces.

Morgan commemorates the vanished ancestors, folklore, and wildlife of North Carolina's Blue Ridge as if writing were "payment on a vast unpayable obligation."

When he depicts a weed entombed in dust blooming "where a bee digs into it," he describes his own project as a writer reclaiming the past. "Passenger Pigeons" recalls a time when the skies were clouded "with the movements of winged pilgrims / wide as the Mississippi," and asks "how can I replace / the hosts of the sky, the warm-blooded jet-streams?" A connoisseur of *le mot juste,* Morgan goes on to describe "the fletched / oceans," *fletching* being the arrangement of feathers on an arrow. Lost words are retrieved in order to retrieve the past. Regionalisms appear ("haints," "shivarees") along with the languages of plowing or of soil. Morgan knows the difference between "a washed- / out Old Field of clay and broomsedge" and the "greasy swamp / and floury bottom soil." "School Ground" compares the land's crop to the crop of churches and schools, which turn out people as fertilizer, literally and figuratively. The symbiosis of life and death informs many of these poems. In "Sunday Toilet" the hogpen is dusted with the "make-up" of lime while women powder their faces for church, covering the evidence of mortality. "I like to think they found in work / a soil subliminal and sublime," Morgan writes of his characters. Much of their labor involves soil, whether in planting or cleaning. Tidiness is a way of restoring memory when the community gathers to groom the cemetery. This is a graveyard's best function—bringing all, living and dead, together. Of course, these poems serve the same purpose.

Nature's worth is sometimes expressed in economic terms: One speaker wants to "gather the clean money of the trees"; in another poem thrown rocks "glide like dollars." The boy of the latter poem is close kin to the swinger of birches, and Morgan's last line, "I had other loves also, and work to do," has a Frostian ring. In fact, both the interests and the exquisite craft of these poems recall Frost. With this material (attics, feather beds, stills) it would be easy to slip into a hayseedy nostalgia. But these poems are no more cornmeal mush than Frost's were crackerbarrel philosophy. Morgan's world is holy rather than hokey. Nature is untainted, and when love pitches its mansion in the place of excrement, excrement is ennobled rather than love defiled. Dirt and dust are sublime sources of generative power, and an outhouse is "the enhoused shrine." Holiness pervades the tiniest as well as dirtiest mote of life. In "Brownian Motion" each particle "is an opal angel." Most poets of the homely would write about a quilt, say, in preference to a manure pile. But here is Morgan on manure:

> Haunted in the hot months by a genie
> of flies, it jewels the downwind.
> Sundays the many purple butterflies
> that suck its inks, shiver off into the sky
> where carillons of convection ring.

The poems are intrigued with all we don't comprehend—from the voices transmitted via radio to voices transmitted via the gift of tongues. A bellrope becomes a metaphor for the strand we can reach—in fireflies, manure, comets—that leads to the divine. A lightning bug is reverently addressed as "Carat of the first radiance" whose "noctilucent syllables" send messages we can't interpret. It's

as if nature is trying to tell us something when we're just
out of earshot.

Morgan's narrative poems often focus upon characters:
Elmer who "sits for years on the bank / above the meadow,
watching his cow / graze"; cousin Luther for whom the
tractor is the equivalent of a three-quarter-cam Corvette;
the matriarch who "chaired decisions / to keep the land
and refused welfare." This woman is something of an exception since Morgan primarily reclaims men's lives. I'd like
to see more of the hard labor and everyday heroism of his
female forebears: making soap and clothes, cooking, en-
during childbirth and child death. Through such inclusions poetry gives us the complexity of history, rather than
the bravura of patriarchy.

I hope I've conveyed the pure pleasure to be had in this
book. There isn't a weak moment—and how often can that
be said? Morgan resurrects ancestors who "left no more /
trace than a cloud shadow," whose pastoral America was
effaced by agri-biz and TV. How fortunate we are to have a
poet so amply able to reclaim these people, this past.

~~

While the other poets under review have one eye on the
hereafter, Carolyn Kizer is concerned with how to improve
and live this life. Although her robust appreciation of the
world is akin to Whitman's, the wit, urbanity, and classical
balance of her best poems recall Pope. An irreverent, un-
romantic stance distinguishes her from many of her peers.
Perhaps Hecht and Wilbur are most similar in style. *Mer-*

maids in the Basement collects work from three out-of-print books, along with a few new poems and translations. It's a joy to have the work of a major poet readily available; however, the number of duplications in Kizer's recent volumes make me wish for a single *Collected Poems.* Although the book is subtitled "Poems for Women," it's more important that men read these poems. Women are well acquainted with both women's and men's writing: As Annette Kolodny notes, "for survival's sake, oppressed or subdominant groups always study the nuances of meaning and gesture in those who control them." But the reverse is not true.

Kizer's early poems tend to be formal and well crafted. They seldom make a false move. The later work is less rigorously structured; the tone is more varied; the form often analogous. Kizer was analyzing the image of women well before the second wave of feminism took hold. *Mermaids* begins by exploring relationships between mothers, daughters, and women friends. In one delightful narrative, the poet's mother is a juror during the trial of a dentist accused of drilling through his patient's tongue while flirting with a nurse. Kizer's mother "with eleven good men in her pocket" reads Voltaire during the trial, knowing "before she half-heard a word, the dentist was guilty." The rift between Kizer's worldview and that of her strong-willed mother adds a fine complexity. Although men poets often bespeak a rugged fly-rod camaraderie, less has been said about the bonding rites of women. It's refreshing to see women swim, sun, run, drink, dance, joke, and exchange confidences with one another as they do in these poems.

The book's centerpiece, "Pro Femina," recalls Pope's

"Essay on Man" in its summary of a major issue, although Kizer's topic is "the fate of women." The first three sections of "Pro Femina" appeared in 1965, not long after Rich's groundbreaking "Snapshots of a Daughter-in-Law" (1963). Both poems regard women with a critical eye, untempered by the revisionary feminism of the seventies. Kizer notes the tactics of women scabs "Impugning our sex to stay in good with the men"; of "sleek saboteuses" who "try to be ugly by aping the ways of men / And succeed"; of "Quarterly priestesses / Who flog men for fun, and kick women to maim competition"; of "cabbage-heads" who "vague-eyed, and acquiescent, worshipped God as a man"; and of those good girls who "took notes in rolling syllabics, in careful journals, / Aiming to please a posterity that despises them." The latter assessment echoes Rich's "Snapshots": "Mere talent was enough for us—/ glitter in fragments and rough drafts." In Kizer, however, "us" becomes "they," turning women into others. The poem does praise women as peacemakers "Disdainful of 'sovereignty,' 'national honor.'" And it angrily recounts the price independent women have paid under patriarchy, the damned-if-you-do-or-don't quality of the choices. Of course, women accomplished more great work than either Kizer or Rich admit in these early poems. And the fourth section of "Pro Femina," added in 1984, presents a female hero as corrective. "Fanny" acquaints us with the pluck, resourcefulness, adventurousness, and physical strength of the indomitable Fanny Osbourne Stevenson (wife of Robert Louis) during 1890, when she lived in Samoa. Kizer's diaristic narrative reveals details gradually. Rather than defining Fanny at the onset as wife to the famous man, the identity of "RLS" dawns slowly. "I have been planting," Stevenson writes, in a colossal understatement. Her life was a farmer's nightmare: The strawberry plants rot; horses trample the corn; the lettuce gets too much sun; rats eat the second crop of corn. After reading of her relentless physical labor, one is amazed to learn Stevenson was fifty years old and ill at the time. "I cured my five ulcers with calomel," she says. Although Louis writes every morning, Fanny has little time for her hidden journal, which someone continually finds and censors. To further complicate matters, she lives among headhunters. A tale that could easily have sunk into melodrama or martyrdom is saved by a matter-of-fact tone. "Mr. Haggard begged us to stay in town / Because he bitterly wanted women to protect," she notes. I suspect that Fanny Stevenson's actual diary is *not* a delight to read. But I am glad her fascinating life has been retrieved from a fragmentary obscurity through Kizer's art.

The book also contains translations of Chinese love poems, and poems based on Greek myths. "Hera, Hung from the Sky" shows a woman punished for ambition. Venus is "The Dying Goddess" since no one makes sacrifices to her anymore and "Odd cults crop up, involving midgets." In an imaginative retelling, Semele describes her transformation into "altar, oracle, offal, canoe and oars" after seeing Zeus in his immolating blaze of glory. Section Six, a prose journal interspersed with haiku, focuses on love and self-destructiveness. The entries are sometimes insightful: "Perhaps at the extremes of happiness or unhappiness, one should take care that only inferior works of art will be contaminated by nostalgia." This cautionary tale of pain and self-exposure casts woman in the familiar role of sufferer. Reading it, I wondered why it is so hard to think of long poems by contemporary men poets on the pain, rather than the blame, of divorce.

The final section, "Where I've Been All My Life," is largely autobiographical. The former poem contains the line "Love, become feminized, tickles like a feather," "feminized" being synomymous with "weakened" or "trivialized." Such disparagement makes me feel that Kizer regards women with some ambivalence. I also was ready to dislike a poem called "Bitch." There's certainly no analogous term for a spiteful man. However, rather than depict the bitch as a destructive force, Kizer shows her to be a result of causes. In this poem, bitchiness is the honest anger people feel for those who misuse them. Thus, the civil woman carrying on small talk while the bitch rages within is something of a hypocrite. Another fine poem shows a "large lady" climbing a gun emplacement in hope of damaging the weapon. After failing in her attempt, she leaves an eggshell from her lunch on the gun. Kizer captures the endearing (perhaps lifesaving) goofiness of this symbolic gesture, which embodies pacifism more effectively than the bravado of heroism. "A Muse of Water," the concluding poem, builds a witty conceit in which female creativity is made to serve as reflecting pool, cofferdam, fountain, and reservoir. "And you blame streams for thinning out, / Plundered by man's insatiate want?" Kizer asks. No wonder there are "Dry wells, dead seas, and lingering drouth," or that women's creativity sank "To silent conduits underground." Once

found, however, female imagination "Is water deep enough
to drown." This is the ambiguous, final warning of *Mermaids in the Basement.*

Although Kizer's new book, *The Nearness of You,* explores
such themes as "Manhood" and "Fathers," it is not subtitled "Poems for Men." And the section of poems about
men friends is called simply "Friends," unlike the parallel
segment of *Mermaids* designated "Female Friends." Although the slight difference in subtitles might have been an
oversight, the distinction is like the one commonly made
between "women poets," who are of course female, and
"poets," who are of course male. (How often does one encounter the term "man poet"?) Thus, women are singled
out for difference, and men assumed as the norm.

This book, like *Mermaids,* is a compilation of old and
recent poems. And again, I marvel at Kizer's technical skill
and inventiveness. Her fondness for wordplay, puns, and
extended conceits recalls seventeenth-century aesthetics:
"We will be well, and well away / until our pulse and pallor
tell / That we are ill, of being well." While the metaphysical strategies occasionally work, they often feel overdetermined, and the language is conventionally poetic at
times: Lovemaking becomes "hushed rapture" and drown-
ing. On the other hand, a witty prologue poem describing
the difficulties of writing about happy love succeeds in
doing just that. And "By the Riverside" makes good use of
puns to imply connections between a child's idea of Christ
and of Indians. This poem of recollection bears a fine
epigraph from a telephone directory: "Do not call from
memory—all numbers have changed." Although the adult

recalling a memory is not put off by an operator "Saying, 'Sor-ree, the lion is busy,'" the child would have trembled "seeing a real lion / Trammeled in endless, golden coils of wire, / Pawing a switchboard in some mysterious / Central office, where animals ran the world." "Streets of Pearl and Gold" eloquently laments the demolition of America's historical buildings and suggests art as a hedge against the wrecking ball. The mutable imagery finds subtle correspondences between the X that stands for kisses, the X of destruction on condemned buildings, the hairs crossing in a gun sight, and the figurative crosses artists are to America.

Kizer is as critical of men as she was of women. She casts a canny eye at the sad lechery of a visiting poet, and a "Promising Author" is something of a male bitch. "I watched you curl your lip / As you ran down every writer in the place," she says, but by the last stanza she realizes that this "great white shark" is "Vulnerable, whiskery, afraid." Kizer's extraordinary insouciance and confidence can make one forget her compassion. She is able to capture the excessive, sentimental foolery of a happy drunk seeing the world in a mug of beer ("Tying One on in Vienna"), or to mourn "gentle heroes" of good conscience ("The Death of a Public Servant"). The latter poem addresses an ambassador who killed himself after being accused of Communism in the fifties. Here she describes the breakdown of men who wounded in name are wounded in mind:

> Or they, found wandering naked in the woods—
> Numbed from the buffets of an autumn storm,
> Soaked blissfully in its impersonal furies—

Are wrapped and rescued after a long dark night,
Are bustled into hospitals and baths
While the press explains away their aberrations:
"Needed a rest . . . and took no holidays. . . ."
But even so, they have managed to catch their death.

"Thrall" portrays the relationship between an emotionally remote father and an outwardly obedient, inwardly rebellious daughter. The most moving exploration of paternity is occasioned by a letter from a man writing a study-club paper on Kizer's father. Her reply forms an affectionate, insightful portrait, and its prose is a graceful change from the density of poetry. The poems to male friends are sometimes interesting only as literary gossip. However, two with strong moral implications are quite fine. "The Good Author" contrasts Malamud's advice to be "pure in spirit" with the vain posturing of a predatory male writer. "To an Unknown Poet" shows a scruffy, uninvited bard arriving at Kizer's door with wife and kids. Annoyed at first, she then remembers Rimbaud and the tenuous relation fame bears to genius or justice. In poems like these, Kizer is loving, smart, and as tough on herself as she is on others. Her work addresses one of the "main things" of twentieth-century literature: "Merely the private lives of one-half of humanity." In its size, integrity, and finesse, her canon is comparable to Bishop's. For these reasons, as well as for her blithe spirit and rigorous mind, Kizer deserves our esteem and readership.

1988

VI

Premises

The Tongue as a Muscle

A Poetry of Inconvenient Knowledge

I HAVE TWO INTERRELATED WISHES FOR THE FUTURE of poetry. First, I would like to shift the emphasis of our collective conversation. The formalist debate has had American poetry in its grip since the early eighties. It's as if our aggregate imagination has been buttonholed by an obsessive, cocktail-party bore for fourteen years. When I mentioned this to a friend she seemed doubtful. Until recently, I shared her sense that formalism had played itself out. I no longer believe this, however. Should questions concerning meaning and structure come up, someone inevitably posits their indivisibility. In service to this belief, responsible discussions of content always invoke form. I've noticed, however, that interrelatedness does not work both ways: Discussions of form seldom include content. This hidden program is one symptom of form's ascendency. Why has poetry allowed itself to be so monopolized? Can we talk about something else? I'm not recommending reductive explications. I am advising that we turn our thoughts from the poem's lineation to its lining: the most reclusive values and unobvious ardours—the snobbery or loneliness, complicity or courage—alive in its lungs.

I refer to the poem's content. In an effort to distance myself from naive or literal readings, I (and other poets) often go to some lengths rather than begin a sentence "this poem is about." After years of circumlocution, perhaps it's time to admit that, yes, poems are about something. Because of the engagement entailed in creating an aesthetic, all poems worthy of the name evince a praxis that amounts to meaning, however metatextual or self-reflective such investments might be: however embedded. What poems are saying—and what they are failing to say—are issues of considerable complexity. Although the struggle to address content unreductively would foster new areas of debate, formalism, as constituted within American poetry, has excluded such intricacies of meaning. In doing so, it has served to deflect anxieties created by the fraught and frightening problems poetry would otherwise confront.

From the start, the form wars seemed a bit spurious. In 1983, I wrote:

> Until recently, I believed that Pound (along with Blake
> and Whitman, among others) had managed to establish
> beyond all argument the value of vers libre as a poetic
> medium. I thought that questions concerning the validity
> of free verse could be filed along with such antique quarrels
> as "Is photography Art?" and "Is abstract art Art?" (*Ecstatic
> Occasions, Expedient Forms,* ed. David Lehman)

Despite my impatience, the early eighties concern with structure was arguably a corrective response to the generic poem of the seventies. But the necessary statements—on all sides of the issue—had been made by 1986. Few fresh or urgent thoughts have been added since. In her 1996 essay, "Arguing Poetry: How Contemporary Poets Write about Poetry," Sharon Dolin describes the form wars and poses the following questions: "Isn't it time for poets to cease labeling free verse as merely poetry with a conspicuous absence of meter or metrical consistency?" And "Isn't it also time for there to be a clearly elaborated poetics of free verse?" A decade earlier, my essay "Of Formal, Free, and Fractal Verse: Singing the Body Eclectic" (pp. 43–59) spoke to these concerns and cited other works that did so. Recent commentators, however, seem unaware of the temporal breadth of the debate they've chosen to enter.

New books and essays on form present warmed-over arguments as bulletins from the front. If poet-critics extended their reading beyond the usual suspects, if they did some scholarly research of the old-fashioned, exhaustive sort, they might be dissuaded from reiterating. As it is, the ongoing debate has ceased to be ongoing. Rather than forwarding the discussion into otherscapes and whichaways of difference, the vocal factions practice a karaoke poetics in which existent opinions are mimed with alarming energy by new performers.

I pause again to wonder: Why this fetish for form? The evidence—and it's purely empirical—suggests that the old free-versus-metered rivalry still makes some poets' hearts beat faster. "Like everyone else engaged in the argument about poetry, I will take sides," Sharon Dolin writes. The polarized debate encourages a frothing and brouhaha comparable to the excitement of sports. Poets form teams, ring nugatory changes on the standard themes, and achieve therapeutic catharsis. Of course, structural discussion need not be limited to a specious battle between traditional and nonce forms. But even when essays explore opinions more oblique, what is at stake? What do we talk about when we talk about form?

One recurring argument is whether formalist poetry must be a vehicle for reactionary values. As I see it, nothing prevents poets from using received forms to express radical points of view. More importantly (and less evidently), structure allows poets to imply content without resorting to words. But the national concern with a poem's "shape" has not included the substantive possibilities of form. And if formalism becomes a means of avoiding content, it deserves the charge of conservatism. Aren't there subjects of greater moral, ethical, philosophical, or intellectual weight we could honor with our energies? The formal debate does not concern itself with class, race, or gender; it does not consider cruelty; it does not think about the locations of power in the world or poem. In sum, I am not wishing for deeper, fresher considerations of form's substance. I am wishing that poets would actively construct, rather than passively inherit, the dominant discussion. "Karaoke" means "empty orchestra." I would have us frame a new conversation rather than reframe a vacuous debate.

"Us?" Who is this third-person plural, anyway? As I understand it, the Language poets have been considering the nexus of power and form for some time. Yet there should be a multitude of discussions on the subject. The MLA convention has welcomed many papers and panels concerned with class, gender, and race over the past decade. Few of those papers were concerned with contemporary poetry, however, and few were given by poets. It is the Associated Writing Programs, not the MLA, that speaks to and for a majority of poets. And my informal survey of the *AWP Chronicle* for 1996 suggests that its membership is terribly interested in form. The March/April National Poetry Month issue, billed as "A Symposium on the Shapes of Poetry," featured an interview with formalist Marilyn Hacker and essays on "Modernism & Continuing Myths of Closure," "The Multiplicity of Form," "The Inner Meaning of Poetic Form," and "Karezza & Closure." The October/November issue included Paul Lake's article on "The Shape of Poetry." In December, the journal published an interview with formalist Molly Peacock and Sharon Dolin's previously cited essay.

But the formal fixation is not limited to members of AWP. A search of the University of Michigan libraries (and my own bookshelves) under the keywords "poetry and form" disclosed twenty-six books published between 1987 and 1997, most of them written by poets. Three separate searches, linking "poetry" by turns to the broad subjects of "gender," "class," and "race," turned up eighteen books in the last ten years, only one or two of which were written or edited by poets. Although they feast on form, poets evidently became sated with "political" issues before those suasions had a chance to spasm and sunder the national discussion.

Let me temper that assertion: Poets of color write about race, yes. But how many "colorless poets" give race the time of day on the page? Inscriptions of class and gender also tend to be unwitting: accidental rather than mindful inclusions. The issues occur as side effects of autobiography, but relatively few poets make them a conscious part of the poem's reach and saying. Although the national *discussion* has fastened on form, the national *poem* evinces an overriding obsession with the shape of the poet's life rather than the shape of the poem. Practice speaks louder than precept. Rather than being concerned with conscience, responsiblity, power, cruelty, or *form*, in practice American poetry is relentlessly concerned with the self. Its investigations are not ontological or epistemological so much as solipsistic.

This view of poetry's topography is based on my reading over the last five years as a judge of the National Book Award; the Lamont Prize; Sarabande Books Award; the Akron Poetry Prize; the Loft Awards of Distinction; the Walt Whitman Award; and other, smaller prizes. From this immersion, I conclude that the generic contemporary poem is built of diaristic, confessional anecdotes; its failure springs not from didacticism but from narcissism. Of course, autobiography and social engagement need not be mutually exclusive. And poetry of immoderate freshness can spring from private worlds. But neither of these transformations is taking place. The poet's experience does not embrace spheres beyond the self; neither is it transformed into a rich imaginative realm: Experience does not levitate into illuminations above and beyond the slice-of-life.

Most commonly, the poem tries to move the reader by recounting personal trials. The mortal illness of friends or relatives becomes a showcase for the poet-speaker's sensitivity. Erotic content provides another means of self-display. There is little interest in language per se. As a result, much contemporary verse reads like failed short-short stories rather than failed poetry. The generic lyric—in which readers are denied even the salacious, spying pleasures of narrative—draws on a day-old vocabulary of *angel, wild, sweet, dark,* and *desire.* Diligently troping through prefabricated landscapes of loss, these elegies are here to tell us—and tell us—that "absence is presence." That formulaic phrase seems all too apt. Poets lip-sync old hits— "Dark Angel," "Wild Desire," "Sweet Wings"—that once upon a long ago had life.

Yet rather than acknowledge poetry's perfunctory involvement with "engaged" tropes, poets express a weariness with "political" issues, as if verse had devoted itself to nothing else for decades. The jaded stance seems somewhat prophylactic. Or perhaps poets are annoyed by the practical applications of "diversity." A poet friend comments: "The world of poetry (which encompasses publications, teaching positions, reading series, essays, anthologies, etc.) pays tribute to the god of 'diversity.' 'Diversity' is concerned with sexual preference, political standpoints, ethnicity, and is completely unconcerned with 'form.'" One could argue, however, that without a concern for diversity, literary politics would revert to what they were before the lately enforced sensitivity: An unacknowledged affirmative action program for white men.

I can sense the hackles rising even before this comes to print, even as I write it. The excised is by definition dangerous. Perhaps poets avoid discussions of content because the issues stirred by such a conversation would involve more peril than those engendered by debates on form. Elias Canetti notes that "Survival is at the core of everything that we—rather vaguely—call power." The wish to survive turns poets into poeticians, mincing their words lest somebody—at the Academy or University, in the men's room or locker room, on the board or committee—take offense. Rather than being "the only Kangaroo among the Beauty," in Dickinson's self-descriptive phrase, poets tend to align themselves with accepted notions of the seemly. Such fealty to "Beauty" or aesthetic correctness is rewarded and admired. But as Tadeusz Borowski writes, "There can be no beauty if it is paid for by human injustice, nor truth that passes over injustice in silence, nor moral virtue that condones it." If we refuse to consider the implications of our words, our poems will reflect rather than revise aesthetic and cultural norms. If, on the other hand, we focus on content, we might notice—and counter—the complacency and complicity within poetry of every shape.

The dominant culture is as invisible as it is invidious: We partake in its assumptions unthinkingly. To write mindfully, however, we must disinter and interrogate its premises, revising or accepting as necessary. One can try to oppose the behemoth of American culture independently, without a community of like-minded others, but it is lonely work. When I began writing in the mid-seventies, the notion of a counterculture was still alive. The second wave of feminism was at its height. It was a time of thought made deed, the age—or more accurately the end of the age—of activism. Practical feminism had a few basic tenets, one of them being that the personal was political. Suddenly, what happened to women in private and in silence was seen to be part of a vast social fabric. Biological fatalism gave way to cultural determinism. Gripping frayed copies of *Sisterhood Is Powerful*, women met to scrutinize their heretofore unexamined lives. Consciousness-raising groups. Does anyone remember them with honor? Or have they been consigned to the nostalgia heap, along with mood rings and platform shoes holding dead goldfish?

The purpose of consciousness-raising was not self-fulfillment so much as knowledge. With awareness came the wish to revise existing assumptions concerning women and redress the balance of power. Consciousness, when purposefully pursued, encourages conscience. I don't believe in golden ages. The seventies certainly did not constitute a positive utopia—in poetry or nation. But I do miss the cultural resistance that thrived in that decade. Of course, we are engaged with a slightly different social context today. While a new counterculture might have some interests—nonviolence? human rights?—in common with the old one, this historical moment contains its own issues and possibilities.

This brings me to the second half of my wish: I hope that considerations of content encourage a poetry of mindfulness rather than compliance: a poetry with the strength to be culturally incorrect. One of Elias Canetti's demands for a poet is that "he stand against his time."

Against his entire time, not merely against this or that;
against the comprehensive and unified image that he alone
has of this time, against its specific smell, against its fate,
against its law. His opposition should be loud and take
shape; he cannot simply freeze or resign himself. . . . He may
wish for sleep, but he must never attain it. If he forgets his
opposition, he has become an apostate. (*The Conscience of
Words*; translated by Joachim Neugroschel)

Canetti adds that "this is a cruel and radical demand."
To poets endowed with the niceties of America, it might
seem a perverse and contrarian one. It certainly entails
some inconvenience. You'll notice that the preceding excerpt (written in 1936 and reissued in the seventies) does
not oppose the assumption that all poets (*"der dichter"*) are
male. Elsewhere in the same piece, Canetti says, "The
writer who is able to take part in many lives must also take
part in all the deaths that threaten those lives." Surely our
participation must extend beyond physical death to its
spiritual, emotional, aesthetic, and cultural instances. The
quoted passage, by means of its own blind spot, enacts the
difficulty of writing against the prevailing grain, against
cultural correctness.

I devised the term *culturally correct* as a synonym for *politically incorrect. Culturally incorrect* by extension becomes syn-
onymous with *politically correct.* Although the paired terms
sound oppositional, they describe the same position. The
need for new labels becomes clear once we consider the
connotations of the existing terms. Political correctness is
associated with doctrinaire humorlessness and a neurotic

sensitivity to trivial concerns. Political incorrectness, on the other hand, carries the following implications: "I am fun-loving, sensible. Not a killjoy, whistleblower, trouble-maker. I'm a regular guy. I rebel against the silliness and tedium of politically correct beliefs. And my rebellion makes me, in the best American tradition, an outlaw."

These popular definitions mask the real issues of power and equity at stake. They encourage ethical forgetfulness. We forget that it is "politically correct" to honor rather than despise gay sexuality; to work toward equal rights for all; to oppose cruelty to animals; to respect the natural environment. In fact, "politically correct" views seek to revise the culture's deep beliefs concerning sexuality and gender; white privilege; male dominance; patriarchy; and human supremacy over nature. Political incorrectness, on the other hand, supports the self-congratulation of American culture—especially as that complacency is defined and disseminated by network television. Rather than being a position of wild independence, an allegiance to political incorrectness is an allegiance to the existent cultural and economic forces, whose well-being depends upon vigilant maintenance of the status quo.

It is a dreary fact of human nature that those in a position of power or privilege usually wish to remain there. It is in their best interests to flatter fellow adherents of "business as usual" by reconstituting that stand in attractive terms. As I have suggested, in the current version of this Orwellian ploy, conventional views are vaunted as "incorrect," while radical positions that suggest the need for social change are denigrated as prissily "correct." The proferred new labels reverse these false constructions by recognizing the orthodox subtext (cultural correctness) of "politically incorrect" views and the maverick aspect (cultural incorrectness) of positions labeled p.c.

There are always attempts to countervail social change with mockery; it is an old technique. Reactionaries dress radical humanist values in costumes so ridiculous that one is embarrassed to be seen with them. The real issues are trivialized in entertaining ways as a means of distracting us from their profound content. Thus, in the 1970s, feminists were labeled *women's libbers* or *bra-burners,* and a great movement for human rights was conflated with underwear, its issues reduced to the right to forego lingerie. Such "politically incorrect" constructions chipped away at the substance and authority of feminism. Afraid of contagion by association, even women and men who supported human rights began their liberal sentences with apologetic demurrals: "I'm not a feminist, but . . ."

In like fashion, attempts to question inequities in the nineties are nicknamed p.c. and used as comedy fodder. Everyone knows it's uncool to be p.c. The breezy abbreviation is a contemptuous epithet by which people of conscience are diminished. Why do people—including poets—comply with such reductive versions of humanist movements? Are we going along to get along? Buying into debased fictions of political correctness is more convenient than not. If we reduce humanist claims to, for instance, a garbage collector's right to be called a sanitation engineer, there is no need to change our lives.

A gloomier, realpolitik view suggests that the majority

sees contemporary humanist values as threats to their own well-being. From my observation, many poets admire great ethical thinkers—Simone Weil, Walter Benjamin, Elias Canetti, and others. Of course, literary lions and icons go in and out of fashion. Simone Weil was à la mode in the early eighties, and Walter Benjamin seems the latest philosopher of choice. I don't for a minute mean to denigrate the achievements of these writers. I mean to indicate the factor of literary chic that colors poetry's excursions into thought and morality. It is easy to take the high moral ground retrospectively. Thus, the ethical dilemmas and heroics of previous ages, as confronted by Weil, Benjamin, Canetti, are replayed and honored in poetry, while present-day problems of moral complexity are avoided or ridiculed.

Seamus Heaney notes that "In ideal republics . . . it is a common expectation that the writer will sign over his or her venturesome and potentially disruptive activity into the keeping of official doctrine, traditional system, a party line, whatever." (*The Government of the Tongue*) American writers regard themselves as servants of their own imaginations rather than of any ruling party. We tend to believe our views will emerge if we look in our hearts and write. This school of thought denies the immense pressure of the cultural surround. Unless we write mindfully—interrogating received beliefs—the imagination of American poetry will serve the "traditional system" or "party line" of American culture.

By refusing to encounter unspoken premises, we reify them. As Elias Canetti notes, if we forget our opposition, we become apostates. "From the very start," he writes, "we oppose the idea that a great writer is above his time. No one, in himself, is above his time." Imagination, in other words, cannot be decontextualized; it does not exist in a vacuum; it is always indentured to some notion of the world. To ignore this seems at once convenient and willfully naive.

As an example of active reimagining, consider what is involved in writing toward the other. People sometimes have a hard time understanding the concept of alterity. At the risk of being obvious, I'll try to clarify. The group that holds cultural, economic, or numerical sway defines itself as the norm (the One, the Subject) while singling out differing groups as deviant (the Other, the Object). Simone de Beauvoir notes that woman "is defined and differentiated with reference to man, and not he with reference to her." Thus women take men's names in marriage rather than the reverse; people speak of "women poets" but not "men poets"; female writers are asked how being a woman affects their work, while men writers seldom hear the analogous question. To pose the other/one binary in racial terms, African American writers are routinely identified as writers of color, while Caucasian writers are not categorized as "white writers" or "writers of no color" every time their names are mentioned.

Since the dominant culture is omnipresent as air, subordinate groups learn about it simply by being alive. The divested also become unwilling anthropologists, studying the empowered in order to anticipate—and if necessary manipulate—their behavior. The enfranchised, on the other hand, do not inevitably learn about those on the margins;

the culturally endorsed, if they are to know, must actively pursue awareness of the unendorsed. To approach otherness, not clinically but heartfully, is difficult; it takes humility. A poetry of inconvenient knowledge asks men to think deeply about women's historical and biological situation, a request that entails some empathy, if not self-effacement. And as a white woman, I am asked to think about race; as a member of the middle class, I must encounter poverty; as an American, I can't efface the third world.

The process of learning toward, leaning toward the other is in itself a good thing. There are ethical and practical difficulties, nonetheless. How do white writers speak inclusively without appropriating, stealing other people's thunder? How do heterosexuals write an erotics that is inclusive of gay sexuality? How do poets write across class hierarchies without slumming or stereotyping? Let me be clear: I am not asking for a didactic or polemical poetry. On the contrary, I'd like poetry to unhinge the prevailing culture with the same degree of subtlety—insidiousness, if you will—that it has used to uphold that culture.

Yet reticent techniques that discount readers' assumptions are ineffective. In my first two books, for example, I left some speakers unmarked by race, sex, or gender. I thought this a subtle way of opening the poem's possibilities: Readers could choose various races for the speakers while envisioning them as female or male. I learned, however, that voices created by a white writer will be read as white unless the writer inscribes them racially. And if readers are given no clues as to a speaker's sex or gender, they will imagine those details along culturally correct lines.

A scientist or a diver working on an oil rig will be pictured as a man, and the speaker of a lyric poem will be engraved with the poet's gender and sex. Indeterminacy, in other words, does not create inclusivity.

I've continued to try the problem in various ways. In a recent long sequence, "Give," I wanted the mythic Daphne to exist between categories of color. As my creation, I knew that she—automatically, unquestioningly—would be read as white. Fair enough. Without denying her whiteness, I offered slant suggestions—linguistic, metaphorical, narrative, emblematic—of her darkness. By such means, I hoped to insinuate Daphne between binaries: a figure who is neither one nor the other.

Difficult as it is to address the issues, to write without considering otherness in any of its forms is to write a poetry of narcissism. The most offensive poetics creates White World, Straight World, Man World and calls it Universal World. In an interview, artist Sandra Lopez describes the need to scrutinize our suppositions concerning the universal or natural:

> If you fit the norm in your culture, whatever that norm is, it rarely occurs to you that not everyone is like you. If you are a white male within our culture, the structures of knowledge, language, education, and power are things you are more likely to feel comfortable with, because they are languages made by those who probably are similar to you. A person in that position, or even an acculturated person like a white educated woman, can only begin the questioning if something happens in life and he or she is outside for just one second. . . .

> And then you may begin to think about the fact that while our methods of transmitting knowledge are very good, they can also exclude a great many things which could be of importance to us. Thinking about this, you may begin to ask whether many of these things were willfully excluded, not on a level of individual but cultural will. Was the exclusion necessary to allow and maintain dominance over those whose voices were and are excluded? (*Listening to the Land*, ed. Derrick Jensen)

In order to write and read mindfully, we must become cultural outsiders. By hovering on the perimeter of the circle, we can see its full circumference. Imagination is the transfiguring force. But it is imagination as a thorny rather than lazy maelstrom. Imagination as an active rather than passive metabolism, pressing against cultural assumptions in order to reinvent them.

Reading much contemporary poetry, you could conclude that while most poets think poetry should have imagination and emotion, they don't think it should have ideas. Yet even purely autobiographical poems rest upon assumptions suffused with ideology. Poetry has ideas whether it wants them or not. Usually they remain in the background, a quiet chorus behind the starring subject. When ideas do take center stage, the thinking in poetry favors the canon of Western culture: the Great Ideas of Great Men. This dialogue with emininence often constitutes a bid for authority and a borrowing of intellectual weight. Poets might deny such an agenda, but the effect is there whether intended or not. It would be hypocritical to dismiss the self-serving aspect of the company we keep on the page. When I bolster my words with those of Canetti or Heaney, I effectively say, "These aren't just my own trivial concerns; Nobel prize winners have written on the subject." There is no risk in citing those who are invested with legitimacy, and there can be gain: Such inclusions can dismantle resistance to unpopular ideas.

Poetry (and essays) is more valuable, however, when it calls attention to those whose remarkable histories and thinking would go unremarked otherwise. It also is refreshing to include thinkers who are not favored among poets. Poetics certainly could benefit from an infusion of contemporary thought from other fields. Rather than considering current theories, however, contemporary poetry tends to rehearse the past. In its prizing of the prized and honoring of the honored, poetry supports a winner-takes-all ideology. Whose poetry do I have in mind?

To resist a winner-takes-all framework, one must read across the field rather than limit one's reading to the successful few. It follows that my impressions are not gleaned from "stars" but from an engagement with a much broader spectrum of endeavor. In some cases, I don't know the names of the poets who inform my observations. For instance, I currently am judging an award that requires me to read forty-five anonymous manuscripts, and those submissions will tint my perceptions concerning praxis.

Winner-takes-all is a trickle-down aesthetic in which a largely invisible majority is influenced by a visibly large minority. Rather than conflate the two spheres, I mean to suggest their reciprocity. My approach is comparable, perhaps, to that of "history from the bottom up," a method of inquiry that focuses upon the nonelite. Historian Thomas C. Holt writes, "Major activities are born of germs contained in everyday practice." He notes that power can be *realized* only at the quotidian level, and that "it is dependent . . . on the reproduction of the relations, idioms, and the worldview that are its means of action. In short, the everyday is where . . . politics, economics, ideologies . . . are lived." ("Marking: Race, Race-making, and the Writing of History") I would add that the everyday is where poetry is "lived," where it acquires the force of majority. The zeitgeist is expressed more clearly by the obscure many than by the acclaimed few. It is within the ordinary gossip and buzz, within the thousands of unacclaimed poems, that poetry takes shape.

The visual arts provide a specific instance of the "winner-takes-all" climate. Lately, museums have begun publishing anthologies written in response to art in their collections. In one recent project, the museum commissioned writers—mostly poets—to respond to any work in its holdings. Despite this carte blanche, nearly all the contributors chose to write about a work currently on exhibit. Only two or three delved into the museum's archives, a repository far larger and more varied than the current show. All the writers found surprisingly fresh approaches to their chosen subjects, and the anthology is a feast of startlingly good works. I'm troubled, nonetheless, by the contributors' preference for those artists already preferred by the museum.

Museums legitimize art by exhibiting it. Whether an

artist's work is shown or stored has less to do with its inherent importance than with economic factors and the cartel that is the New York art world. By limiting themselves to the work on display, the writers colluded with institutionalized opinions. Although they had the power to confer visibility upon one of many fascinating and relatively neglected artists from the archives, the contributors chose to reward the work already rewarded by exhibit: Winner takes all. Were the writers convinced that the curator's small selection included the artist best suited to the urgencies of their work? In some cases, this was undoubtedly so. And in others, the poem's subject probably was determined by intellectual convenience. The writers didn't *imagine* an alternate. Rather than think beyond the given, they accepted the world on exhibit as the available world.

Poets often write in response to visual art, and they usually focus on acclaimed, widely collected painters. The well-known artist's reputation has been constructed and authorized: Everyone agrees that van Gogh is important. Poems about him can draw upon a huge store of existent writing, secondary sources. Historians, curators, and collectors have done the groundwork; the poet has only to digest some art books and create a poem in accord with what-is. Things might become interesting if poets chose to excavate the cellar of art history, in search of "the mermaids in the basement." Writing about lesser-known or uncommodified artists requires primary research and first thinking. It entails a deeper engagement with art than is needed to write toward a canonized artist. A broader, more confident knowledge is required to read a work by an obscure contemporary painter than to read a painting by van Gogh. Art history offers so much help with the van Gogh and so little with the unknown.

Georgia O'Keeffe and Frido Kahlo number among poetry's darlings. I have the impression that poets think they are making a feminist gesture and questioning inequity by choosing a female painter—any female painter—as their subject. Such a view is based on biological essentialism: It assumes that people of the female sex are alike in other fundamental ways. In the case of O'Keeffe and Kahlo, the false premise associates their female sex with cultural disenfranchisement and assumes their aesthetics contain elements common to all women artists. The last notion, by suggesting a purely sexual base for intellect and imagination, equates anatomy with destiny. As for marginality, O'Keeffe and Kahlo number among a very few female painters who are culturally and institutionally endorsed. I am not arguing against the quality of their marvelous work. I am observing that writing exclusively about canonical female artists supports systems of power that authorize a few tokens while effacing the rest. It reifies, rather than unsettles, existing hierarchies.

I mentioned emotion as a normative value of mainstream poetics. Emotions are subjective—yes. But their subjectivity is shaped by cultural, autobiographical, and biological happenstance. Readers' emotive responses to poems are determined, in part, by their prior experiences with poetry: how much of it they've read, whether they've written it themselves. As a poet who reads poems by the pound, I am moved by work that does one or more of the following: includes emotions seldom found in contemporary poetry; unsettles the limitations of genre and convention; subverts cultural complacencies; articulates emotional states for which there is no noun; enacts the reader's sublime.

In longing for "emotions seldom found in poetry," I am not longing for a poetry of exposure that exhibits "shocking" inclusions in hope of evoking a response. Such emotive displays are *often* found in poetry. Contemporary poems frequently rely on scandalous or tragic auto/biographies as a means of eliciting empathy. There seems to be a concomitant preference—among poets and readers—for anecdotes recounted in ordinary language. Simplicity is prized as a symptom of sincerity: straight, no chaser. Linguistic effects are suspect since they intrude upon the telling. This array of preferences has turned the plain-style lyric narrative into another karaoke performance. In a twist of intention, the poem's prefabrication undermines the "sincere" effect it set out to create. I notice the poet pulling the familiar rhetorical strings, and I resent the "guileless" manipulation.

The pulling of unfamiliar linguistic strings can disarm my cynicism, however. If the poem is wayward—even to the point of awkwardness, excess, error, or eccentricity—I might be moved though the poet gave no thought to emotion. If the poem presses language against its limitations, if it countervails assumptions, refuses flatness, ease, excuses, and strategies calculated to move me, I might be moved. I hope this is true for others because it seems fundamental: The intellectual and structural wonders of the poem can create emotion. As a reader, I am consoled, made happy, by a poem's courage or strangeness—the uncanny quirks of its saying, the weird spin it puts on craft.

Many poems, perhaps most, want to awaken feeling in the reader. Not just any feeling, of course. The more debased emotions--anxiety, shame, glee, remorse, embarrassment, guilt, dread, jealousy, panic, vengefulness, triumph, humiliation, anger—are unlikely to elicit empathy. The poem does not try to replicate such states within readers. It isn't that poetry is wearing its happy face either: Poems with a sense of humor are dismissed as fluff. (Unless they are written by the critically endorsed "winning" few, to whom different standards are applied.) Readers still expect sorrow and transcendence in poetry, and these are the emotions poems conventionally seek to enact. If a reader feels sad in response to an elegy, the poem is deemed an affective success. If, however, a reader feels disgust or embarrassment in response to a poem concerned with those emotions, the poem is critiqued for its lack of aesthetic distance. Of course, that wished-for distance between poet and subject would be perceived as cold or uncaring if found in an elegy. Clearly, the poet is expected to alter her proximity to content in accordance with the content's emotional ground.

I called "transcendence" an emotion, and some might argue that it is—something else. To transcend is to exceed the natural. But if in doing that, we did not *feel* emancipated, the journey would be more schlepp than levitation. Transcendence seems epiphenomenal in character, although I would not venture to say whether the emotion is derived from the event or vice versa. At a dinner last week, a physicist remarked that understanding, by which he meant comprehension, was an emotion. In fact, it was one of the most powerful feelings he'd experienced, comparable only to familial love. Pressed to elaborate, he described his experience of coming across an important discovery in the magazine *Science*. He always had wondered why we evolved with a need to sleep. The article spoke to this mystery. Reading it, he experienced an understanding that was profoundly and physically affective: his pulse symptomatically accelerated with pleasure. I say "symptomatically" because emotions are drastically embodied thoughts. Our eyes fill with tears, our veins dilate. We blush, we faint.

Desire and grief consolidated into genre long ago: the lyric, the elegy. Poems specializing in other emotions lack categorical titles—a circumstance that points to their relative aberrance. While the melancholy beauty of an elegy or lyric serves as a palliative for loss, the less lofty, more unlovely emotions go unconsoled. I'm interested in poems that engage with those untoward emotions, going off the given emotional scripts to write the peripheral and unvisited. Such poetry will disappoint the genteel expectations of genre, but it stands a chance of surprising me into feeling.

Of all poets, Dickinson most adroitly explores feeling as a foreign language. Her poems express the blanks of sentience: emotions so inconvenient they go unnamed. In *The Dickinson Sublime*, Gary Lee Stonum describes another emotive aspect of her work. He writes that to read all of Dickinson's poems is "to risk the vertigo characterizing the reader's sublime, a bewilderment in the face of some vast surfeit of meaning." The reader's sublime is created by maximalist works of dizzying, mind-defying beauty: works

that stretch into subtler vistas when you thought you'd set-
tled; works that leave no tone unstirred, suspending you between begging for mercy and begging for more; works with
enough intertwining, self-referential, neural complexity to
make you feel both lost and found. Stonum also character-
izes the sublime as "an affective and effective power that
draws attention but also eludes or even disrupts pleasing
harmonies and intelligent schemes." The sublime is gorgeous rather than pretty. It appears as a profligate, lovely
feral force, barely under the poet's—or reader's—control. It
arises from a poetics of inclusivity and synthesis, of gorg-
ing, stuffing to capacity. Of muchness as a means to euphoria. Excess that transcends the natural. Extremes.

The poet cannot build the sublime in thirty lines.
Dickinson's work is vertiginous only when considered
as one long poem. Among contemporary poets, A. R.
Ammons has created such a turbulent, maximalist poetics.
And in the past ten years, poetry enacting the reader's sublime has come to the fore of American verse by way of
Dorothy Barresi, Mark Doty, Albert Goldbarth, Lynda
Hull, Susan Mitchell, Thylias Moss, Pattiann Rogers, and
Stephen Yenser, among others. To feel the head-in-a-whirl
intoxication of the sublime, readers must submit to the
temporal demands of a long poem, which run counter to
the demands of a sound bite. You won't experience the
sublime by channel surfing through a book. And I can't
demonstrate exaltation with excerpts. The poem of the
maximalist sublime creates a sense of plenitude and possibility by orchestrating extended buildups and tear-downs
in your head. Which is to say: The sublime is not pithy.

The sublime is not dainty. But patience—a virtue not encouraged by American culture—occasionally is rewarded by moments of odd, postmodern rapture.

And how does postmodern rapture differ from the old sort? More accurately, how does the poem in pursuit of it differ? What new form does this odd emotive content find? Postmodernism critiques "the natural"; transcendence exceeds it. I suggest that the two relations be collapsed into one technique, an excess that unhinges foundational assumptions. The Romantic transcendence of "Ode on a Grecian Urn" engraves "maidens loth," the "struggle to escape," and the sacrificial heifer into the poem's vessel of foreverness. "Cold Pastoral!" Keats exclaimed, interrupting his appreciation with—what? Petulance? Or is it only reverence for the frigid emblem of his witness? His outburst—the moment at which the poem overmodulates into anger, infatuation, and impatience with the Eternal—is perhaps where we come in.

It is our part to acknowledge the iciness of the artifact's sagas: its latent rape narrative; the unpretty powers that give rise to "struggle"; the human cruelty deflected into the ritualistic slaughter of the calf. By unsettling the "Attic shape" of "natural" truths and the "Fair attitude" of form, we might edge into realms more conscientious and more spacious than poetry has lately allowed.

~~

So—what do I want from poetry? The head notes, heart notes, base notes. The sweatstained. You can have the cold pastorals! But poetry's futurity has a mind of its own: far be it from me.

"The wish to survive turns poets into poeticians, mincing their words. . . ."

Okay. I'd like poetry to remove its leaden eyeliner, wake up to its own blind spots, put its vision through tectonic shifts. I'd like a poetry of unnatural acts. That treats the mind to a mind. Treats the tongue as a muscle.

A poetry of cultural incorrectness, inconvenient knowledge, mindfulness . . . That keeps covenant with old unsettlements. Casts off insulated bliss. Says to human viciousness, I wouldn't if I were you. The poem as epiphany cake sent to prisoners of American culture. The ebon and the flaxen. With a knife baked in it.

Can we talk about something else?

The poem as something else. Language as a foreign feeling. Saying to those who are expatriates in their native land—the fellow travelers, castaways, shipwrecked, exiled, defectors—if you lived here, you'd be home by now.

1997, 1998

About the Author

ALICE FULTON's books of poems are *Sensual Math* (W. W. Norton); *Powers Of Congress* (David R. Godine); *Palladium* (University of Illinois), winner of the National Poetry Series and the Society of Midland Authors Award; and *Dance Script With Electric Ballerina* (University of Illinois), winner of the Associated Writing Programs Award. She has received fellowships from the John D. and Catherine T. MacArthur Foundation, the Ingram Merrill Foundation, and the Guggenheim Foundation. Her work has been included in six editions of *The Best American Poetry* series published by Collier Books/Macmillan. Poems also have appeared in *Poetry*, the *New Yorker*, the *Paris Review*, the *New Republic*, and many other magazines. She is currently Professor of English at the University of Michigan, Ann Arbor.

Acknowledgments

I wish to thank Fiona McCrae, who suggested this book and greatly affected its large and small shapes. Her comments and counsels, over several drafts, were unfailingly perceptive.

I'm grateful to Fred Marchant for his sympathetic close reading of the manuscript. He more than met this work halfway.

My husband, Hank De Leo, has fostered every aspect of my writing. He read and reread these essays in several incarnations over the years. My debt to him exceeds acknowledgment.

"Screens: An Alchemical Scrapbook" (1995) was commissioned by Sven Birkerts for *Tolstoy's Dictaphone: Technology and the Muse* (Graywolf Press). I thank him for inviting and liking this essay. I'm grateful to my sister, Sandra Fulton Carpenter, and to her family, for permission to publish some of the material included here.

"Of Formal, Free, and Fractal Verse: Singing the Body Eclectic" (1986) was written at the kind invitation of Richard Jones for *Poetry East.* The essay also appeared in *Conversant Essays: Contemporary Poets on Poetry* (Wayne State University Press) edited by James McCorkle.

"Fractal Amplifications: Writing in Three Dimensions" (1997, 1998). My gratitude to Kathrine Varnes for suggesting that I elaborate on my earlier fractal essay. A shorter and much-altered version of this piece appears in *An Exaltation of Forms* (University of Michigan Press) edited by Annie Finch and Kathrine Varnes.

Warm thanks to David Lynn who found room for this essay in *Kenyon Review* on short notice. I also thank Tim Kendall, editor of *Thumbscrew* (Oxford, England), for rushing the essay into his pages.

I'm grateful to Lynn Keller, a giving soul, who took time from her demanding schedule for an acute and necessary critical reading. John H. Holland, Cristanne Miller, Kathleen Malone O'Connor, and Stephen Yenser also provided discerning critical readings.

"Unordinary Passions: Margaret Cavendish, The Duchess of Newcastle" (1998) was commissioned by Jonathan Post for *Green Thoughts, Green Shades: Contemporary Poets on Seventeenth-Century Verse* (University of California Press). I'm grateful to Jonathan Post and Stephen Yenser for their early votes of confidence. Many thanks to Jonathan Post for his enthusiastic reception of the completed essay.

"Her Moment of Brocade: The Reconstruction of Emily Dickinson" (1989). Thanks to Herbert Leibowitz, who commissioned this essay for *Parnassus* and provided helpful critical suggestions. Laurence Goldstein, Charles Simic, and Stephen Yenser also gave of their time and minds. Conversations, written and spoken, with Cristanne Miller have enlarged my understanding of Dickinson over the years. To Cris, "appreciation / Out of Plumb of Speech."

"To Organize a Waterfall" (1990). Thanks to Herbert Leibowitz, who invited me to write about my work for a special issue of *Parnassus*. A. R. Ammons, Phyllis Janowitz, Cristanne Miller, Helen Vendler, and Stephen Yenser also read, encouraged, and advised.

"Three Poets in Pursuit of America" (1985) was written at the behest of Laurence Goldstein for *Michigan Quarterly Review*. I thank Larry for encouraging me to begin writing criticism.

"The State of the Art" (1987) and "Main Things" (1988) were commissioned for *Poetry* by Joseph Parisi, who published them as I wrote them. *Grazie tante*, Joe!

"A Poetry of Inconvenient Knowledge" (1997, 1998) was written for *Green Mountains Review 10th Anniversary Double Issue*. Neil Shepherd's sensible editing greatly improved the first version of this piece. Cristanne Miller and Stephen Yenser read later revisions and made indispensable suggestions. I thank Rebecca Scott for her encouragement and for directing me toward Thomas G. Holt's relevant essay.

I'm grateful to the University of Michigan for teaching leaves that made writing possible.

A fellowship from the John D. and Catherine T. MacArthur Foundation afforded me time and incentive. My thanks for their largesse is lifelong.

> More—would be too vast
> For the Soul's Comprising
>
> EMILY DICKINSON, 769

Feeling as a Foreign Language is set in Centaur type.
The roman was designed by Bruce Rogers in 1912–1914
and based on type cut by Nicolas Jenson in Venice in 1469.
The italic was drawn by Frederic Warde based
on a chancery font designed by the calligrapher
Ludovico degli Arrighi in the 1520s.

This book was designed by Wendy Holdman
and set in type by Stanton Publication Services, Inc.
It is manufactured by Maple-Vail Book Manufacturing
on acid-free paper.